IMAGES
of America

COLLEYVILLE

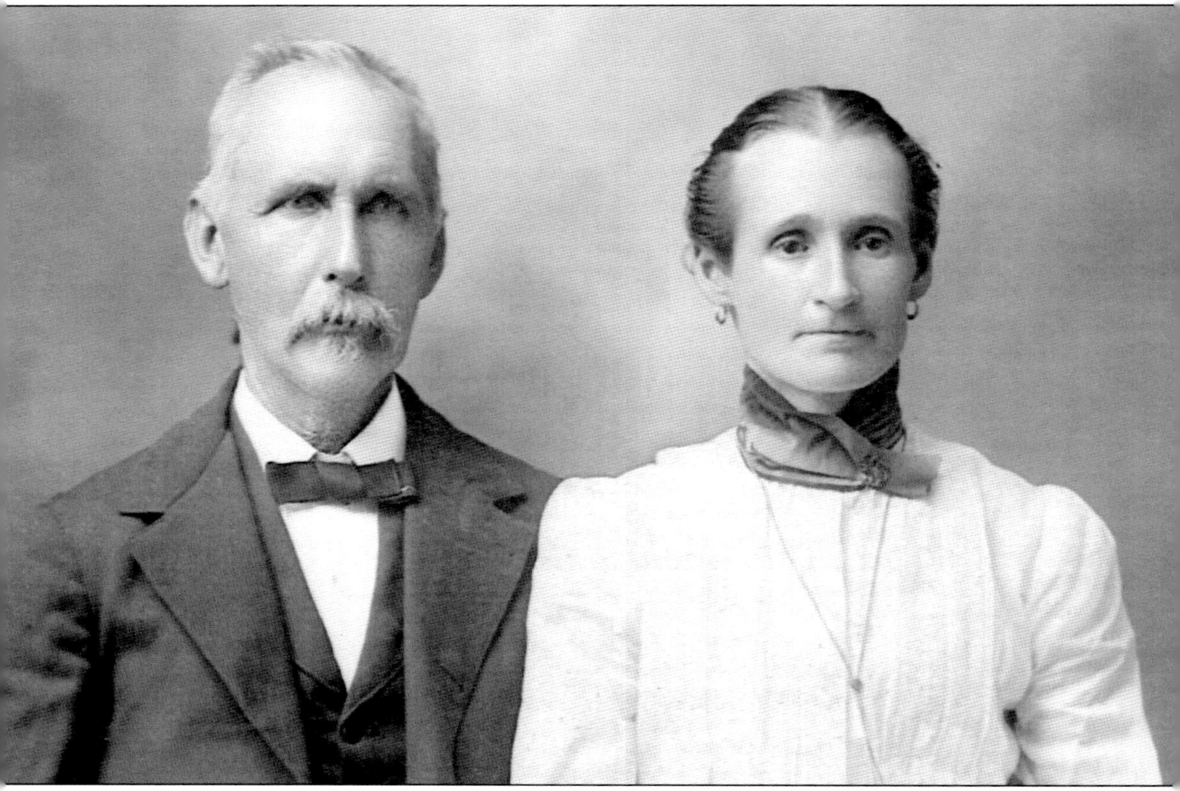

Long before Colleyville was incorporated in 1956, it was a close-knit community. Several small villages, called "parent communities," tied together by commerce, faith, and, most of all, a pioneering spirit, formed the bedrock of the town named for Dr. Lilburn Howard Colley. Dr. Colley is shown here with his wife, Martha Sabrina (Fawkes) Colley, whom he affectionately called "Matt." Colley hailed from Missouri and was a veteran of the Union army before moving to the prospering town of Bransford, situated on a line of the St. Louis, Arkansas & Texas Railway (today known as the Cotton Belt rail line) in northeast Tarrant County. In addition to the rail line, it had a post office, two blacksmith shops, a livery stable, four general stores, and a lodge hall shared by the Masons, Odd Fellows, and Woodmen of the World. Colley was one of four doctors who resided there. Like many towns in that era, a new community formed around a store, in this case opened by W.G. Couch on Glade Road south of Bransford in 1914. Because of Colley's association with that community, it was named Colleyville, and the name stuck when all of the area communities banded together to become incorporated. (Courtesy of Colleyville Historical Preservation Committee.)

On the Cover: This photograph of the Behrens farmhouse captures the essence of what Colleyville was and continues to be. When the Reynolds family first arrived in the pre-Colleyville parent community of Pleasant Run, the Behrens were among the first to welcome their new neighbors. The families helped each other tackle the hardscrabble life over the years. The Behrens house, a typical log cabin of that era, stood on the family farmland, located just off of present-day Behrens Road. The Behrens and Reynolds families have been instrumental in the development of Colleyville. The Behrens owned and operated the Behrens Farm Store, which sold groceries, gasoline, and bait to fishermen. Members of the Reynolds family were very active in the military; 12 grandsons of the original Reynolds settlers served in World War II. Shown here are, from left to right, Henry Behrens, Jim Reynolds, Martha Behrens, Charlie Behrens, and Ella Behrens. (Courtesy of Colleyville Historical Preservation Committee.)

IMAGES
of America

COLLEYVILLE

Mark Fadden

ARCADIA
PUBLISHING

ISBN 978-1-4671-3394-4

Published by Arcadia Publishing
Charleston, South Carolina

Printed in the United States of America

Library of Congress Control Number: 2015935319

For all general information, please contact Arcadia Publishing:
Telephone 843-853-2070
Fax 843-853-0044
E-mail sales@arcadiapublishing.com
For customer service and orders:
Toll-Free 1-888-313-2665

Visit us on the Internet at www.arcadiapublishing.com

Contents

Acknowledgments

While most books contain one or two authors' names on the front cover, the popular phrase, "It takes a village" is appropriate here in recognizing all the people who came together to make this book possible. First, many thanks to the Colleyville Historical Preservation Committee (HPC). William Murtagh, first keeper of the National Register of Historic Places, said, "At its best, preservation engages the past in a conversation with the present over a mutual concern for the future." The members of the HPC keep this quote in mind as they work tirelessly to ensure that the city's historical footprint isn't washed away by the passage of time. Second, thanks to Tom Kellam, who manages the Tarrant County College District Archives and Heritage Room, and Kristy Phillips, who manages the Portal to Texas History at the University of North Texas Libraries, for helping me locate and use several photographs in their extensive collection.

Finally, thanks to all of the individuals who put together the extensive history book *Colleyville Then and Now* as part of the city's 50th anniversary in 2006. At over 600 pages, it is a treasure trove of historical information and family narratives. It was an invaluable research tool and, along with this book, will hopefully be used time and again as a resource for both young and old as they take the important step to reflect on the pioneers, leaders, heroes, and everyday folks who worked together across the lines of history to make Colleyville what it is today.

INTRODUCTION

Cities, like most other organizations, use their logos as part of their branding efforts. Many other cities in the Dallas–Fort Worth Metroplex use elaborate fonts, catchy slogans, or declarative punctuation to show what they are all about. Colleyville's logo features a picture that truly does speak a thousand words. It consists of the silhouette of a horse in a fenced pasture with an airplane taking off in the background. While its wide-open spaces, horse farms, and tree-lined railroad harken back to its rural beginnings, Colleyville has developed into a top-tier community thanks to its location near the heart of the Metroplex and the economic engine that is nearby DFW Airport, but most of all, because of the hard work and determination of Colleyville's citizens.

When pioneering families first began populating the area, not one but six different communities were formed. These "parent communities," which included Pleasant Run, Pleasant Glade, and Bransford, eventually banded together and, in 1956, became Colleyville, named for Dr. Lilburn Howard Colley. He was born in Colley Hollow, Missouri, on September 5, 1843. He was a military man, serving first as a private in Company A, 48th Missouri Infantry in 1864, and then in the Union army, where he was a drummer and the principal musician of his company. He earned his medical degree from the College of Physicians and Surgeons in Keokuk, Iowa, in 1873, which he put to good use after he and his wife, Martha "Matt" Sabrina (Fawks) Colley, moved to Bransford. As a country doctor, Colley served area families by traveling to their homes to attend to the sick and dying and to help birth babies. Beyond providing the community with his medical services, Colley was an active volunteer. He conducted the Pleasant Run School District's trustee election multiple times and was a member of the Smithfield Masonic Lodge. Colley's wife, Matt, died from skin cancer in 1914, but Colley would remain in Colleyville and continued his contributions to the community, both as a doctor and as a volunteer, until his death at his daughter's house in Wichita Falls on October 26, 1924.

Entire generations of Colleyville citizens have displayed Dr. Colley's spirit of hard work, determination, and caring. From a few clusters of pioneering families, to a close-knit community known for its dairy farms, to becoming one of the nation's premier cities, Colleyville's population has grown, from about 1,500 in 1960 to more than 24,000 today.

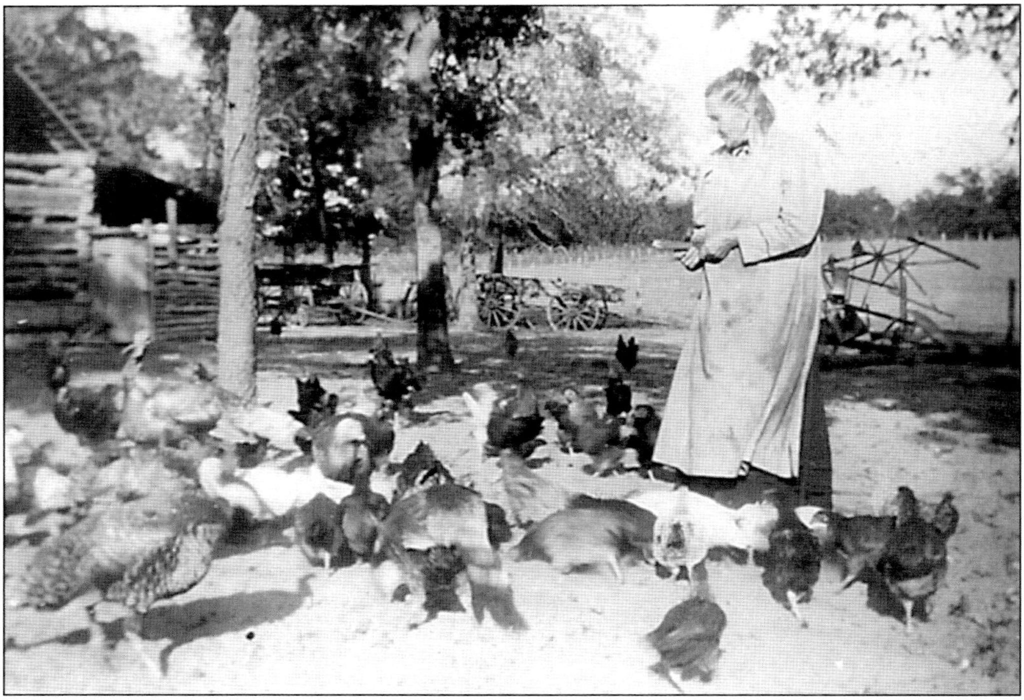

Being able to live off the land was a paramount skill on the open prairies of Texas in the middle and late 1800s. After traveling hundreds, even thousands of miles in covered wagons, settlers had to carve out their existence relying on nothing but what the land provided them and the few animals they brought along. Many of these pioneer families had at least one dairy cow to provide them with milk. They also had chickens that would provide eggs, and turkeys to be butchered on special occasions to provide meat for the family. Above, a woman scatters feed for her chickens. Below, Henrietta Bidault, daughter of Anthelm Bidault, poses with their milk cow on the family farm. (Both, courtesy of Tarrant County College Heritage Room and Colleyville Historical Preservation Committee.)

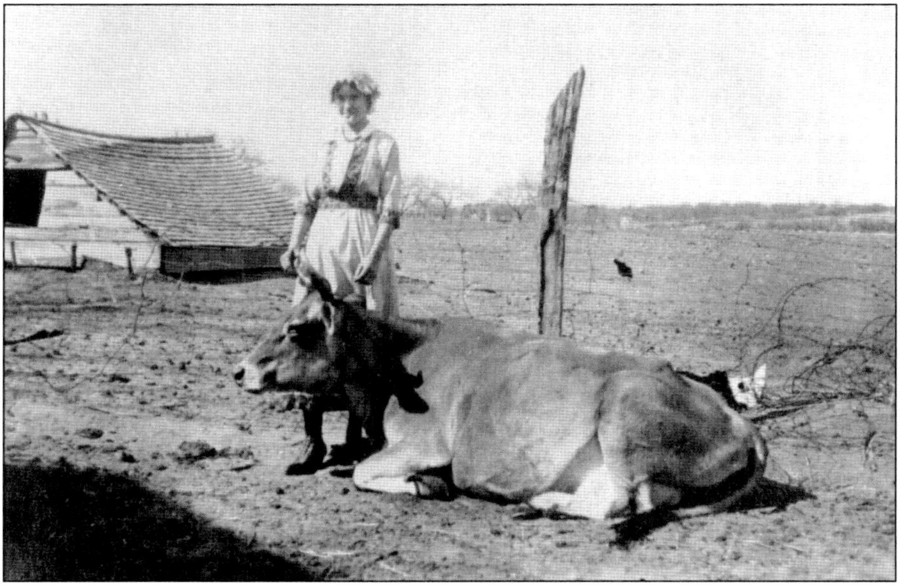

One

Taming the Wilderness

Before the first pioneer families came to settle the fertile land crisscrossed with creeks that would eventually become Colleyville, it was a migratory route for nomadic Indians, including the Comanche, Wichita, and Kiowa tribes. In the mid-1850s, around a decade after Texas became a state in 1845, men like Samuel Cecil Holiday Witten, who established a farm along Little Bear Creek in 1854 and became one of the founders of Spring Garden (one of Colleyville's parent communities), and Jonathan A. Riley, who came from Kentucky in 1856 and settled near the Spring Garden community, flocked to the pre-Colleyville area of Texas from other parts of America and other countries around the world. They left behind exhausted farmlands that were no longer yielding crops, and unrest that would lead up to the Civil War, propelled by a desire to make a fresh start by acquiring new land, which was often free to those who settled it. Untamed lands such as Texas that promised adventures and opportunities proved to be an alluring draw for God-fearing families and rugged outlaws alike. As people banded together to face the harsh realities that pioneer living dished out, they became neighbors who chose to build new communities based on schools, churches, and commerce very similar to the ones they left behind.

While it was a hardscrabble life in the pre-Colleyville era, the land also provided a bounty for these early colonizers. Settlers from the East brought seeds and planted them in the fertile soil, producing various types of vegetables. Wild greens and fruits, such as plums and grapes, were picked from the land, and animals were hunted for meat. Many of the first houses were dugouts, which were essentially mud huts recessed into a hillside, or log cabins, which were two rooms separated by a covered open-air breezeway aptly named a "dog run," where the dogs would bed down during the nights or when storms rolled in.

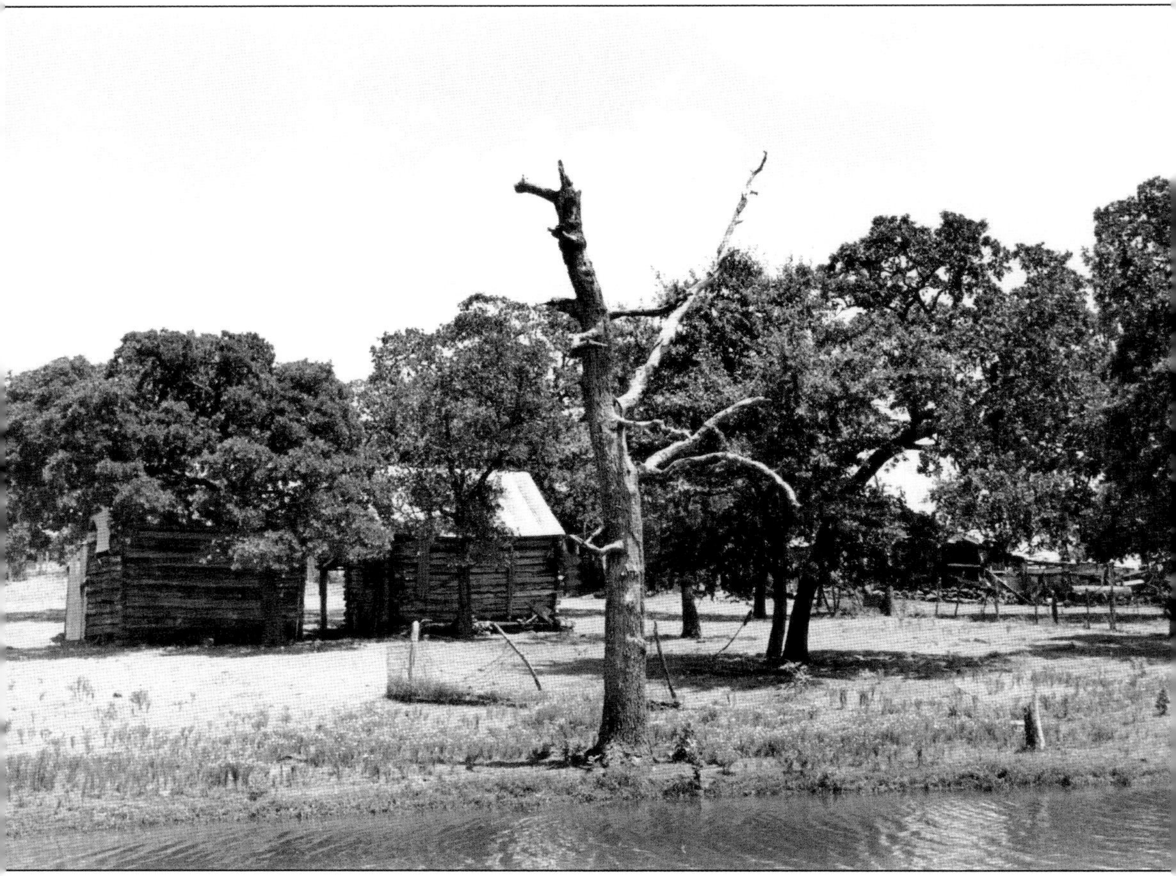

Log cabins such as this one dotted the countryside in the middle and late 1800s in the pre-Colleyville era. The walls and roof were made of logs, and the floors were made of puncheon-style logs, which were split and then smoothed to form an even floor. In these two-room cabins, one room was often called the "big house," or living room, and the other was typically the kitchen. They were separated, in case the kitchen caught fire, thereby sparing the other room. The middle was a covered breezeway, a dog run where the dogs would often lie to shade themselves from the sun or stay dry during harsh weather. These cabins were often shared by more than one family, who welcomed traveling strangers with open arms. The phrase "the latchstring is always out" referred to the practice of pioneers securing their doors only by a string attached to the latch on the outside of the door. If it was out, a traveler only needed to pull on it to gain access to food, lodging, and a warm welcome from the pioneers who lived there. (Courtesy of Tarrant County College Heritage Room.)

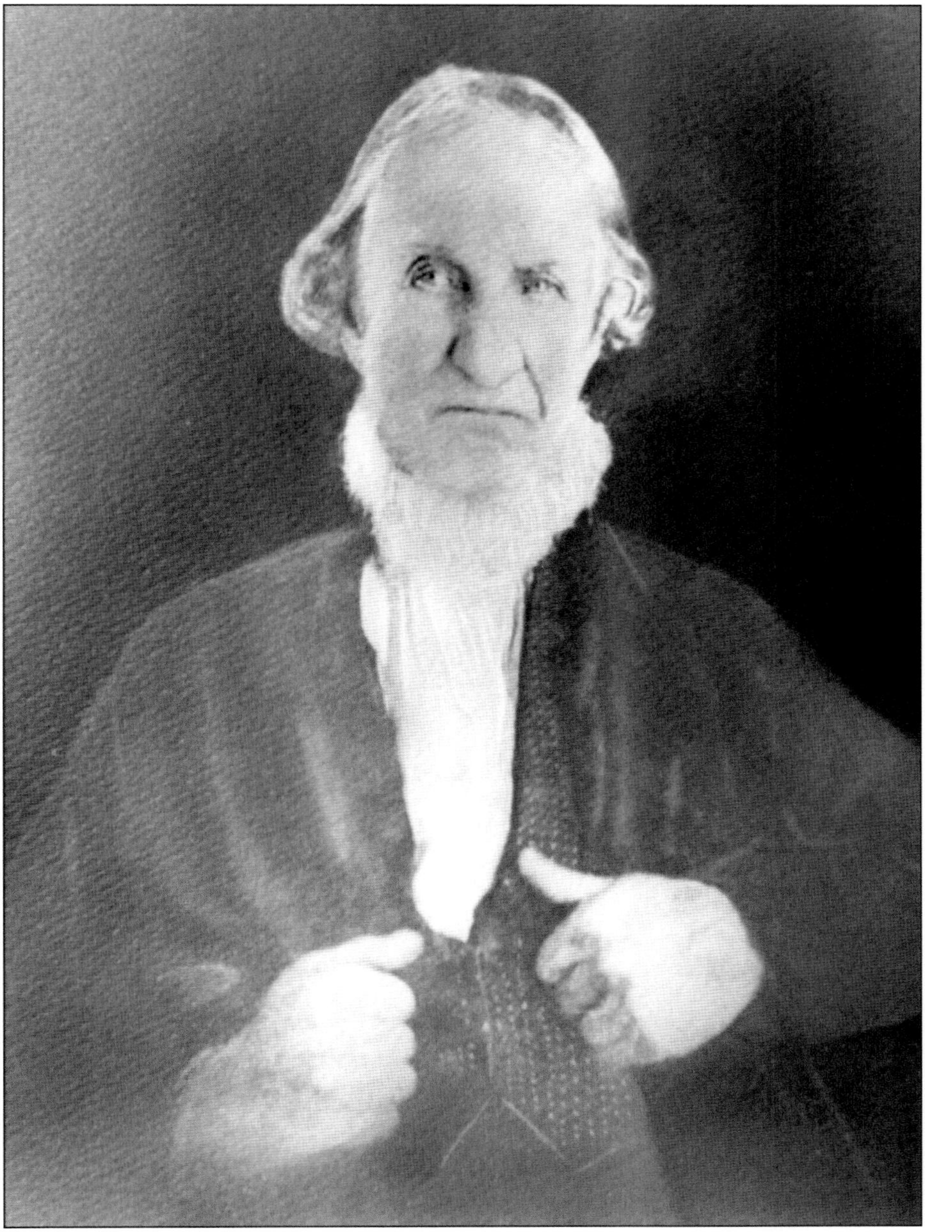

Along with Jonathan Riley, who was one of the largest landowners in Bedford and Colleyville, Samuel Cecil Holiday Witten was an original settler of the Colleyville area. Witten and his wife, Jennetta, picked up and moved from Missouri in 1854 and settled a 1,222-acre farm along Little Bear Creek. They ended up joining Riley as one of the largest landowners in the area. He owned several tracts of land between present-day Glade Road and Cheek-Sparger Road, to the east of present-day State Highway 26 and west of Highway 121. Witten, a cattleman, farmer, and land surveyor, is credited with founding the Spring Garden community, which, like many of the smaller communities in the area, developed around a one-room log-cabin school, which Witten had built. He and Jennetta had 10 children, several of whom are buried in the Witten Cemetery at the end of Jackson Court in Colleyville. Witten died in Corpus Christi in 1891 and was buried there. (Courtesy of Tarrant County College Heritage Room.)

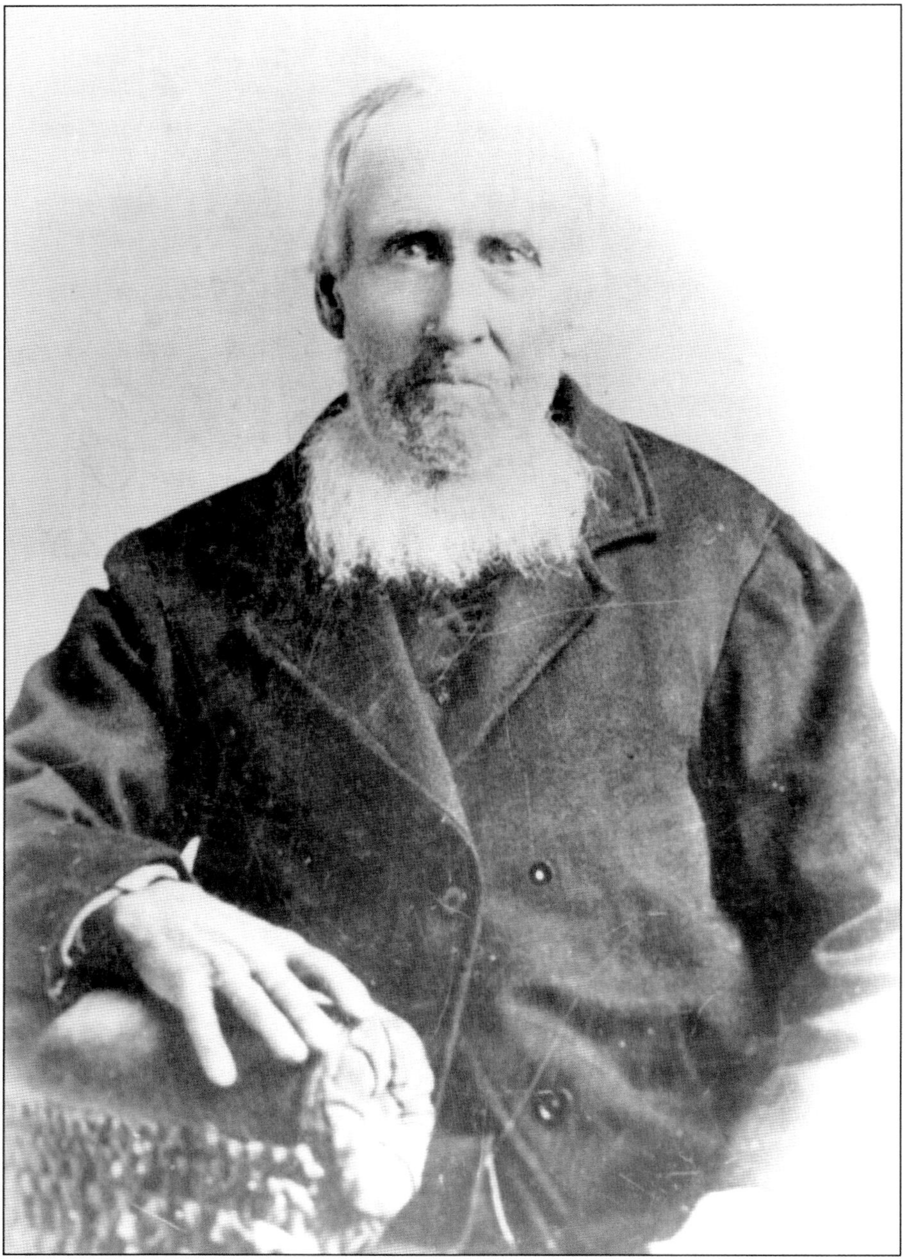

Although Samuel Sparger did not come to the pre-Colleyville area until he was a grandfather, he was the patriarch of one of the most influential pioneer families in Colleyville. Born in 1811 in Virginia, Sparger and his wife, Susan, settled in Tennessee, then Georgia. With the help of his 12 children, Sparger raised crops and livestock, but took on heavy losses in both businesses. In the late 1800s, two of Sparger's sons, Harvey and Thomas, and a daughter, Jane, moved to the pre-Colleyville area. Thomas purchased farmland along Little Bear Creek, where the Tara Plantation neighborhood and Sparger Park now sit. Harvey bought the place from his brother Thomas, and Sparger came to live with him and his family after Susan died in 1890. Sparger died of pneumonia in 1893 and is buried in nearby Smithfield Cemetery, one of the oldest pioneer cemeteries in Texas. (Courtesy of Tarrant County College Heritage Room.)

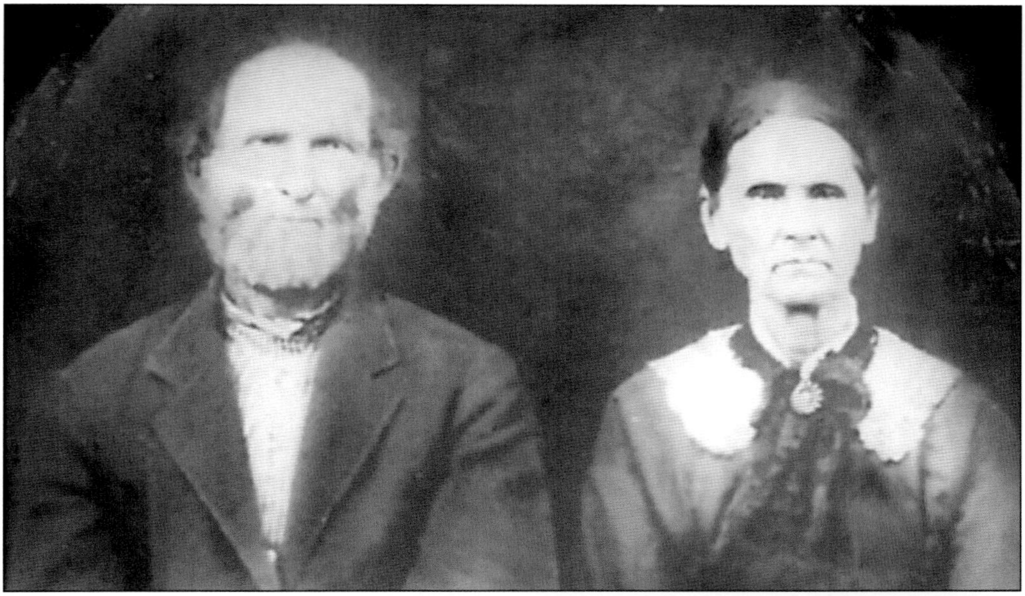

William Milton Dunn and his wife, Fannie Caroline (Steen) Dunn, were among the first documented settlers of the Colleyville area in 1875. The Dunns, shown above, moved to Grapevine from the Carolinas and then went to the Colleyville area, where they were granted 360 acres of land by the State of Texas along present-day John McCain Road. William farmed the land from 1875 until 1890 and used his barn for hay storage. Wagons pulled up onto the roofed runway, and the hay was offloaded and stored in each of the log cabins, also known as "cribs," connected to the runway. The Dunn/Tirk Barn is the oldest building still standing in Colleyville. At right is a portrait of Sudie McCain, daughter of William M. Dunn. (Both, courtesy of Colleyville Historical Preservation Committee.)

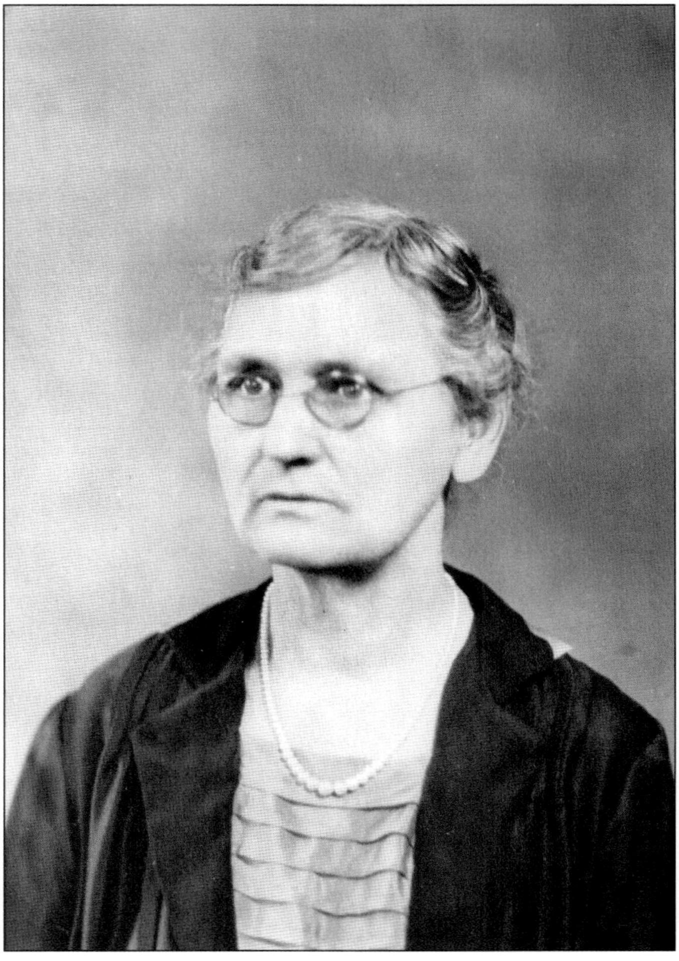

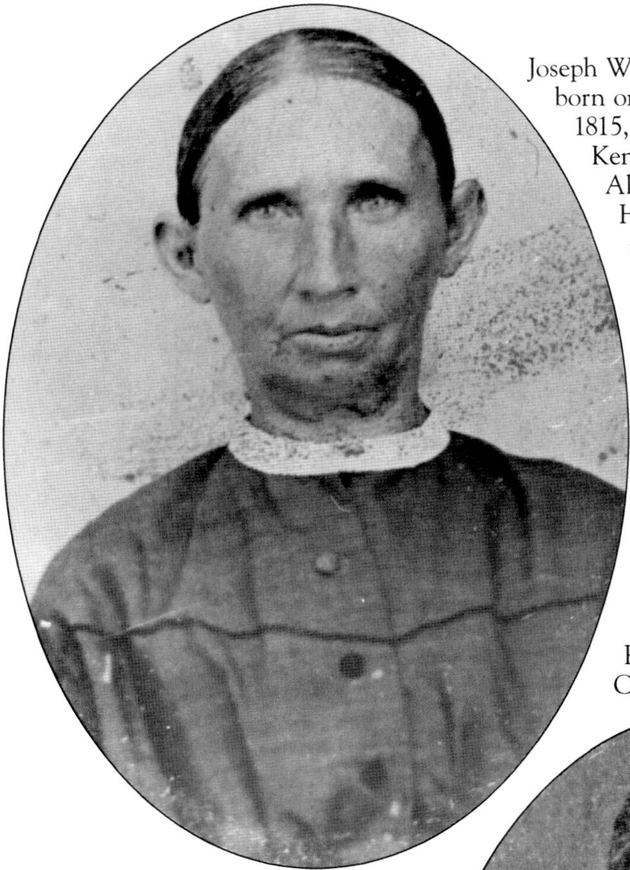

Joseph White and Sarah (Smith) White were born on October 3, 1812, and November 5, 1815, respectively. They were married in Kentucky in 1837 and had four children, Alexander Franklin (born 1840), William H. (born 1841), Mary E. (born 1843), and Lewis Cass (born 1848). Seeking their fortune by heading west, as many pioneering families did in that era, Joseph and Sarah moved the family from Kentucky to Missouri, first to St. Louis and then to Trenton. They then joined a wagon train bound for Texas in October 1858. They lived in the parent community of Bransford, where they acquired 160 acres of land, which would today stretch from the north end of Bransford Road north to John McCain Road and east to Pleasant Run Road. (Both, courtesy of Tarrant County College Heritage Room.)

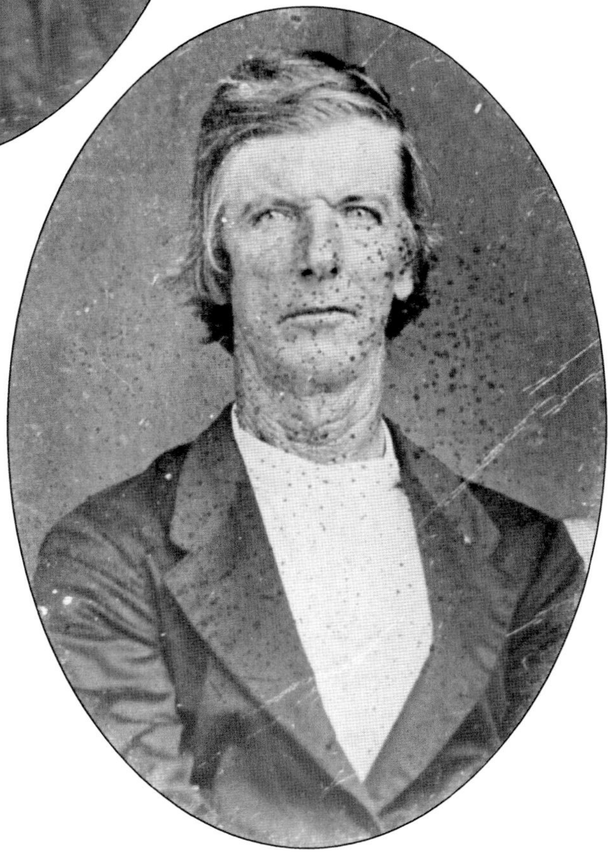

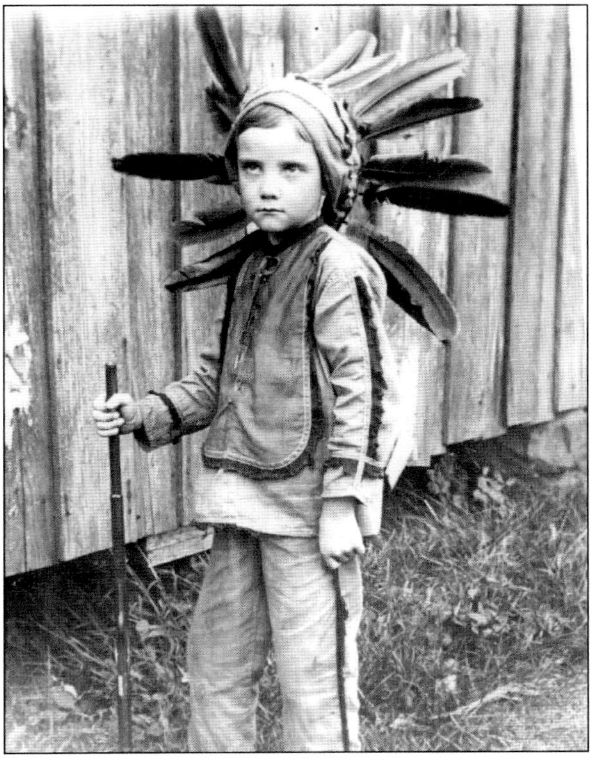

A.W. White is seen here at age five, just after moving from Fort Worth to a farm in Bransford. (Courtesy of Tarrant County College Heritage Room.)

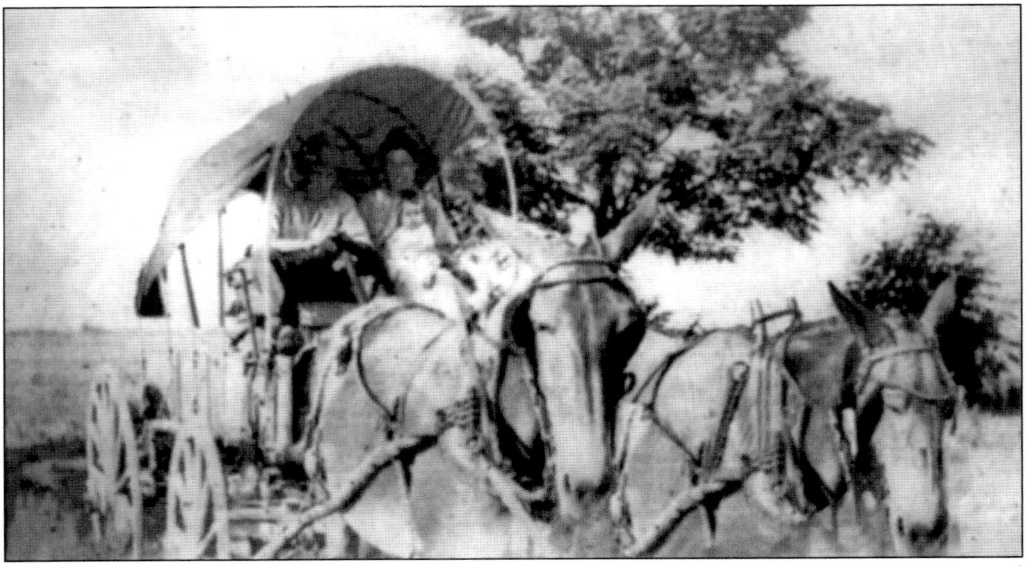

Like most of rural Texas in the late 1800s, the land was the epitome of "wide-open spaces." Instead of paved roads or even rutted dirt trails, Texas was wide-open prairie land, where it took the average settler days to traverse just a few miles in a covered wagon. While these early settlers needed to be as self-sufficient as possible and be able to live off the land, their wagons were filled with those essential items that the land could not provide. Beyond clothing and keepsakes, settlers brought with them beloved cookware, typically made of cast iron, to use with an open fire. Tom Sheppard, pictured here with his widowed daughter, was one of the early settlers of Pleasant Glade, one of Colleyville's parent communities. (Courtesy of Colleyville Historical Preservation Committee.)

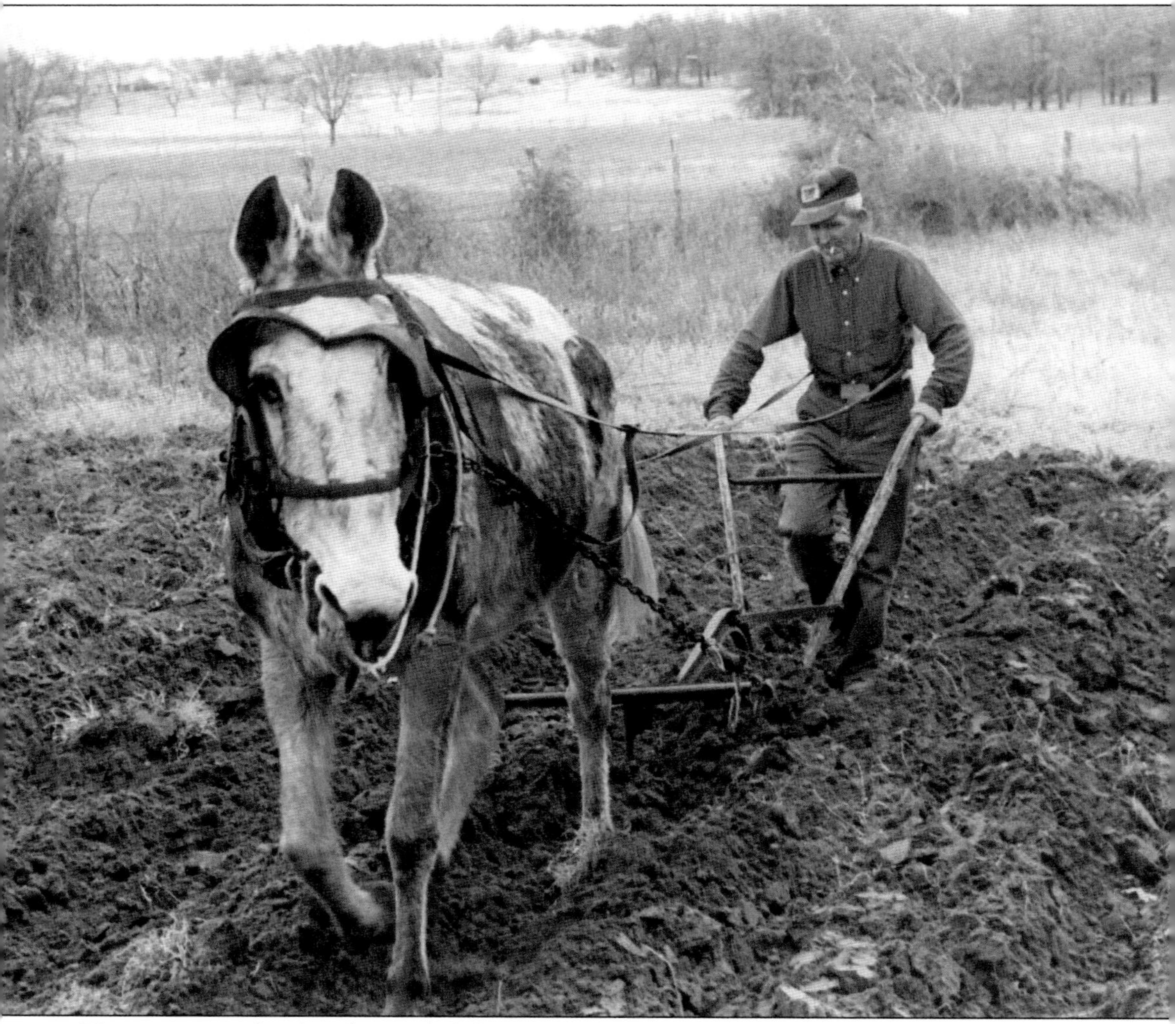

The pioneering families that settled the area in the late 1800s were enticed with stories of fertile land that was abundant, cheap, and promised to be fruitful for generations to come. Whether leaving the failing soils of eastern America, wanting more land than they could afford in pricey California, or escaping social and political unrest in their European homelands, pioneer hopes were pinned on these stories of a land of plenty. And when they arrived, they were not disappointed. Hard-working settlers in the pre-Colleyville area, using plows and cultivators to plant the right vegetables and fruits, were rewarded with a bounty of produce that they could both sell at the markets in Fort Worth, Dallas, and Grapevine and feed to their families. (Courtesy of Tarrant County College Heritage Room.)

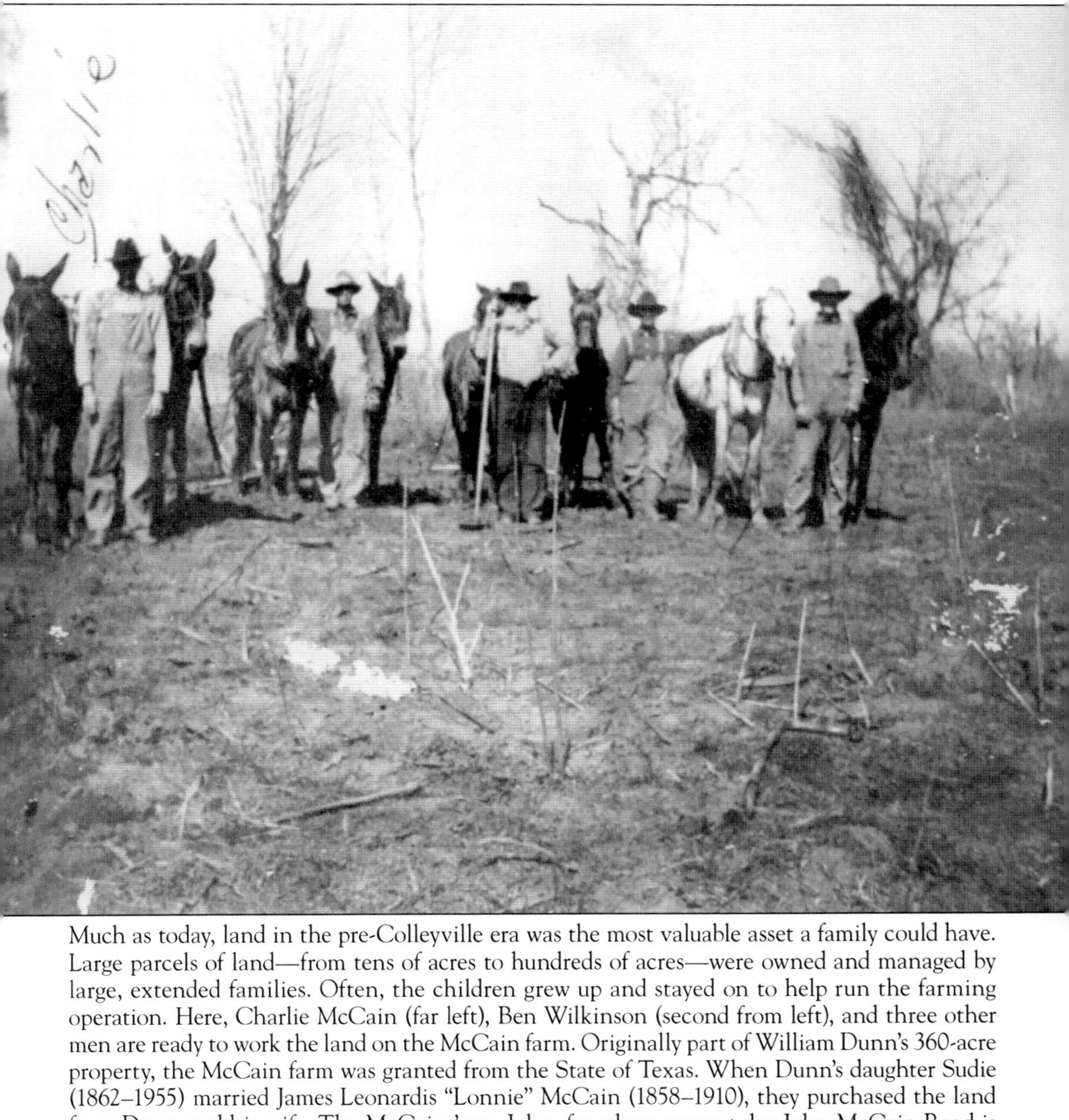

Much as today, land in the pre-Colleyville era was the most valuable asset a family could have. Large parcels of land—from tens of acres to hundreds of acres—were owned and managed by large, extended families. Often, the children grew up and stayed on to help run the farming operation. Here, Charlie McCain (far left), Ben Wilkinson (second from left), and three other men are ready to work the land on the McCain farm. Originally part of William Dunn's 360-acre property, the McCain farm was granted from the State of Texas. When Dunn's daughter Sudie (1862–1955) married James Leonardis "Lonnie" McCain (1858–1910), they purchased the land from Dunn and his wife. The McCains' son John, for whom present-day John McCain Road is named, then purchased that land from his mother, Sudie. (Courtesy of Tarrant County College Heritage Room.)

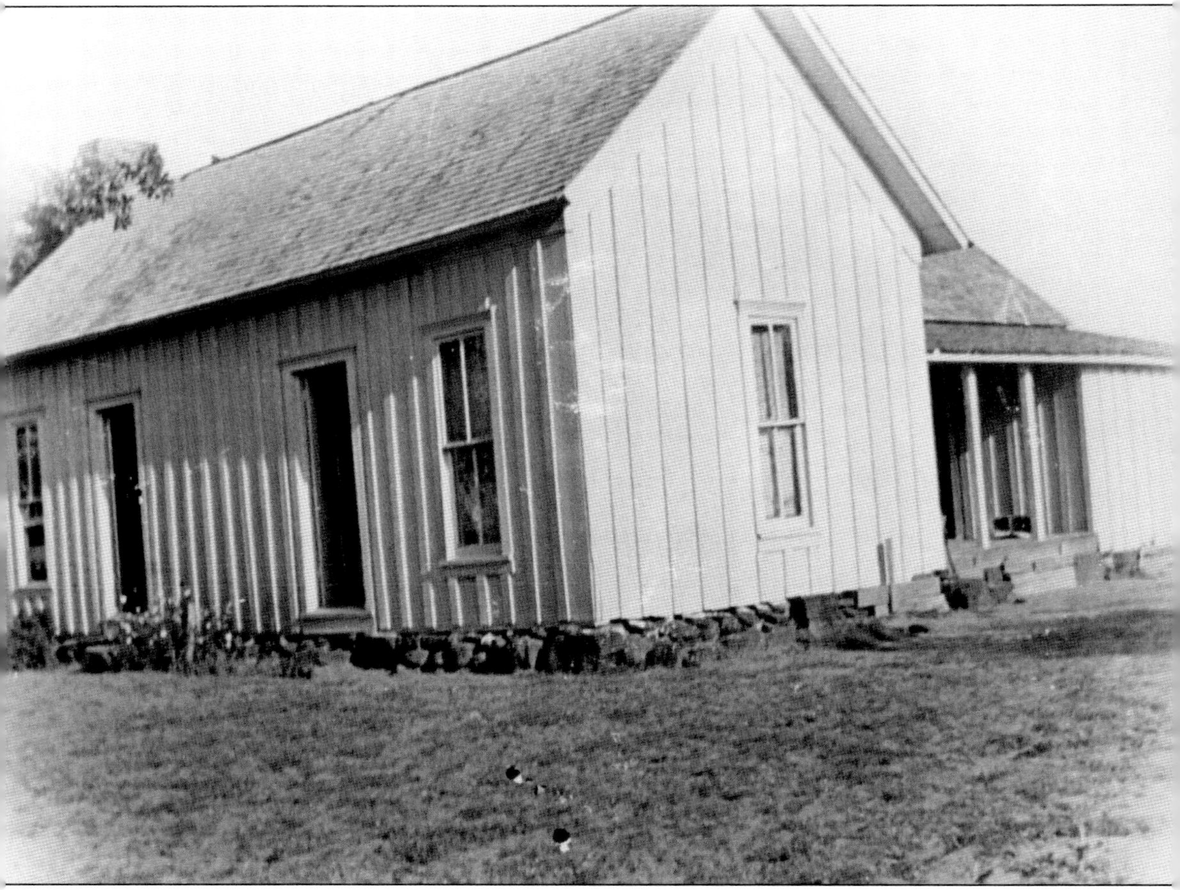

The dawn of a new century brought significant changes to the homes in the pre-Colleyville area. As more people arrived, they brought with them the knowledge and skills to build better shelters. The early homes, cave-like structures called dugouts, had been dug out of hillsides. These were no longer acceptable places to live. Log cabins, even those that had two rooms connected by a dog run, were considered the best shelter at the time. But these were quickly becoming too small and too primitive for a growing family's needs. Many homes began to resemble those of today. This one was built in 1902 by William Dewitt Cavender, who lived in it with his wife, Leona, on their 106-acre farm along Glade Road. They were erected from milled board wood, had windows, and often featured a central hallway that allowed breezes to ventilate the house. (Courtesy of Tarrant County College Heritage Room.)

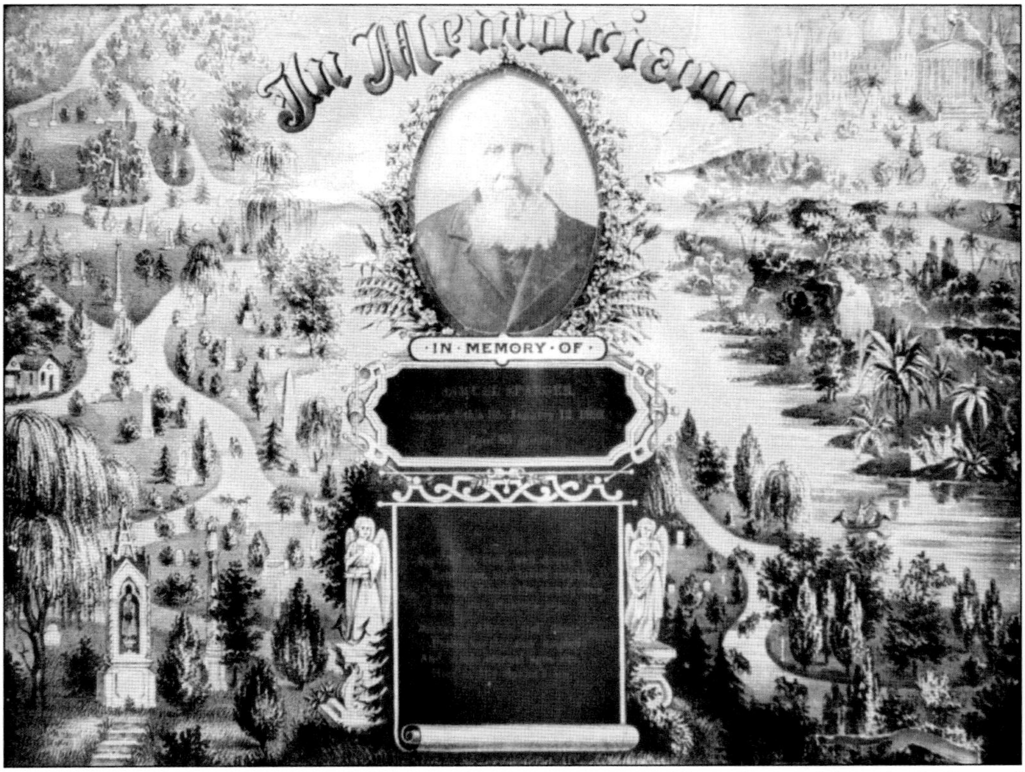

Life was hard in the 1800s, and illnesses that are very treatable today could be fatal. Samuel Sparger died of pneumonia on the morning of January 12, 1893, at his son Harvey's house, located in the present-day Tara Plantation neighborhood. Memorials such as this one were typically made to show important religious aspects of the person's life. (Courtesy of Tarrant County College Heritage Room.)

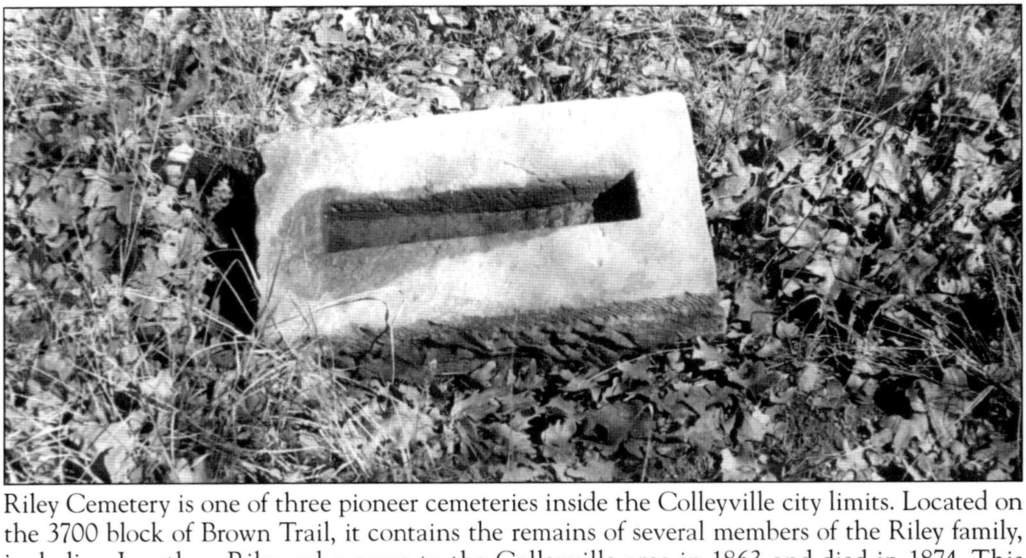

Riley Cemetery is one of three pioneer cemeteries inside the Colleyville city limits. Located on the 3700 block of Brown Trail, it contains the remains of several members of the Riley family, including Jonathan Riley, who came to the Colleyville area in 1863 and died in 1874. This unadorned headstone is typical of those from the pioneer era. (Courtesy of Tarrant County College Heritage Room.)

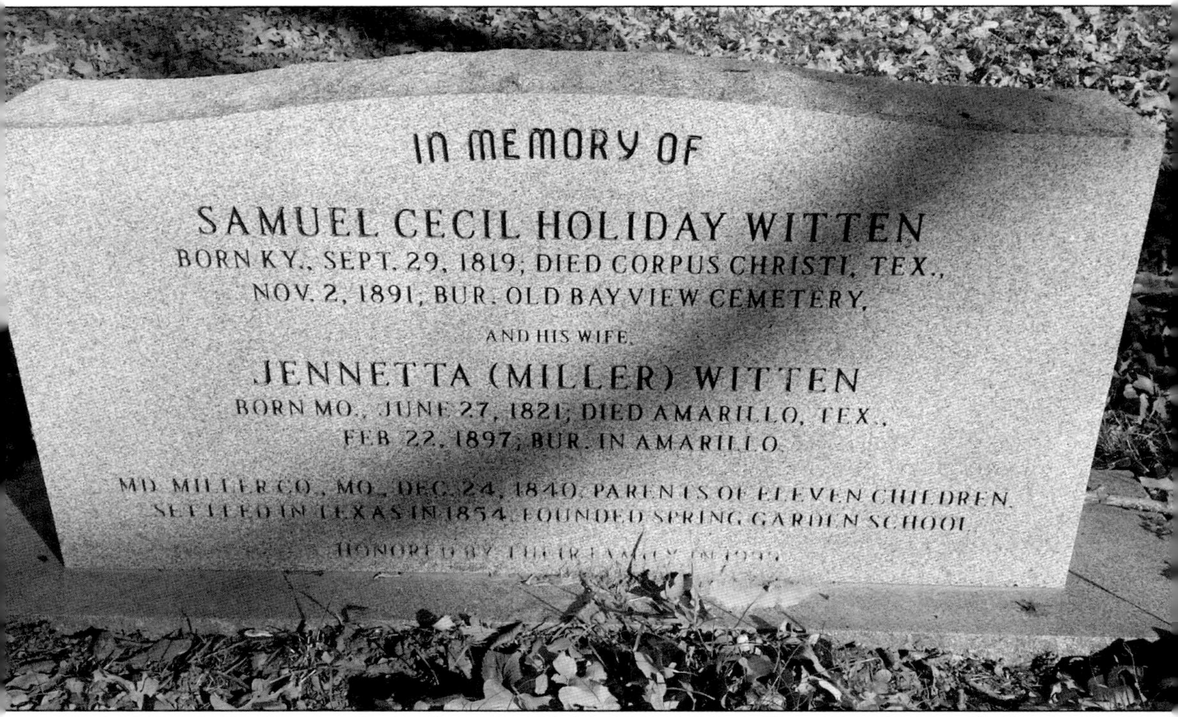

The Witten Cemetery is located on part of the former Witten homestead, just off of Jackson Court in the Brook Meadows neighborhood. Samuel C.H. Witten's son William, who died in 1857, was the first to be buried in this plot, and Witten made the land surrounding his son's grave a family cemetery. Ironically, even though there is a memorial stone honoring Witten and his wife in Witten Cemetery, Samuel Witten is buried in Corpus Christi, and his wife, Jennetta (Miller) Witten, is buried in Amarillo. Unlike many of the pioneer cemeteries in Texas that have vanished over the years, history has not forgotten the Witten Cemetery. In 1981, it was awarded a Texas Historical Marker, and in 2004, Eagle Scout Andrew Sylvester marked several of the unmarked graves. (Courtesy of Mark Fadden.)

Lilburn Colley was the grandson of Dr. Lilburn Colley, namesake of the city of Colleyville. (Courtesy of Tarrant County College Heritage Room.)

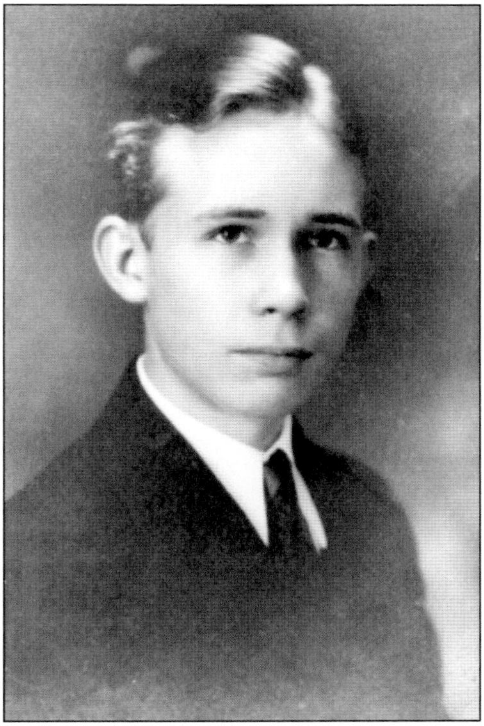

Mary Gulledge poses with five children. Joining her, standing in a barnyard on Bransford Road, are, from left to right, Cecil Hill, Sybol Hill, J.E. McCain, Juanita McCain, and Arnita McCain. (Courtesy of Tarrant County College Heritage Room.)

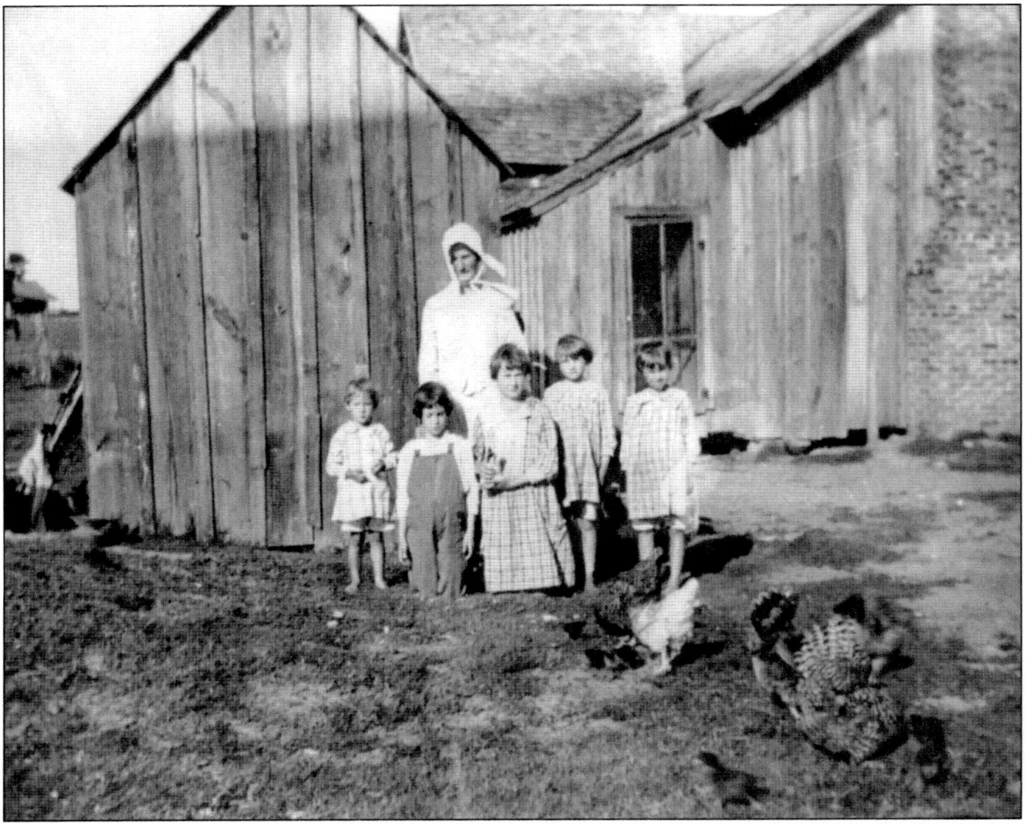

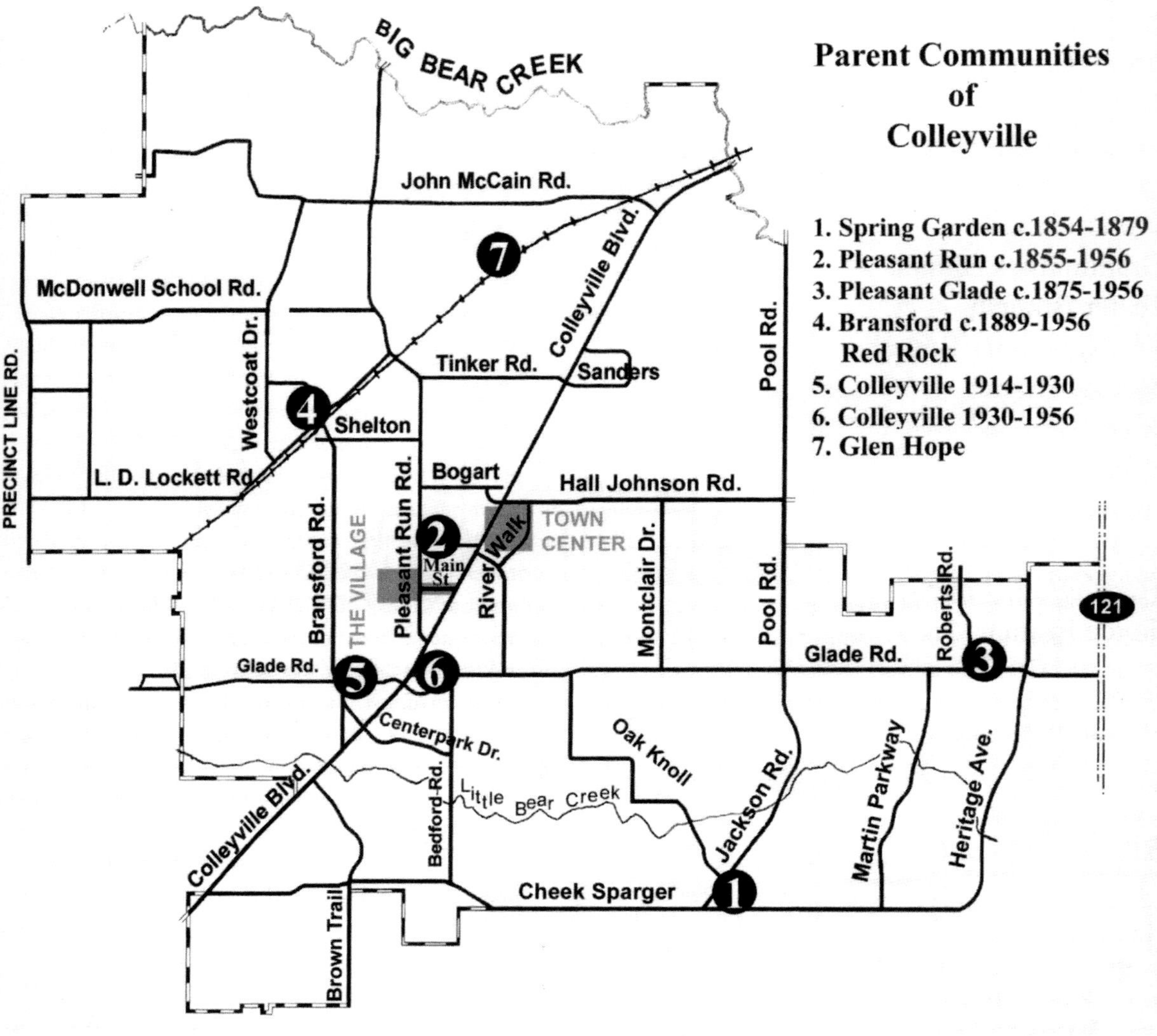

This map of the parent communities that existed before the City of Colleyville was incorporated in 1956 shows present-day roads, allowing today's history seekers to see exactly where these communities once existed. Note that the towns of Red Rock and Glen Hope, which are on this map, are generally not included in the list of parent communities. Glen Hope existed on a section of the Cotton Belt rail line where there were double tracks. As the trains moving in different directions often met there, it was a brief stop for travelers and railroad workers to get a hearty meal or warm conversation from the settlers. Red Rock, which would later become Bransford after the Bransford Post Office moved there, started off as a gravel pit where railroad workers got the gravel to repair failing rail beds or create new ones along the Cotton Belt line. (Courtesy of Colleyville Historical Preservation Committee.)

Two

Parent Communities

Before the city was incorporated in 1956, several different parent communities sprang up in the area. These parent communities were clustered near the creeks that crisscrossed the area, including Little Bear Creek and its many tributaries, often named for the family that owned the land that it crossed. To the first residents of these communities, the waters from these creeks and tributaries were the lifeblood of the community, as they were the only source of water before wells could be dug. A very close second was the need for a church, school, or store to draw residents into their community, to have a place where they could worship, provide an education for their children, or conduct business.

Spring Garden (1855–1875), which is located just north of present-day Bedford, was the first of these communities to be formed by Samuel C.H. Witten. It was named for Witten's hometown in Missouri. A bit of mystery surrounds how Pleasant Run (1855–1956) came to be named. Some claim that it was named for the tributary that flowed through it; others said it was named after Pleasant Run, Ohio. Legend has it that Pleasant Glade (1875–1956), which existed near the corner of present-day Glade and Roberts Roads, was named by early settlers who looked out over the vast prairie before them and declared, "This is a pleasant glade. Let's stop here." Besides being pleasant to the eyes, the land was highly productive; the farmers living there raised prize-winning produce for more than 50 years. Both the Bransford community (1889–1956) and its post office were named for Felix Grundy Bransford, a veteran of the Mexican War who lived in the area in the 1870s. The Colleyville parent community was actually considered two separate entities. The first, known as Early Colleyville (1914–1930), existed at the corner of present-day Glade and Bransford Roads along the major thoroughfare through town. Then, in 1930, that thoroughfare was straightened to present-day State Highway 26, causing Colleyville (1930–1956) to shift its location to be along that route.

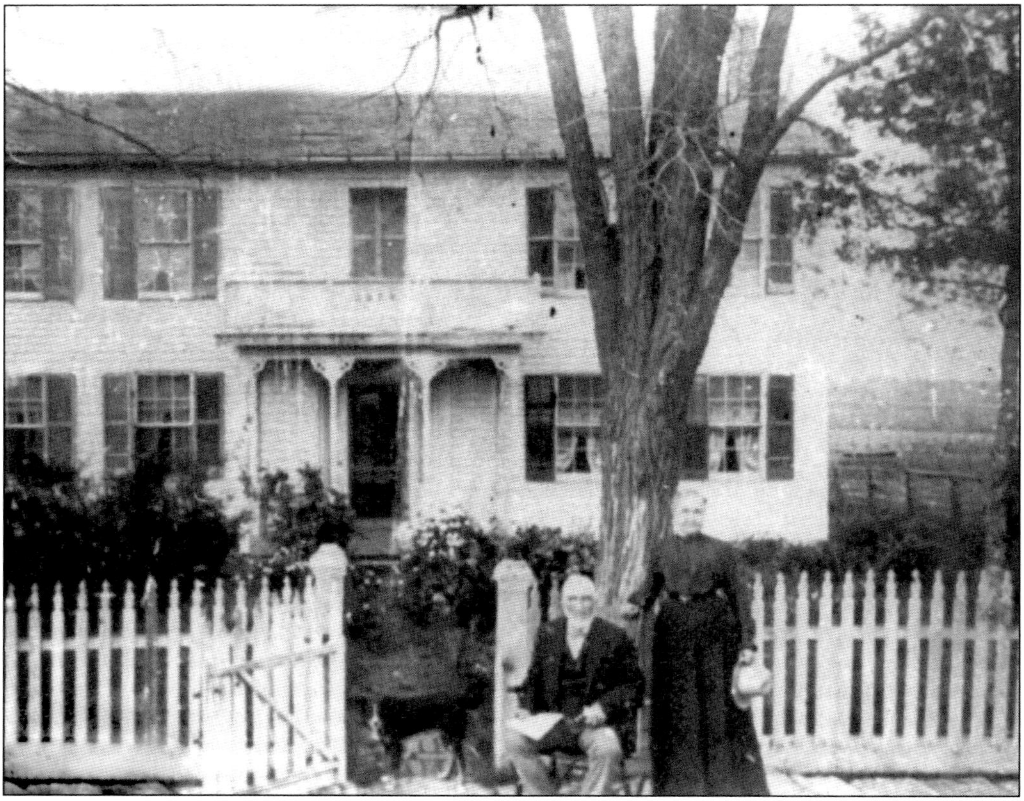

Samuel C.H. Witten and Jennetta Witten are pictured in front of their house just off of present-day Jackson Road in the Spring Garden community, which he founded. A large residence for its time, it housed the Wittens and their 11 children, was made of milled boards, and featured windows and a central hallway for ventilation. (Courtesy of Colleyville Historical Preservation Committee.)

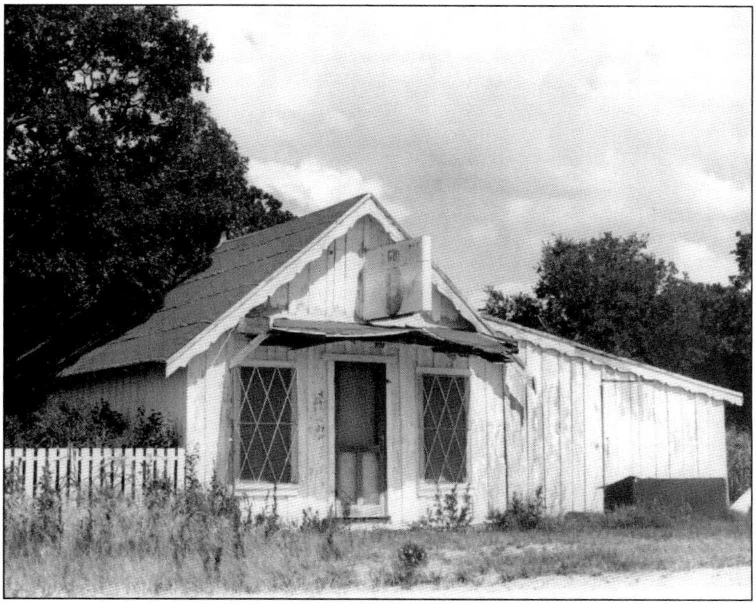

This is Board's Grocery Store, which was the last remnant of the Old Union Community, located near the Colleyville parent communities. (Courtesy of Tarrant County College Heritage Room.)

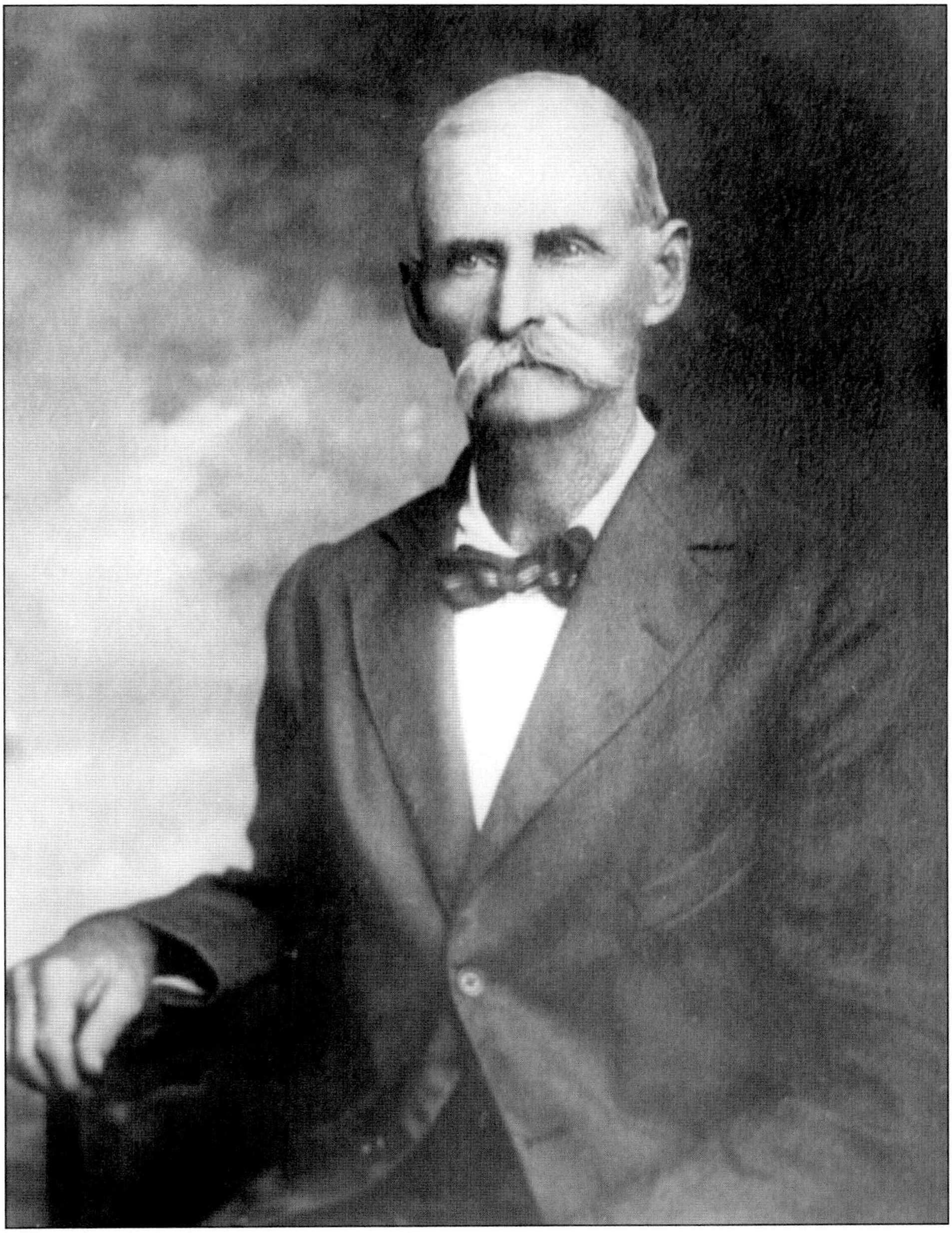

Born in 1846, William Burgess Cheek and his wife came to Spring Garden in 1869. With business partner Lon Weddle, Cheek operated gravel pits and helped build many area roads, such as Brown Trail and Cheek-Sparger Road. He was also an ordained Methodist minister who loved to walk with his family to the Glade Baptist Church for Sunday service. On land along present-day Heritage Avenue, William Cheek built a log house and then converted it to a frame house. Cheek-Sparger Road also ran through the Cheek property. Originally, the road ran east to F.M. 157, but the land was too low, and the bridges would flood. Cheek allowed the road to be turned up north to Glade Road on his property. In 1990, this north/south portion was renamed Heritage Avenue, and the east/west portion of Cheek-Sparger Road from Heritage Avenue to F.M. 157 was reconstructed and is still called Cheek-Sparger Road. Cheek died in 1930. (Courtesy of Tarrant County College Heritage Room.)

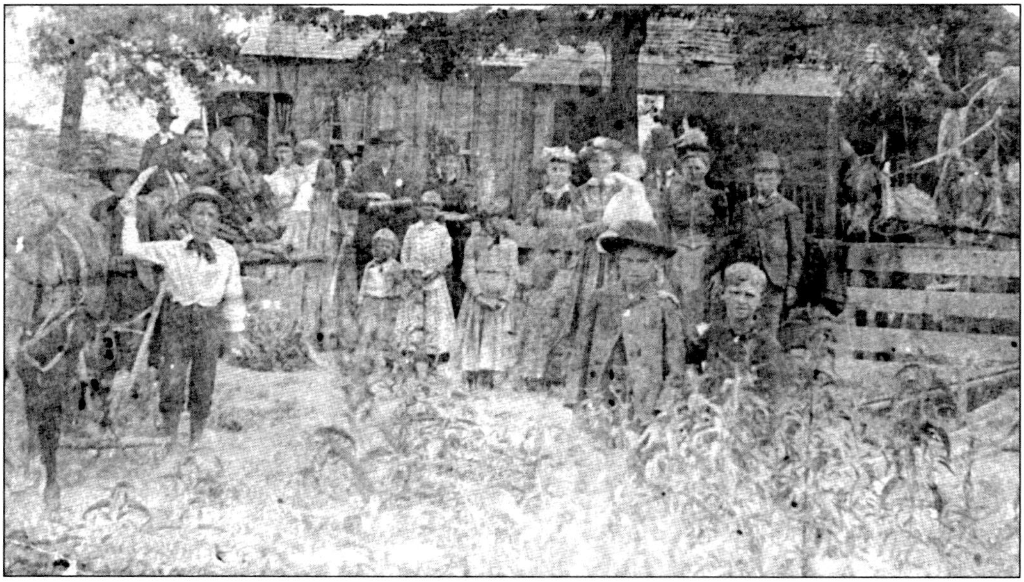

In the late 1800s, the Sparger family farm was located south of Little Bear Creek. Of Samuel and Susan Sparger's 12 children, three lived in the Colleyville area at this time. Generations of the Sparger family raised cattle and crops on the land until it was developed into the Tara Plantation neighborhood along Cheek-Sparger Road. (Courtesy of Tarrant County College Heritage Room.)

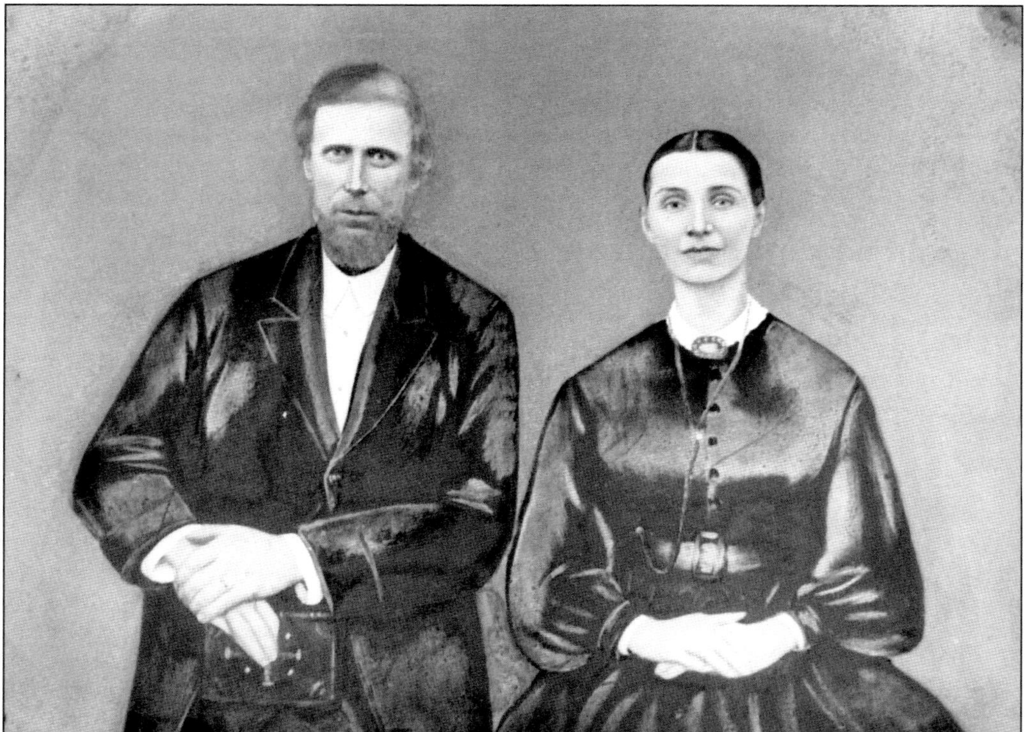

Harvey Sparger is seen in this portrait with his wife, Mary. (Courtesy of Tarrant County College Heritage Room.)

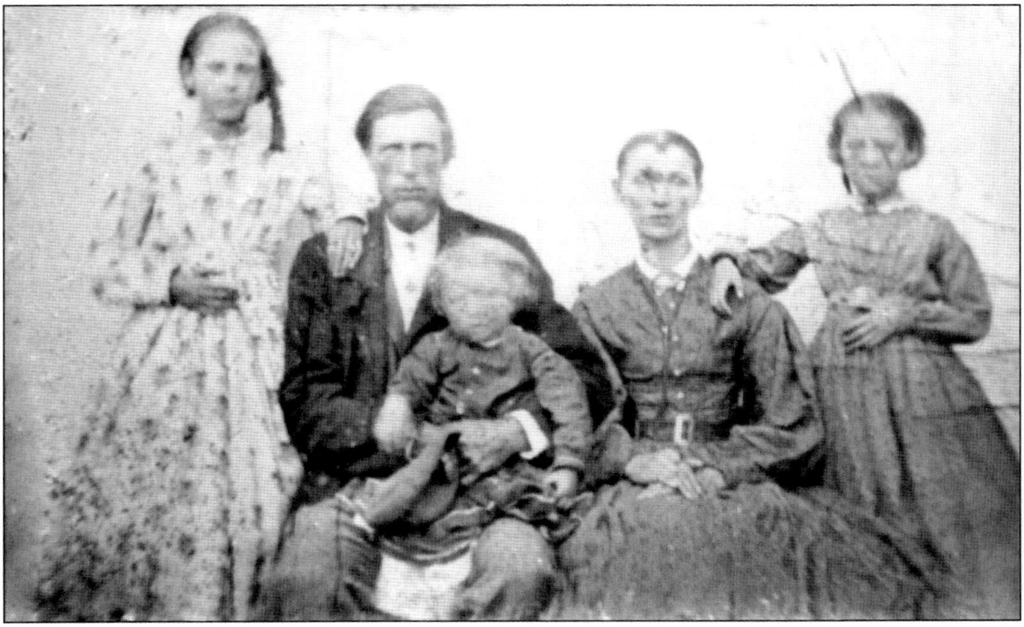

Seen here is the Harvey R. Sparger family. In 1879, Harvey "Harv" Richard Sparger bought several hundred acres in Spring Garden from his brother for $500. The original house on the property was a log cabin. Harv added a frame room and kitchen, complete with a dog run. Present-day Sparger Park, located on Bedford Road, sits on part of the Sparger family land. (Courtesy of Tarrant County College Heritage Room.)

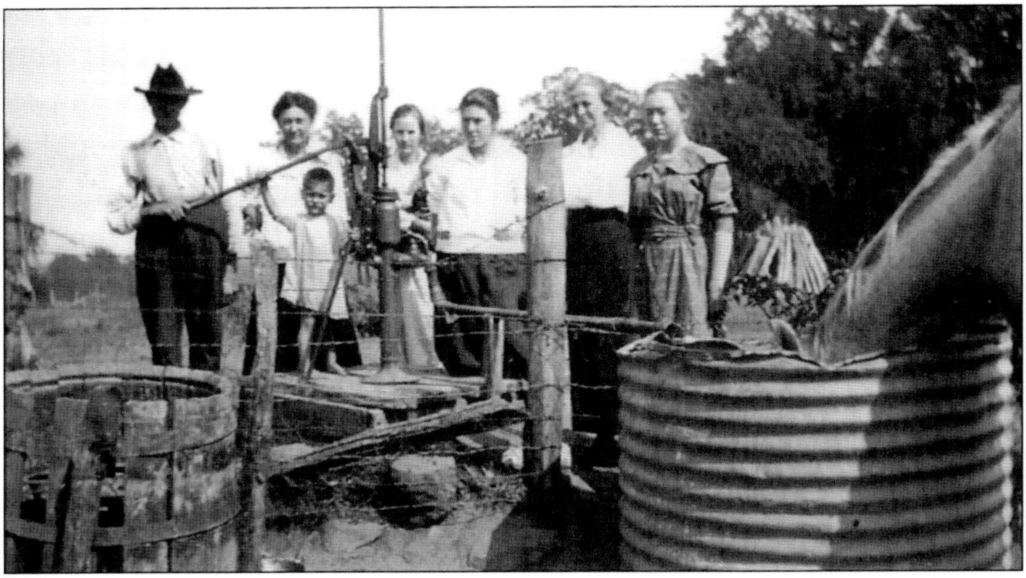

The Sparger "waterhole" was used to water the horses and cattle on the farm. The waterhole was fed by a well with a hand pump. Pictured here are, from left to right, Samuel Hamilton Sparger, Emily Prather Sparger, Cletus Sparger, Pearl Sparger, Kate Bailey, Leona Cavender, and Annie Smith. (Courtesy of Colleyville Historical Preservation Committee.)

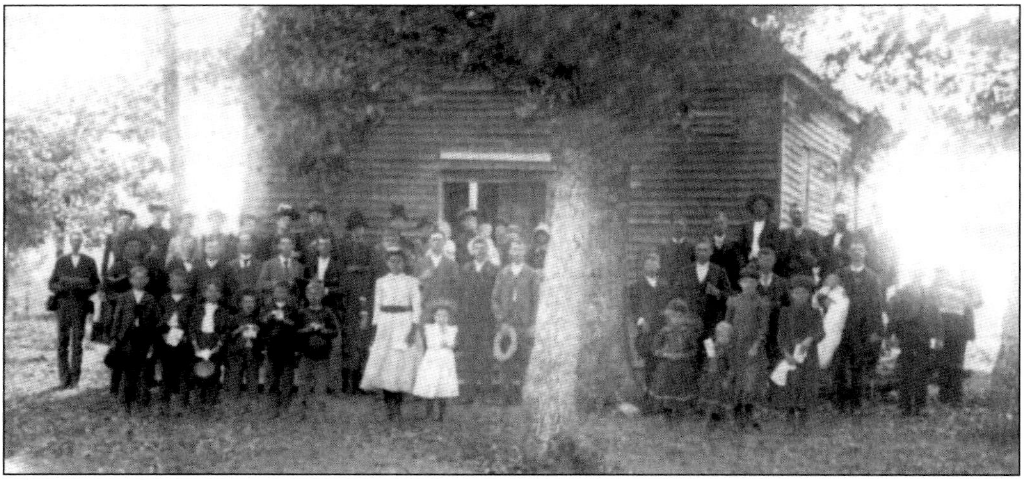

This group photograph was taken in front of Oak Grove Methodist Church. Known throughout the community as a spiritual man, Harv Sparger was a staunch Methodist who took his family to several area churches before deciding to build a church in Bedford in 1886. Together with M.D. Arthur and J.F. Moody, Sparger purchased two acres of land for $15 per acre and built the Oak Grove Methodist Church. (Courtesy of Colleyville Historical Preservation Committee.)

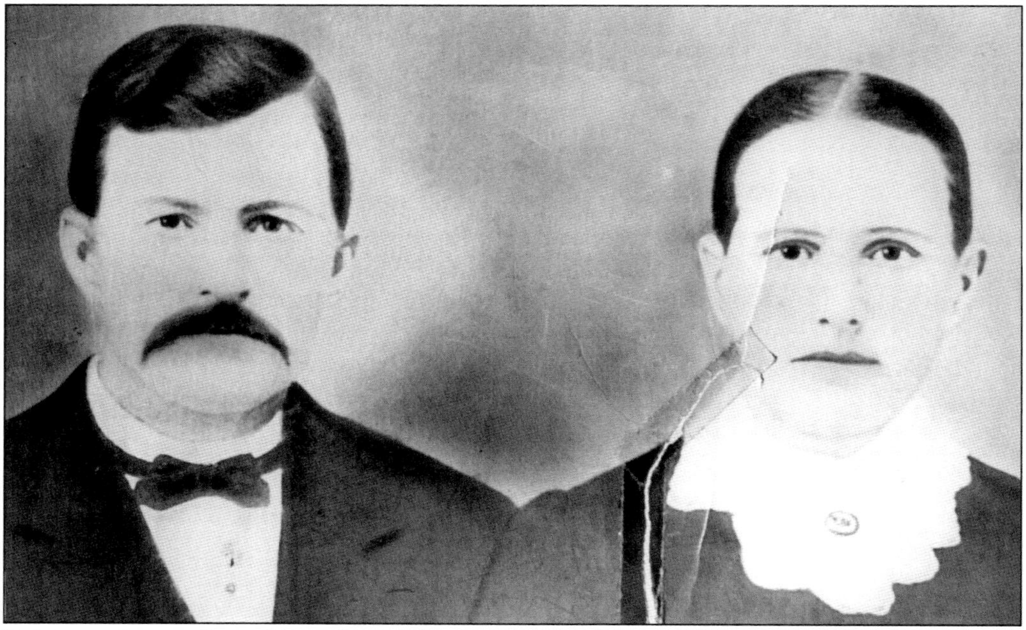

Robinson Crusoe Reynolds and his wife, Annie (Miers) Reynolds, moved to the Pleasant Run community from the town of Renner, Texas, located in Dallas County, in 1902. Together, they had nine sons and one daughter and bought 179 acres of land along present-day State Highway 26, which Rob farmed until his death in 1928. During World War I, the telephone exchange for the Pleasant Run area was housed in the front room of the Reynolds house. Several of the sons married and raised families in the Pleasant Run community, and descendants of the family live in the Colleyville area today. Most of the Reynolds farmland was sold off to develop the present-day Ross Downs subdivision, but several street names, such as Frances Lane, Kyle Court, Reynolds Drive, and Wallace Lane, bear the names of Rob and Annie's 10 children. (Courtesy of Tarrant County College Heritage Room.)

Lewis Cass White lived in Pleasant Run for most of his life. He was born on May 11, 1848, in Grundy County and moved to Texas with his family in October 1858. He and his wife, Nancy, were charter members of the Pleasant Run Baptist Church, and White remained a church leader for more than 50 years. He died on February 14, 1929. (Courtesy of Tarrant County College Heritage Room.)

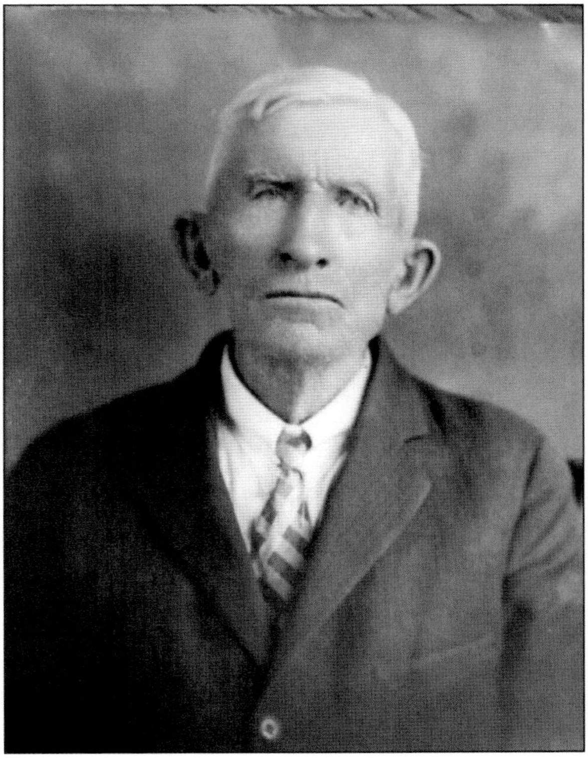

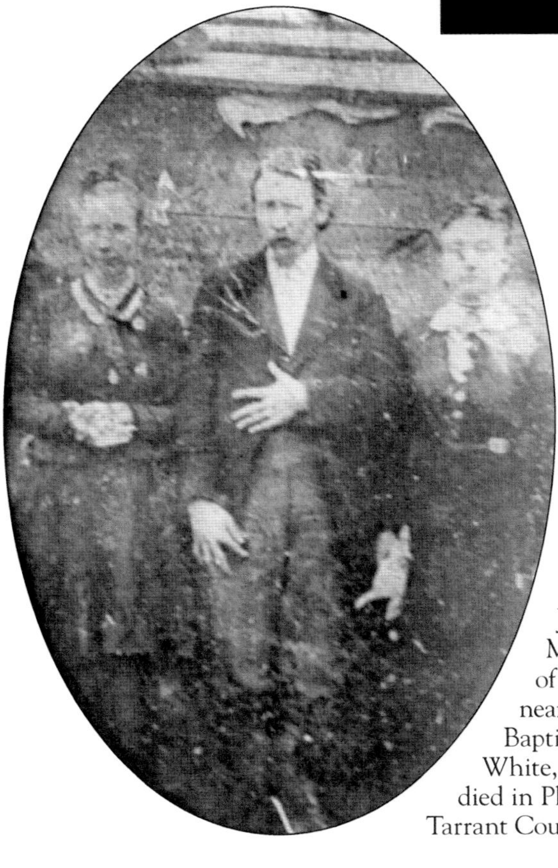

Posing here are, from left to right, Nancy Jane (Grimes) White, Robert Grimes, and Mary Grimes. These siblings were members of the pioneering Grimes family that settled in nearby Keller. Robert K. Grimes was a well-known Baptist minister. Nancy, who married Lewis Cass White, was born in Tennessee on July 1, 1847, and died in Pleasant Run on April 10, 1889. (Courtesy of Tarrant County College Heritage Room.)

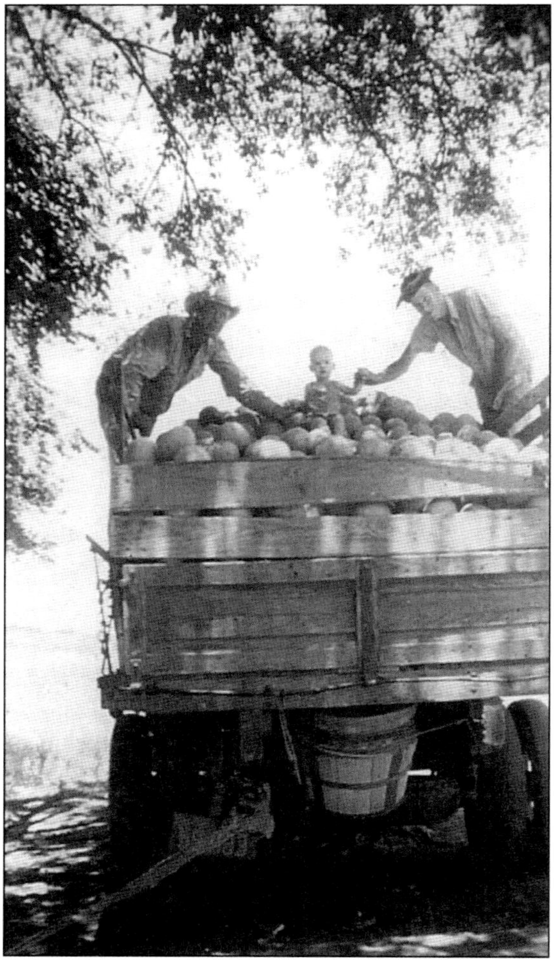

The McCains, early settlers, became a prominent family not only in the parent community of Pleasant Run, but also once Colleyville became an incorporated city. The McCain farm, which was once part of William Dunn's 320-acre property, was a labor of love for several generations of the McCain family. They raised many types of vegetables, and the farm also had a large dewberry patch and a grape vineyard. The photograph at left, taken around 1940, shows Joy McCain sitting on a truckload of cantaloupe that was probably bound for the markets in Fort Worth. Holding her hands are Ollie McCain and Ford Reynolds. The photograph below, also taken around 1940, shows that preparing produce for market was a McCain family affair. (Both, courtesy of Colleyville Historical Preservation Committee.)

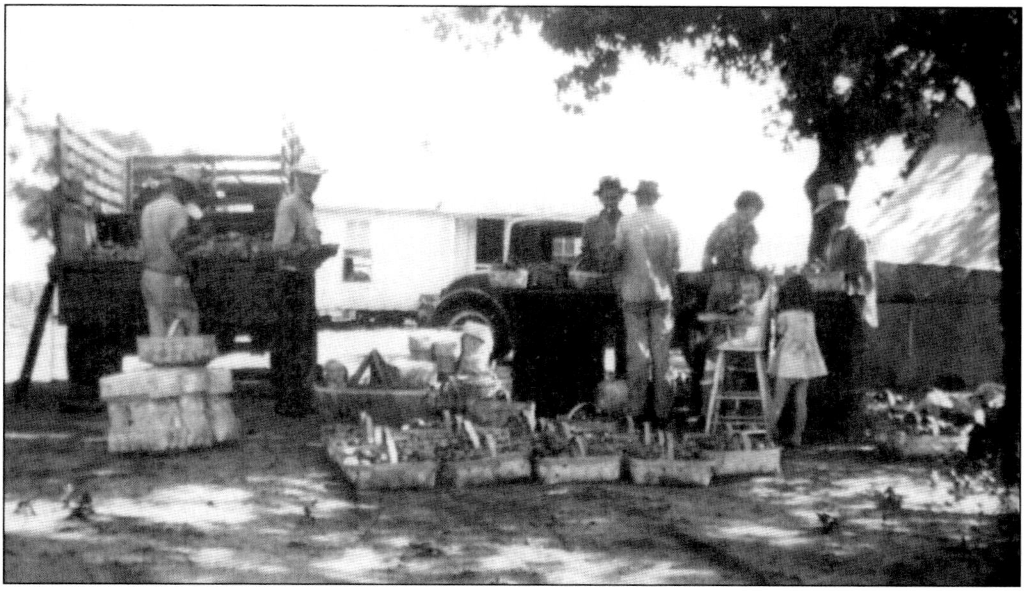

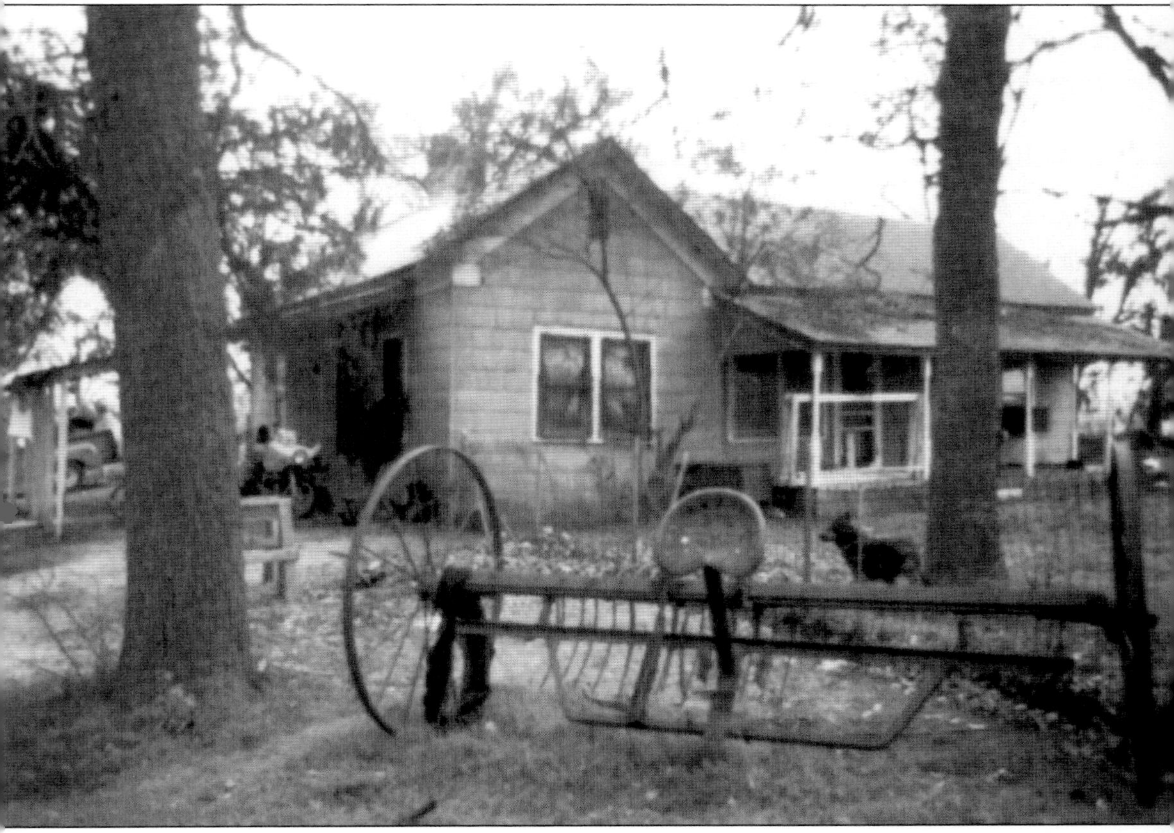

James and Mollie Forbes, pioneers of Pleasant Run, made not one, but two perilous journeys to Texas in the late 1800s. In 1877, they joined a 15-wagon train and made the two-month-long journey from Tennessee to neighboring Grapevine, Texas. After staying a short time in Grapevine, they trekked back to Tennessee to retrieve their belongings, including their children, and made the hazardous journey back to Texas. This time, in 1887, they settled in the northeast section of current-day Colleyville, on a farm that provided all that was necessary for them to live. This house replaced the log cabin that the Forbes family first lived in on their Colleyville farm. (Courtesy of Colleyville Historical Preservation Committee.)

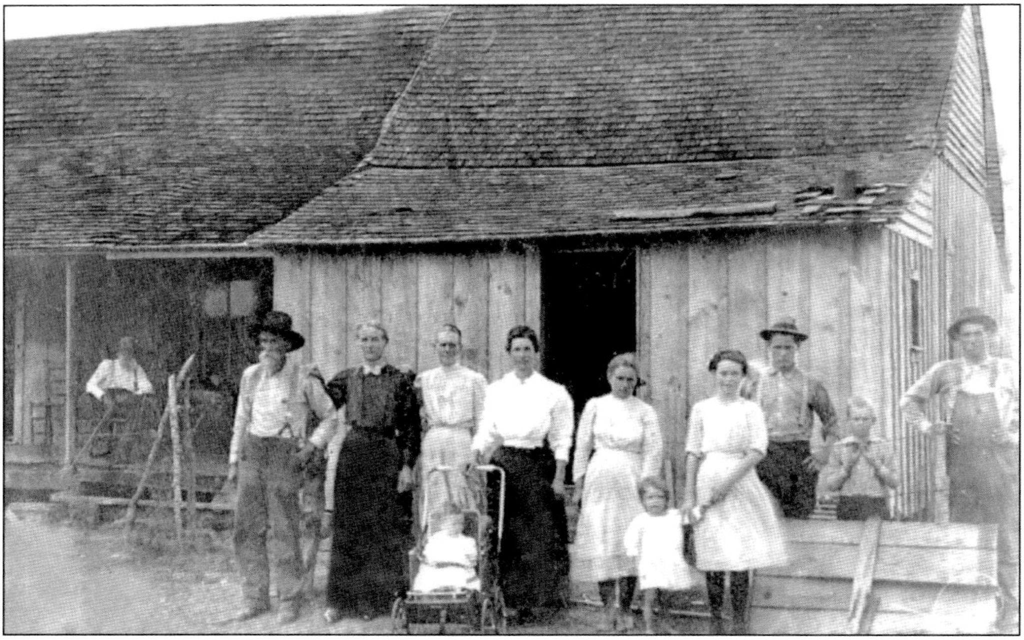

Calvin Crow's route to Colleyville was anything but a straight line. Born in 1848 near Dalton, Georgia, he and his first wife, Betty Margaret Bouldin, lived in Alabama and then Palo Pinto County, Texas, where Betty died. Crow then moved to Alabama, where he met and married Mary Jane Chambers in 1881. From Alabama, they moved to Spanish Fort, Texas, then to Oklahoma, and then finally to their farm in Pleasant Run. The Calvin Crow home is pictured above around 1910. Calvin Crow and Mary Jane (Chambers) Crow are seen at front left with members of their extended family. Erskin Crow, their son, had a four-room house (below) near the family farm. Posing below are, from left to right, Harold, William, E.J., and Floyd Crow, and R.K. Reynolds. (Both, courtesy of Colleyville Historical Preservation Committee.)

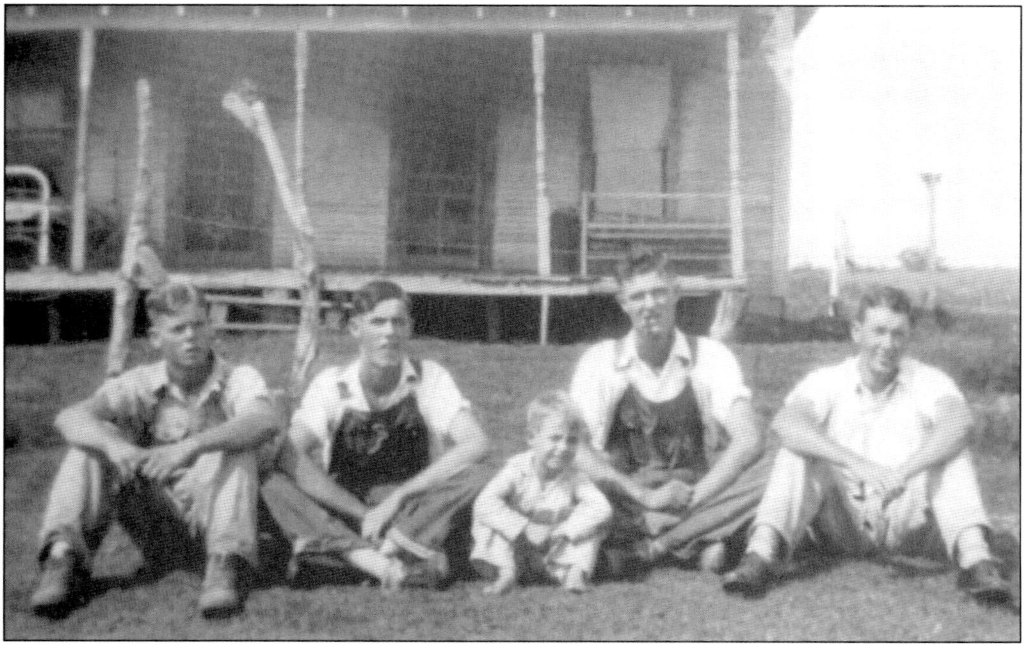

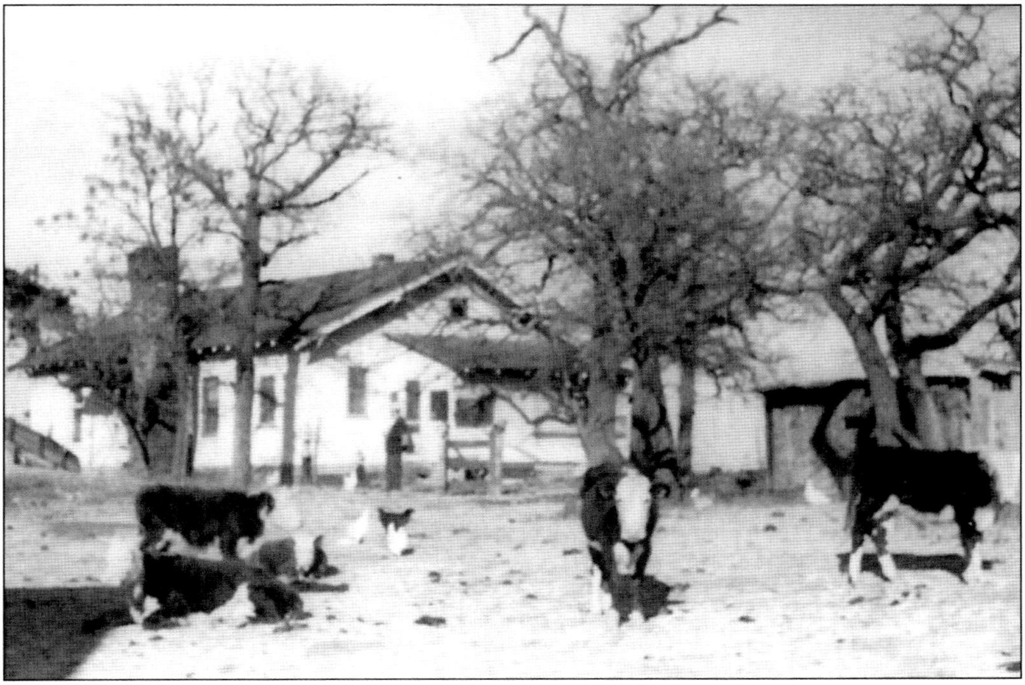

After running away at age 21 from his home country of Poland because he did not want to get drafted into the Russian army, Anton "Tony" Tirk arrived in the Port of Galveston in 1913. He made his way to Fort Worth, where he worked as a blacksmith. Tony met his future bride, Frances, at a Sokol picnic that celebrated gymnastics, and they were married soon after, in 1916. In 1924, they moved to a 150-acre farm at the southeast corner of present-day John McCain and Pleasant Run Roads. The house on the Tirk farm is pictured above. Shown below are, from left to right, Frances, Lydia, and their mother, Mrs. Tony Tirk, on the family's wagon. (Both, courtesy of Colleyville Historical Preservation Committee.)

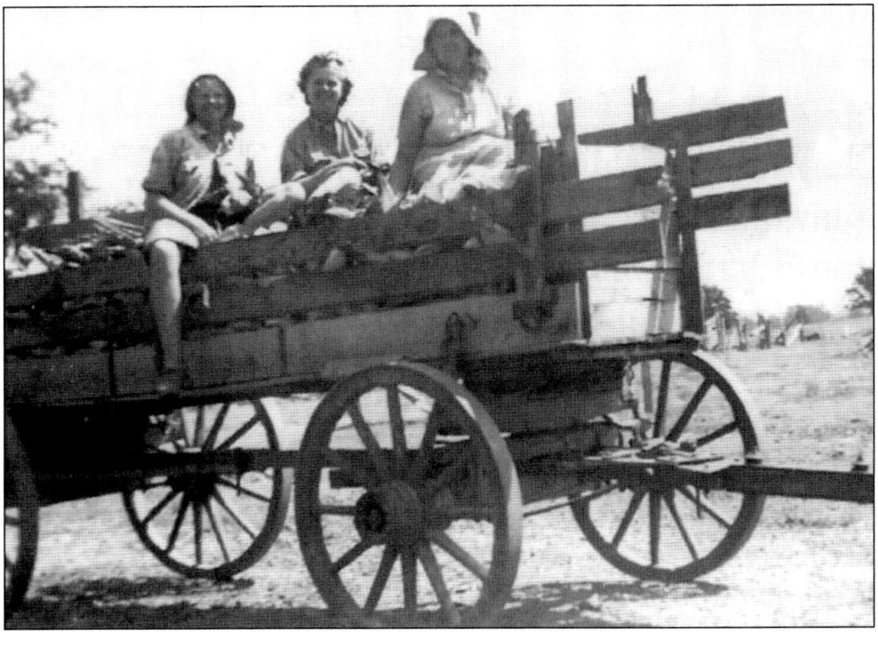

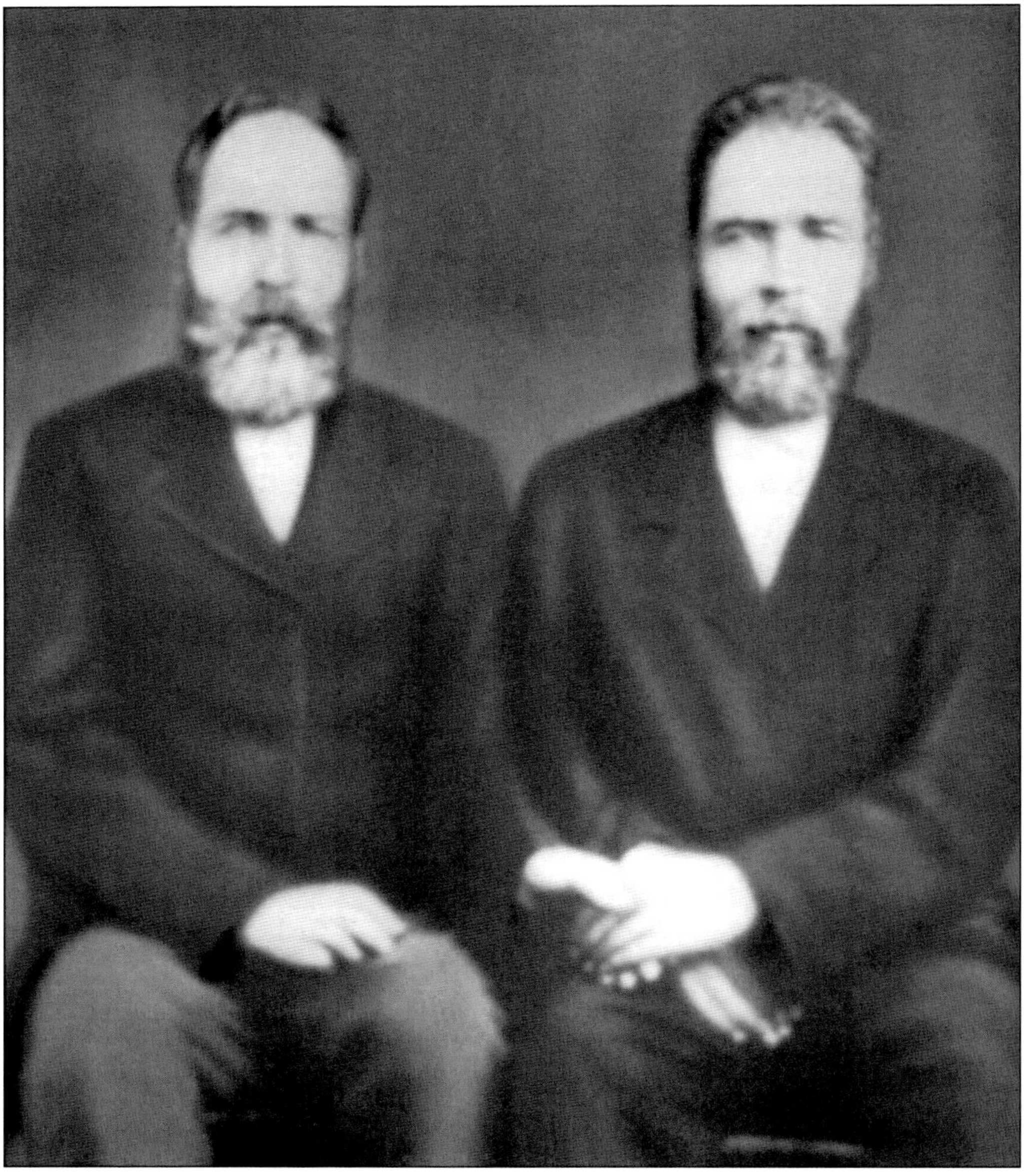

Ryan and Bryant Harrington, among the first settlers of Pleasant Glade, gave part of their land for the first school in the community. While serving as a Texas Ranger, Ryan Harrington helped recover Cynthia Ann Parker, who had been kidnapped as a child by a Comanche war band. Ryan's sons, Ryan and Bryant, built a house in 1906 along present-day Heritage Avenue near Glade Road. While generations of Harrington family members lived in the house and raised produce and animals on the surrounding farmland, the Harringtons were best known for their cantaloupes. Buyers would come from as far away as Missouri and Kansas to buy them. (Courtesy of Tarrant County College Heritage Room.)

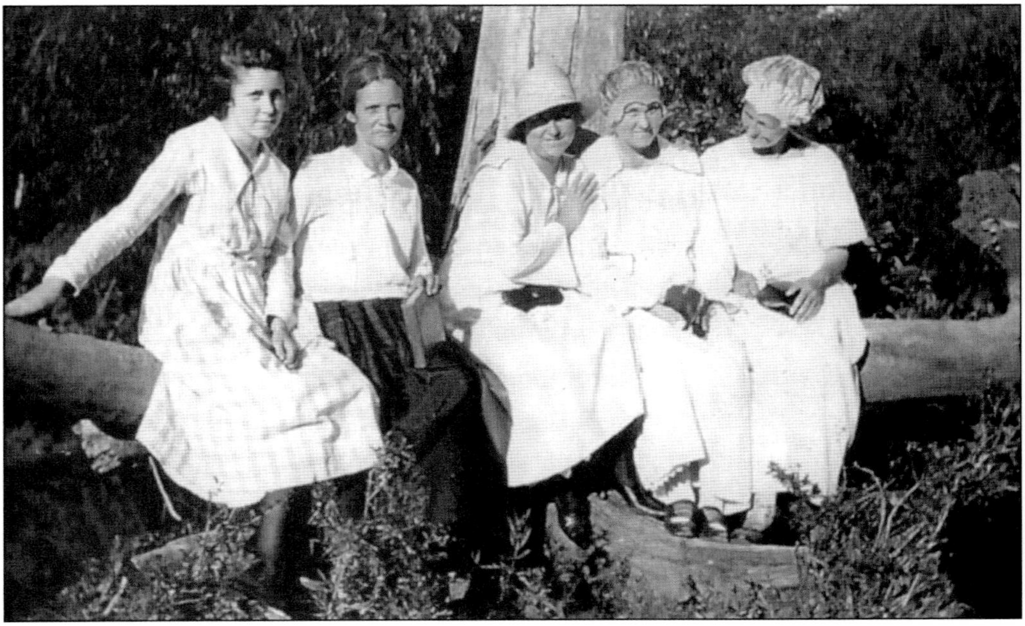

While Big Bear Creek forms the northern boundary of present-day Colleyville, Little Bear Creek is located in the southern part of the city. Once upon a time, it ran by the community of Pleasant Glade. During the long spells of hot temperatures, which could be counted on to arrive with every summer in North Texas, people would seek relief when they were not working at local shops, in businesses, or on the family farm. Swimming in Little Bear Creek and picnicking along its shady shores were two common ways that people survived the long, hot summers. Above, a group of ladies enjoy the day at Little Bear Creek. Pictured below are several family members picnicking along Little Bear Creek. (Both, courtesy of Colleyville Historical Preservation Committee.)

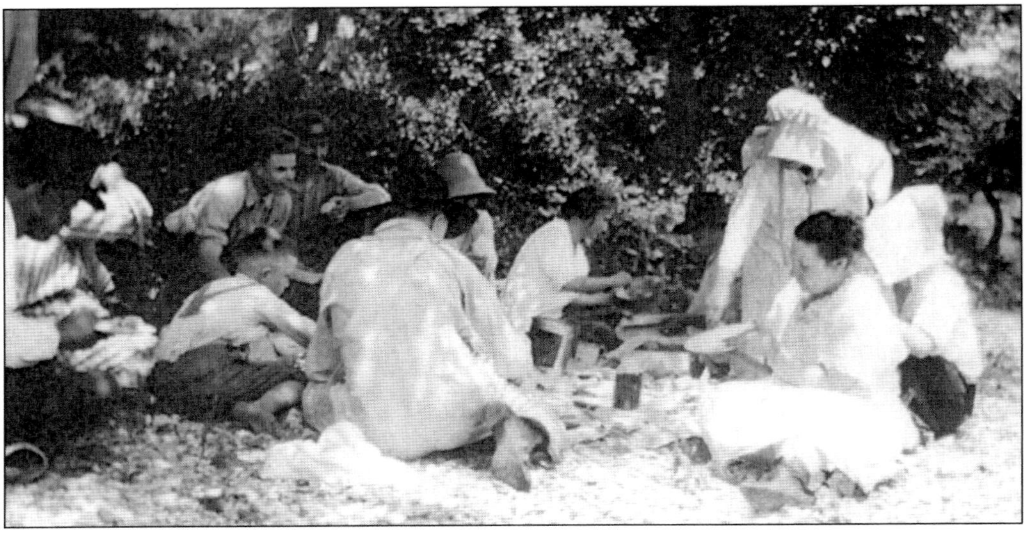

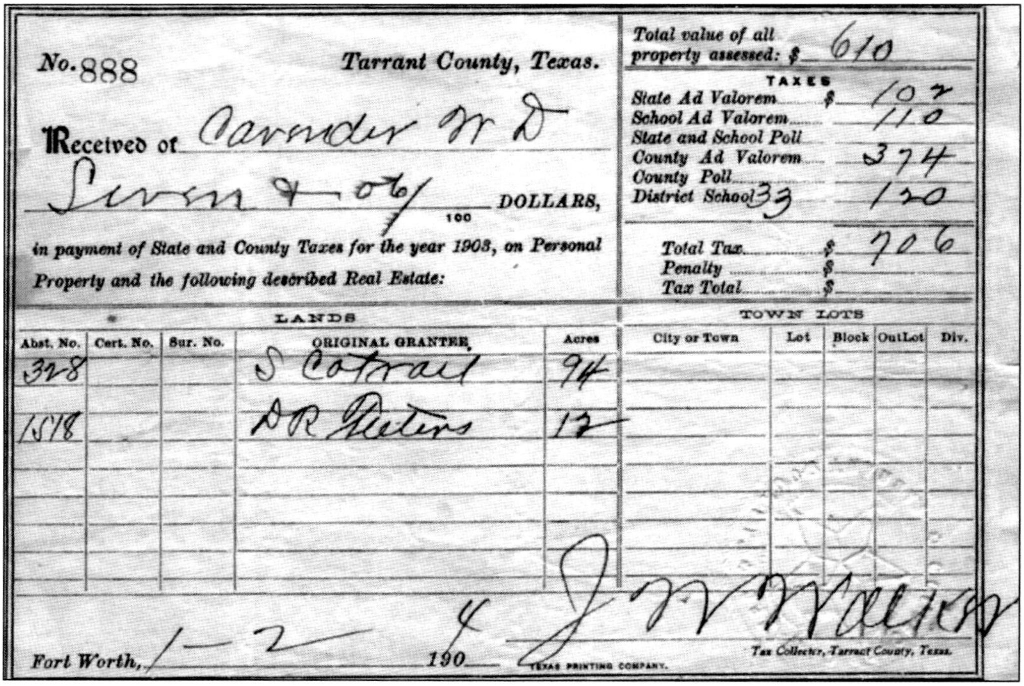

No. 888 Tarrant County, Texas.

Received of Cavender W D

Seven & 06/100 DOLLARS,

in payment of State and County Taxes for the year 1903, on Personal Property and the following described Real Estate:

Total value of all property assessed: $ 610

TAXES

State Ad Valorem $	107
School Ad Valorem	110
State and School Poll	
County Ad Valorem	374
County Poll	
District School 33	120
Total Tax $	706
Penalty $	
Tax Total $	

LANDS

Abst. No.	Cert. No.	Sur. No.	ORIGINAL GRANTEE	Acres
328			S Cotrail	94
1518			D R Peters	12

TOWN LOTS

City or Town	Lot	Block	OutLot	Div.

Fort Worth, 1-2 1904

J W Walker
Tax Collector, Tarrant County, Texas.

TEXAS PRINTING COMPANY.

William DeWitt "Witt" Cavender was born in Georgia and lived for a while in northern Arkansas before moving with his family to the Colleyville area in 1880. He married Leona Sparger on December 23, 1891, at the Oak Grove Methodist Church and purchased a 106-acre farm along present-day Glade Road in 1901. This 1903 tax bill shows that he owes $7.06 on that property. (Courtesy of Colleyville Historical Preservation Committee.)

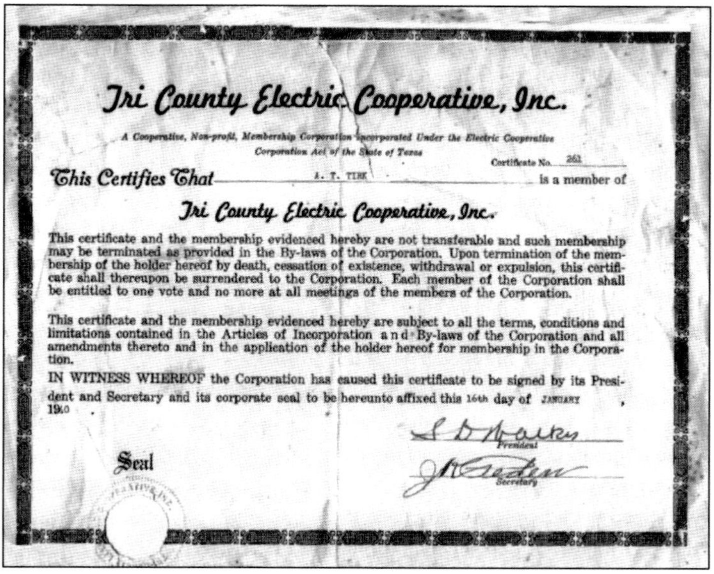

Tri County Electric Cooperative, Inc.

A Cooperative, Non-profit, Membership Corporation Incorporated Under the Electric Cooperative Corporation Act of the State of Texas

Certificate No. 262

This Certifies That A. T. TIRK is a member of

Tri County Electric Cooperative, Inc.

This certificate and the membership evidenced hereby are not transferable and such membership may be terminated as provided in the By-laws of the Corporation. Upon termination of the membership of the holder hereof by death, cessation of existence, withdrawal or expulsion, this certificate shall thereupon be surrendered to the Corporation. Each member of the Corporation shall be entitled to one vote and no more at all meetings of the members of the Corporation.

This certificate and the membership evidenced hereby are subject to all the terms, conditions and limitations contained in the Articles of Incorporation and By-laws of the Corporation and all amendments thereto and in the application of the holder hereof for membership in the Corporation.

IN WITNESS WHEREOF the Corporation has caused this certificate to be signed by its President and Secretary and its corporate seal to be hereunto affixed this 16th day of JANUARY 1940.

Seal

S D Walker
President

J M Graden
Secretary

Membership has its privileges. Electricity came to the pre-Colleyville area, along with most other rural areas in America, in 1936. The installation of electrical lines was done by the Works Progress Administration (WPA). In order to get service, people had to become members of a nonprofit corporation. This certificate of membership was issued to Tony Tirk in 1940. (Courtesy of Colleyville Historical Preservation Committee.)

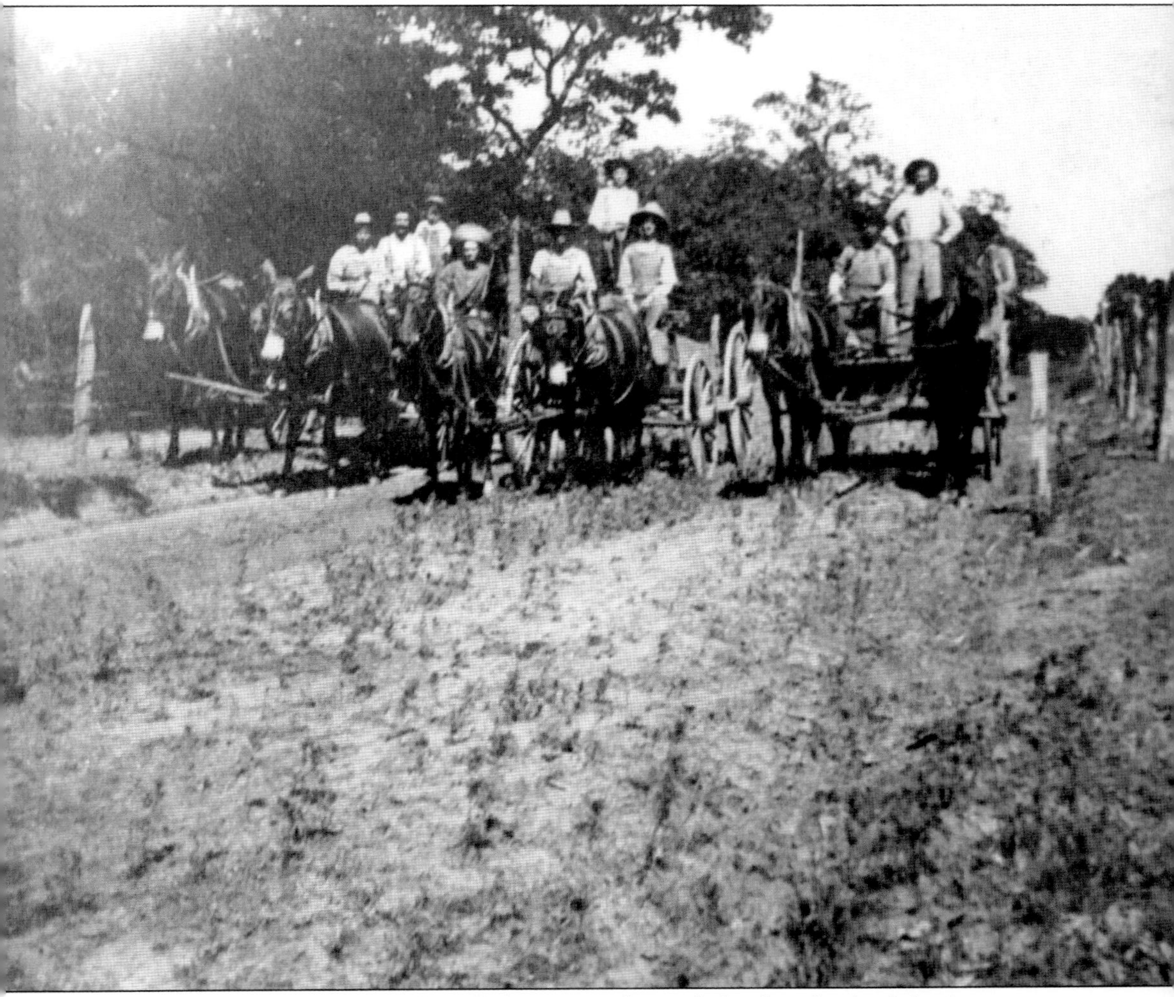

Local residents did not sit by and let all the progress be made for them by the federal government. Farmers, who for years had to haul their goods to markets in Grapevine and Fort Worth, grew tired of the long trips over rutted dirt roads. If farmers wanted to sell their vegetables and fruits in the produce markets in Dallas, the journey to the market, the time selling their goods, and the return trip home would take three days! Local farmers banded together to improve the dirt roads by hauling in gravel by horse-drawn wagons and manually spreading it by the shovelful. The invention of the "dumpboard" wagon made this task significantly easier for the farmers. Various boards that ran along the bottom of the wagon were removed one at a time, allowing the gravel to fall in small amounts as the wagon rolled down the road. (Courtesy of Tarrant County College Heritage Room.)

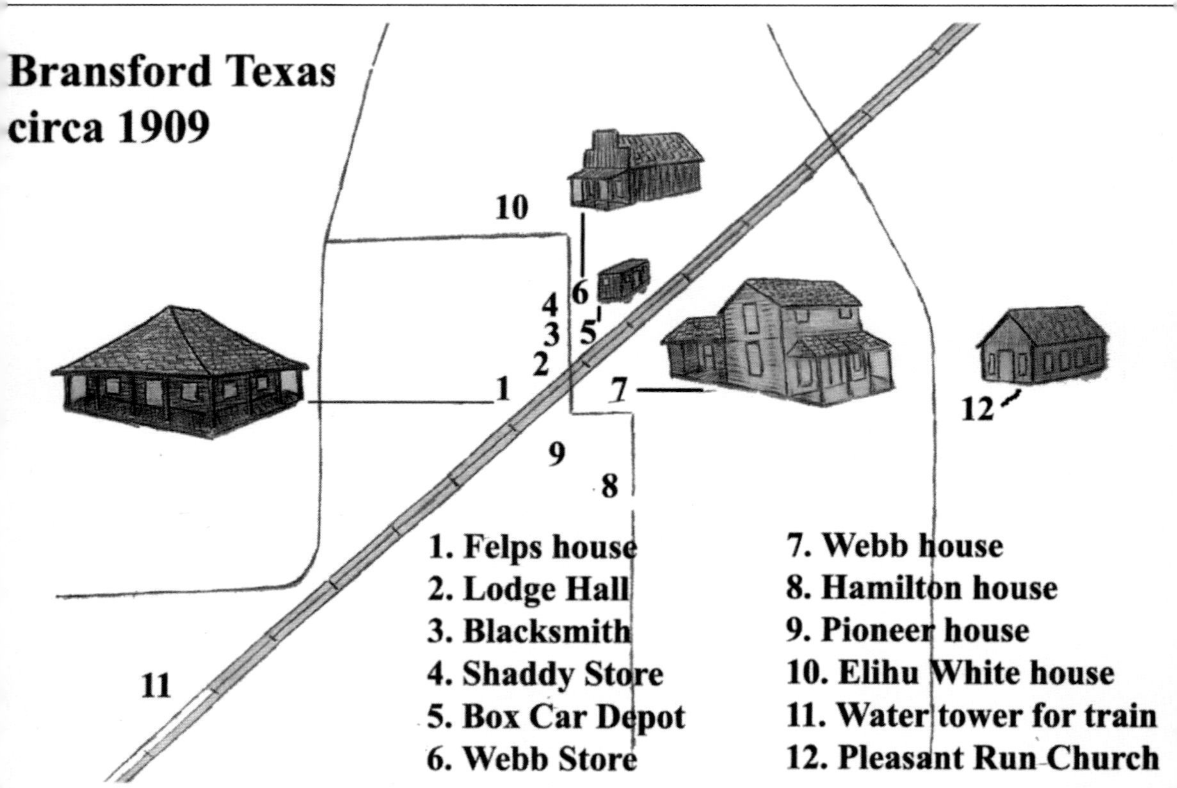

The Bransford community thrived in its location along the Cotton Belt rail line from 1889 until 1956, when it was incorporated into the City of Colleyville. Both the town and the post office were named for Felix Grundy Bransford, a veteran of the Mexican War who lived in the area in the 1870s. This map shows some of the business locations as well as a few prominent buildings and residences in Bransford in the late 1800s. Trains transported both freight and passengers along the Cotton Belt rail line through Bransford on a daily basis. Legend has it that when the St. Louis, Arkansas & Texas Railway purchased three parcels of land from Rev. Elihu Newton in 1887 to be used for a new Fort Worth extension of the railway (the present-day Cotton Belt line), a flag-stop depot, and a gravel pit, members of the Bransford community, which was named Red Rock at the time, loaded their buildings onto long skids and hauled them to their new location along the new railway. (Courtesy of Colleyville Historical Preservation Committee.)

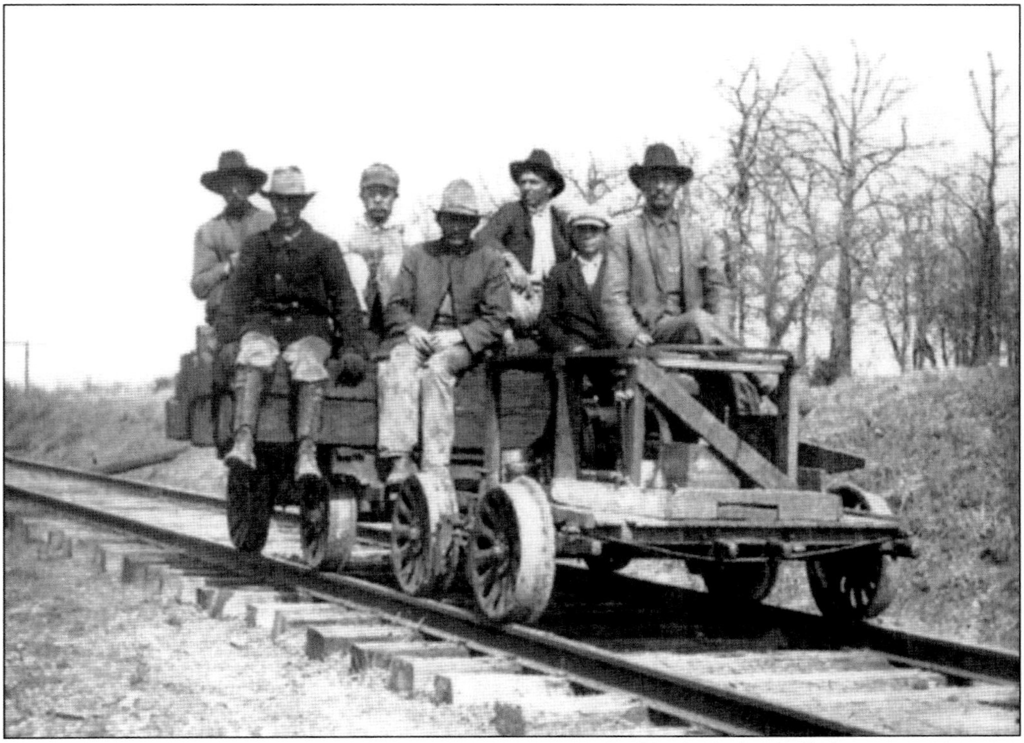

Arguably the busiest of all the parent communities, Bransford had a lodge hall, four general stores, four doctors, two blacksmith shops, a livery stable, and a depot, in addition to its post office. Two passenger trains stopped there daily. Tending to the tracks around 1909 is the "Cotton Belt Railroad Gang," with foreman John Rueben Webb at the front of the car. (Courtesy of Colleyville Historical Preservation Committee.)

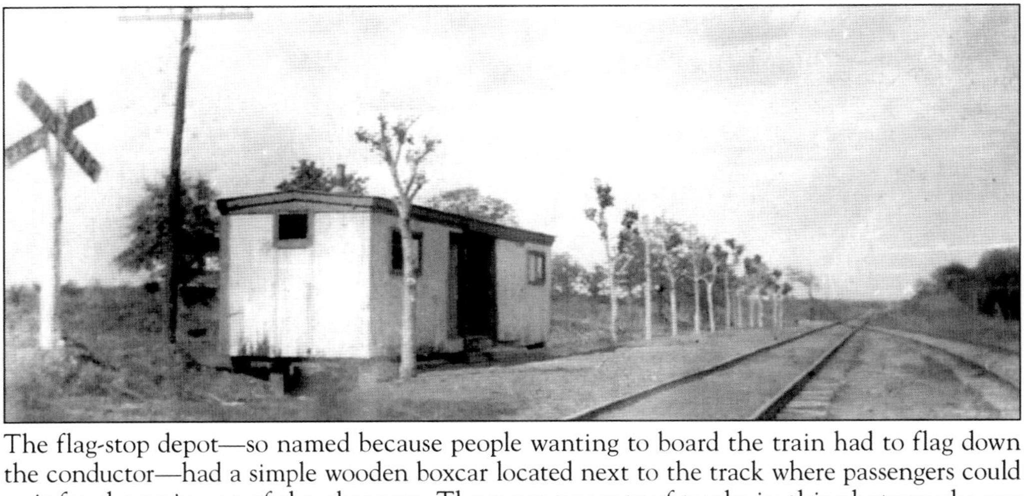

The flag-stop depot—so named because people wanting to board the train had to flag down the conductor—had a simple wooden boxcar located next to the track where passengers could wait for the train out of the elements. There are two sets of tracks in this photograph; one set was the main track, the other set led to the gravel pit. (Courtesy of Colleyville Historical Preservation Committee.)

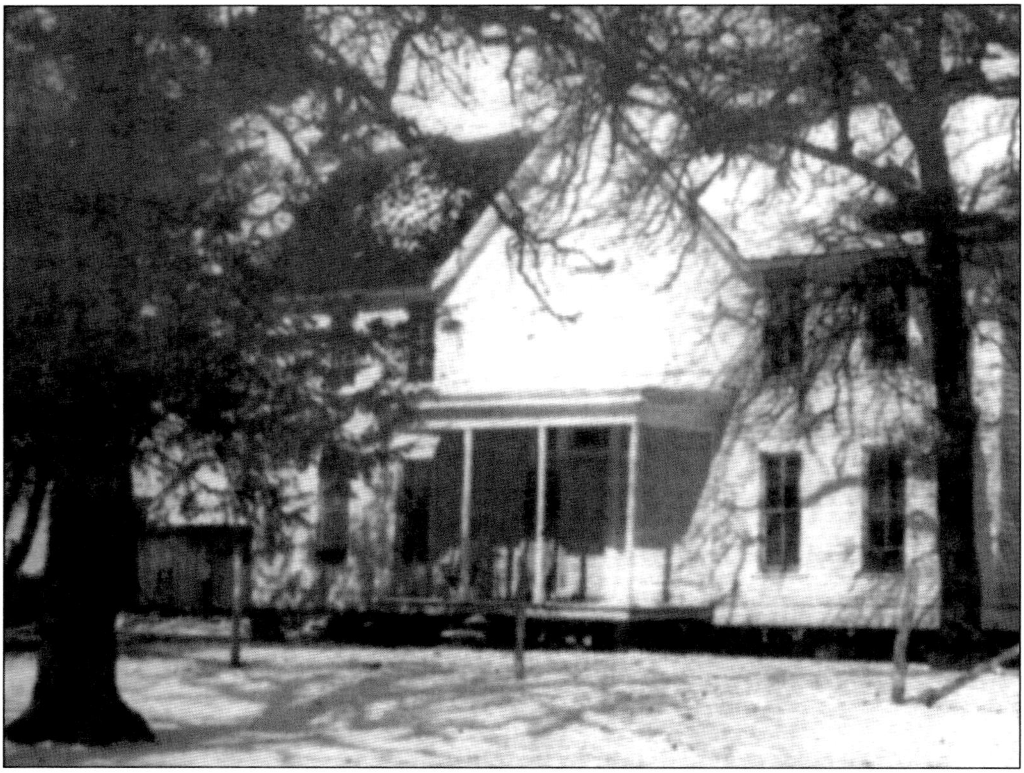

Whether it was its location along the railroad or the skills of its residents, or a little of both, the buildings in Bransford seemed to be a little ahead of their time. Many were board-wood houses, not log cabins like those found in other communities. Houses like the one Elihu Newton built in 1880 (above) were two-story homes that featured a porch and windows. It stood at 212 Oak Crest Hill Drive until 1964, when the owner replaced it with a brick house. Houses like the Felps house (below), complete with a wraparound porch and picket fence, were also a testament to the skilled craftsmanship of the era. (Both, courtesy of Colleyville Historical Preservation Committee.)

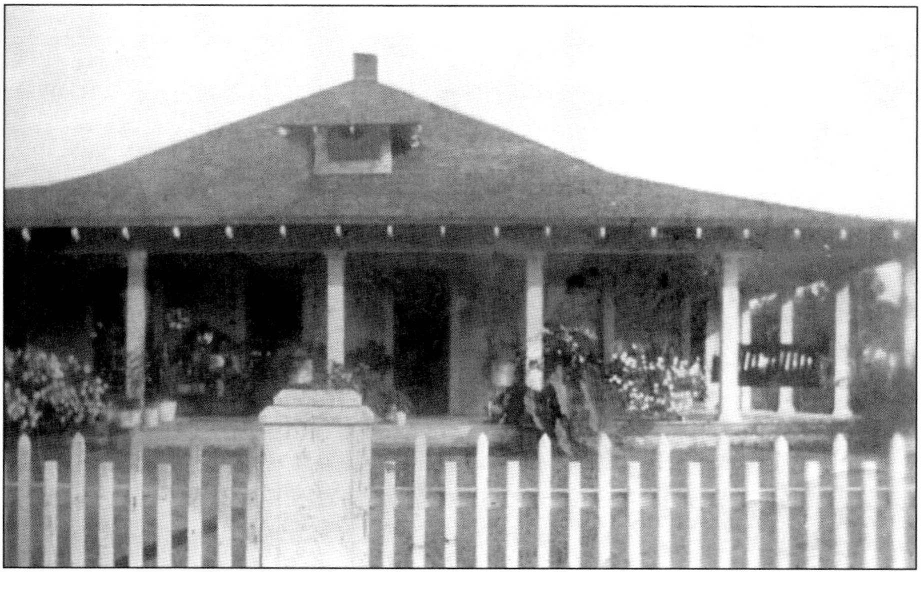

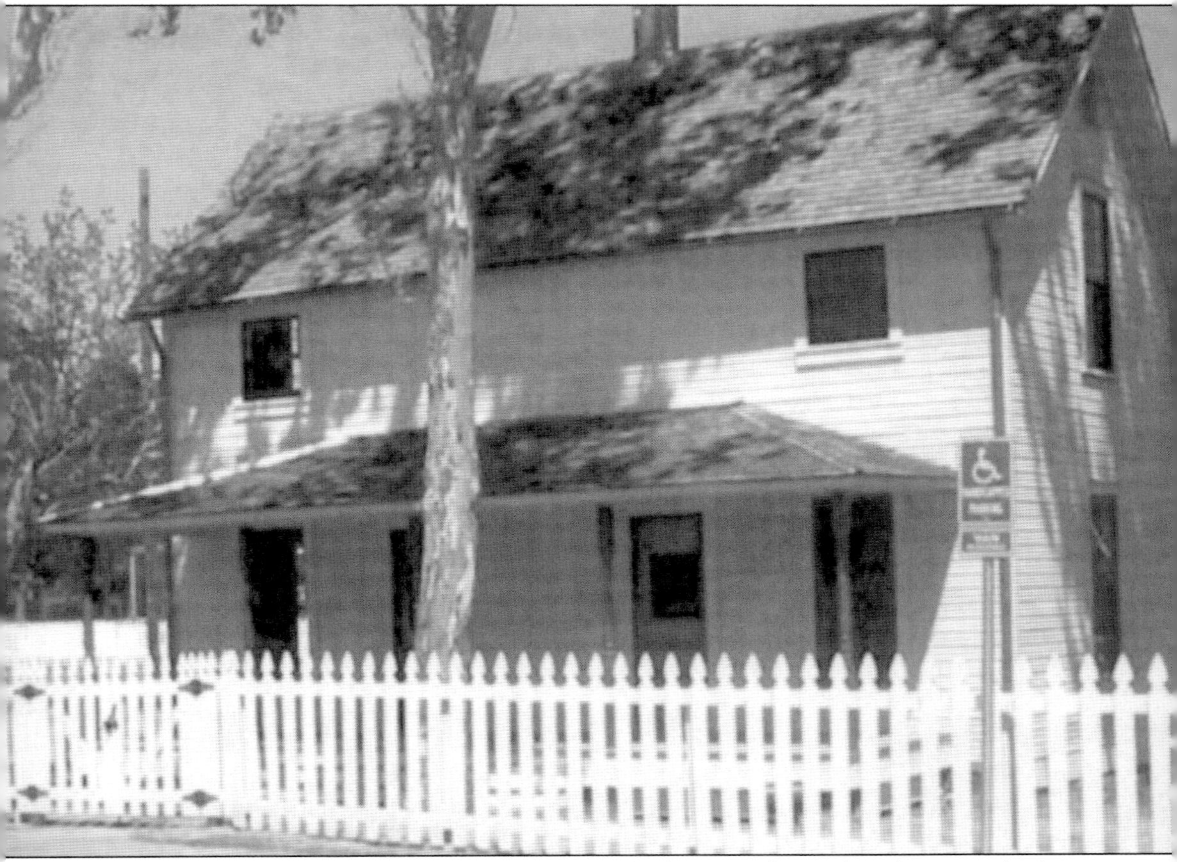

As one of the city's historical landmarks, the Webb house still stands today near the heart of the Bransford community. But, few probably realize that it stands not just as a reminder of Bransford, but also as proof of neighbors helping each other. John Rueben Webb and his wife, Orpha, came to Bransford in 1895. Webb was a jack of all trades; he worked at the gravel pit and then as the railroad section foreman before opening the Webb General Store in 1914. In the fall of 1913, a fire broke out at their home, and the only thing that was saved was the family's prized organ. (It still sits in the restored Webb house today.) While the Webbs stayed with neighbors, everyone in the community helped to rebuild their house, and it was completed in just a few weeks. Shown here is the restored Webb house around 1920. (Courtesy of Colleyville Historical Preservation Committee.)

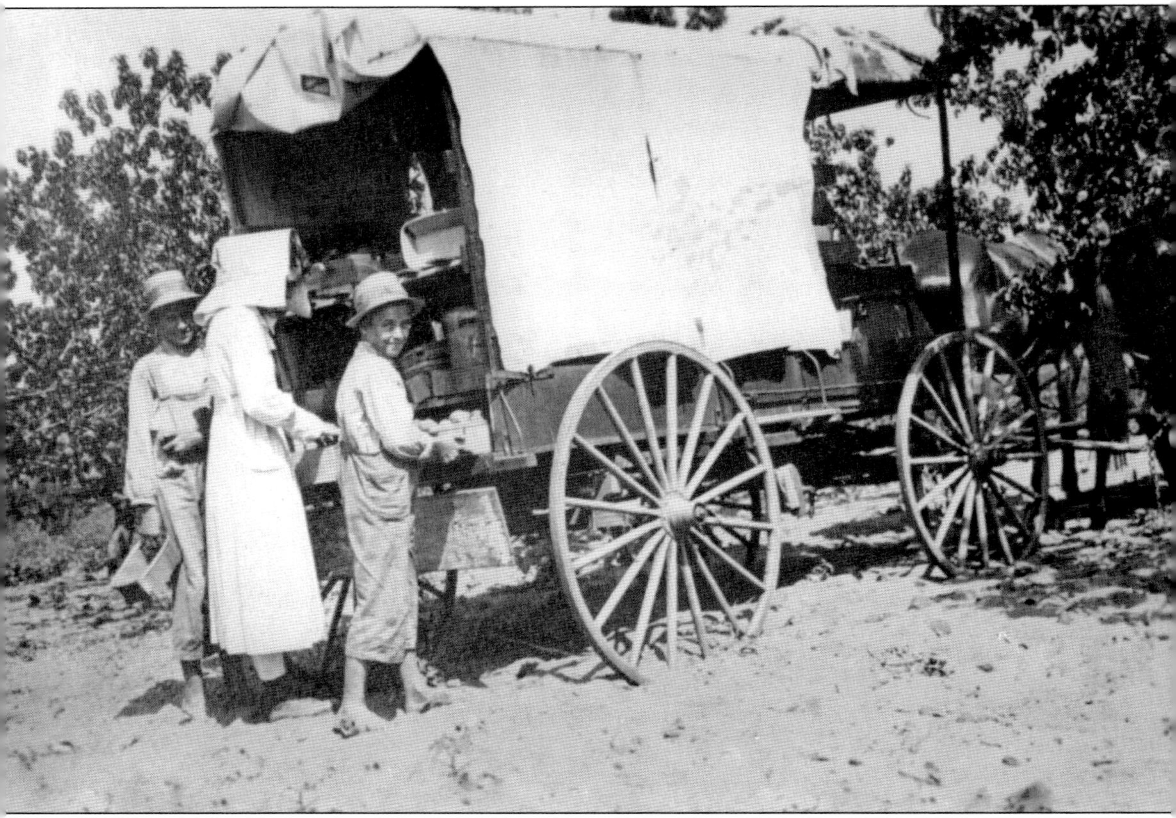

The Bidault family exemplifies the spirit of the people of Colleyville and its parent communities. Born in France in 1862, Anthelm Bidault came to America in 1882 and worked in the restaurant industry in New York, Alabama, and California. He finally came to Texas, where he and his wife, Jeanne, paid $500 for 58 acres of farmland in the Pleasant Run community. After three years of transforming it from barren soil to productive, nutrient-rich farmland, the Bidault farm produced a multitude of fresh vegetables and fruits. The farm also contained many fruit trees, grapevines, and berry vines. The Bidaults became known far and wide for their fruit and berry farming. Here, the Bidault children (from left to right) Ceece, Henrietta, and Pierre prepare their produce for market. (Courtesy of Tarrant County College Heritage Room.)

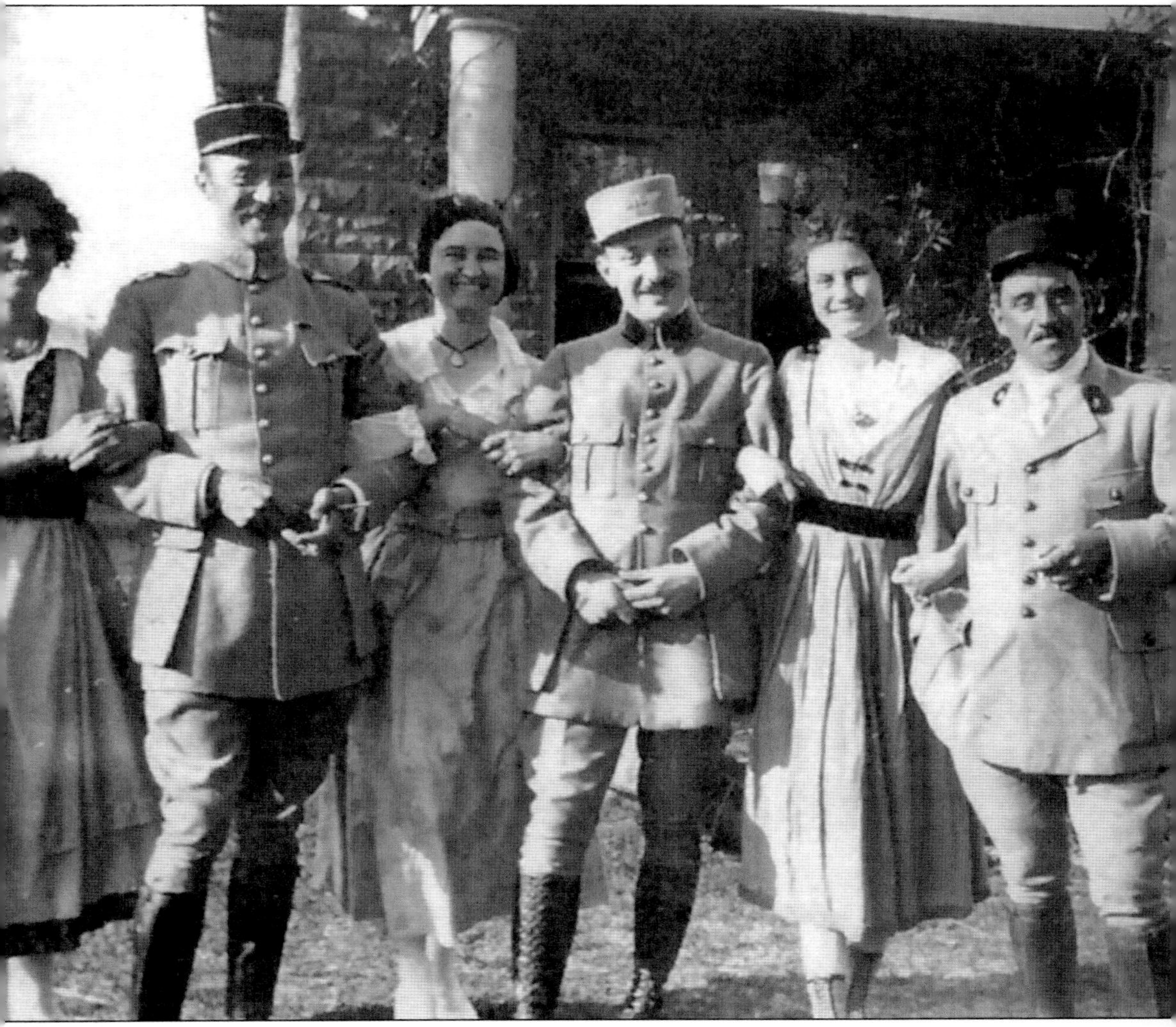

The Bidaults were especially successful fruit farmers, their berries and peaches sent by the wagonload to sell in Fort Worth. They also built 500-gallon wine vats on their property, which were filled each year with their bountiful harvests. But the Bidaults did not keep their success to themselves; they shared much with their friends and neighbors. They were extremely proud of their French heritage. French officers came to the United States from 1914 to 1917 to train at nearby Camp Bowie in Fort Worth to serve in World War I, and many spent their weekends on the Bidault farm. There, on the hilltop overlooking the rolling acreage of grapes hanging on the vines and row after row of fruits and vegetables, the soldiers got a taste of home with hearty food, flavorful wine, joyful music, and soulful friendship. (Courtesy of Colleyville Historical Preservation Committee.)

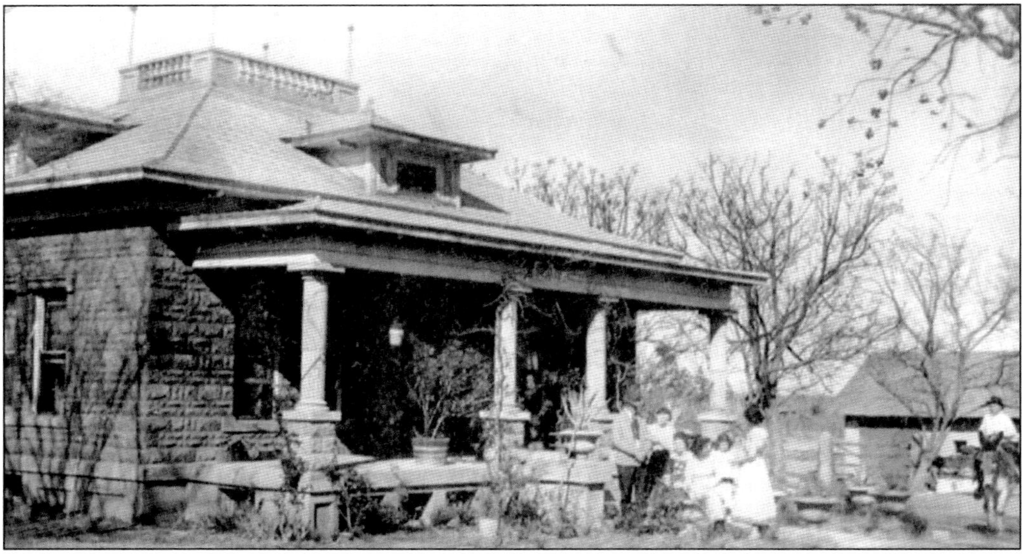

The Bidaults' success allowed them to claim several "firsts" in Bransford. While there was a two-room log cabin on his property when he purchased it in 1897, Anthelm Bidault soon replaced it with a concrete blockhouse (above) that still stands at 1416 Glade Road. Construction began in 1905 and was finally completed in 1911. One of the additions to the house was a garage, built in 1917, for the family's Jackson motorcar (below). The car was the pride and joy of the family and accommodated up to seven passengers. (Above, courtesy of Colleyville Historical Preservation Committee; below, courtesy of Tarrant County College Heritage Room.)

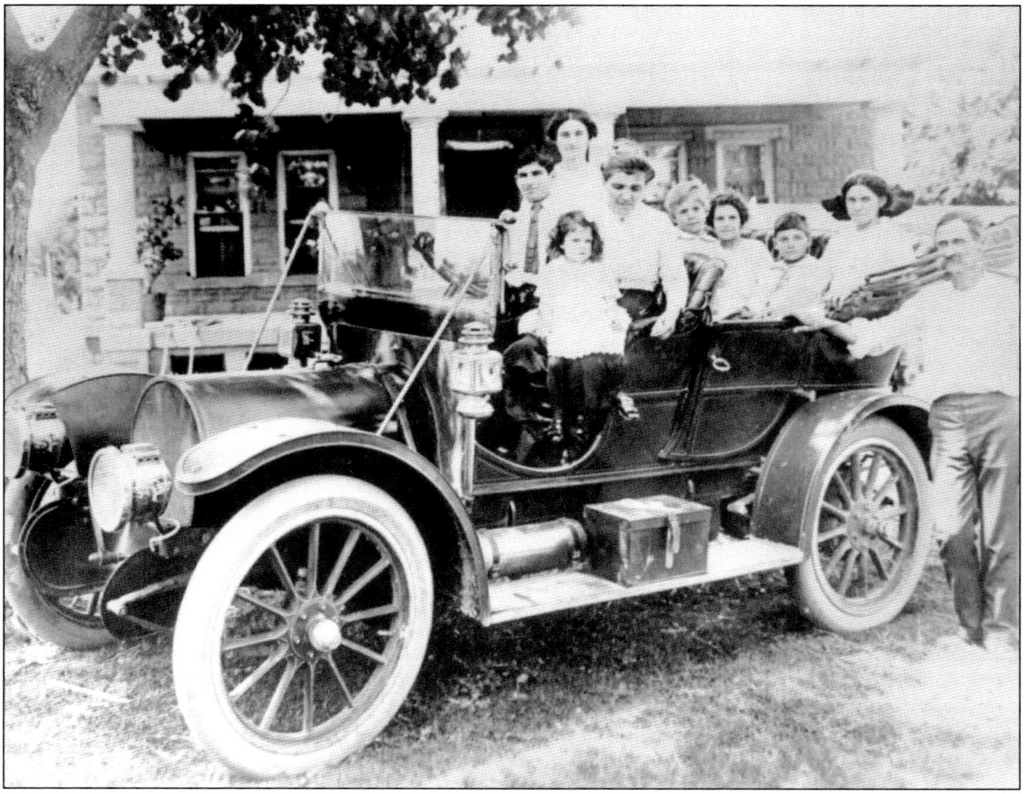

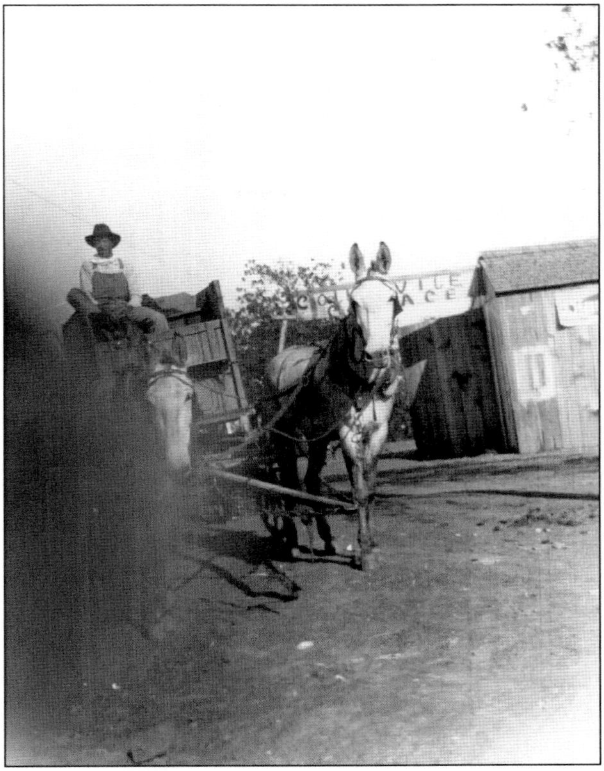

Early Colleyville sprouted up at the corner of Bransford and Cardinal Roads, which is the present-day Glade Road, after George Couch and his son Walter opened a general store there in 1914. This unidentified man is on a horse-drawn wagon in the downtown area. A Colleyville banner can be seen in the background. (Courtesy of Tarrant County College Heritage Room.)

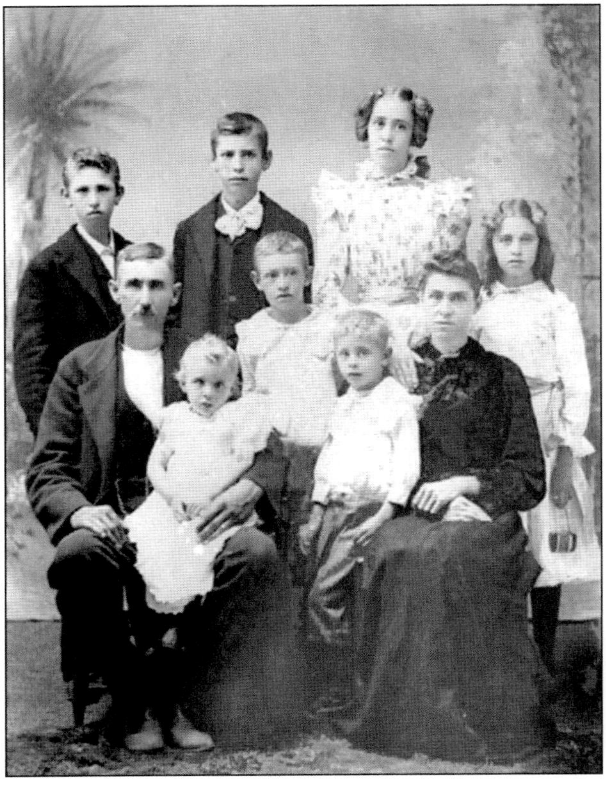

The Couch family was one of the prominent families of the Early Colleyville community. This photograph shows the family while they were living in Early Colleyville. Shown here are, from left to right, (first row) George (holding Lloyd), James T., Walter, and Alice; (second row) Sam, John and Laura. (Courtesy of Colleyville Historical Preservation Committee.)

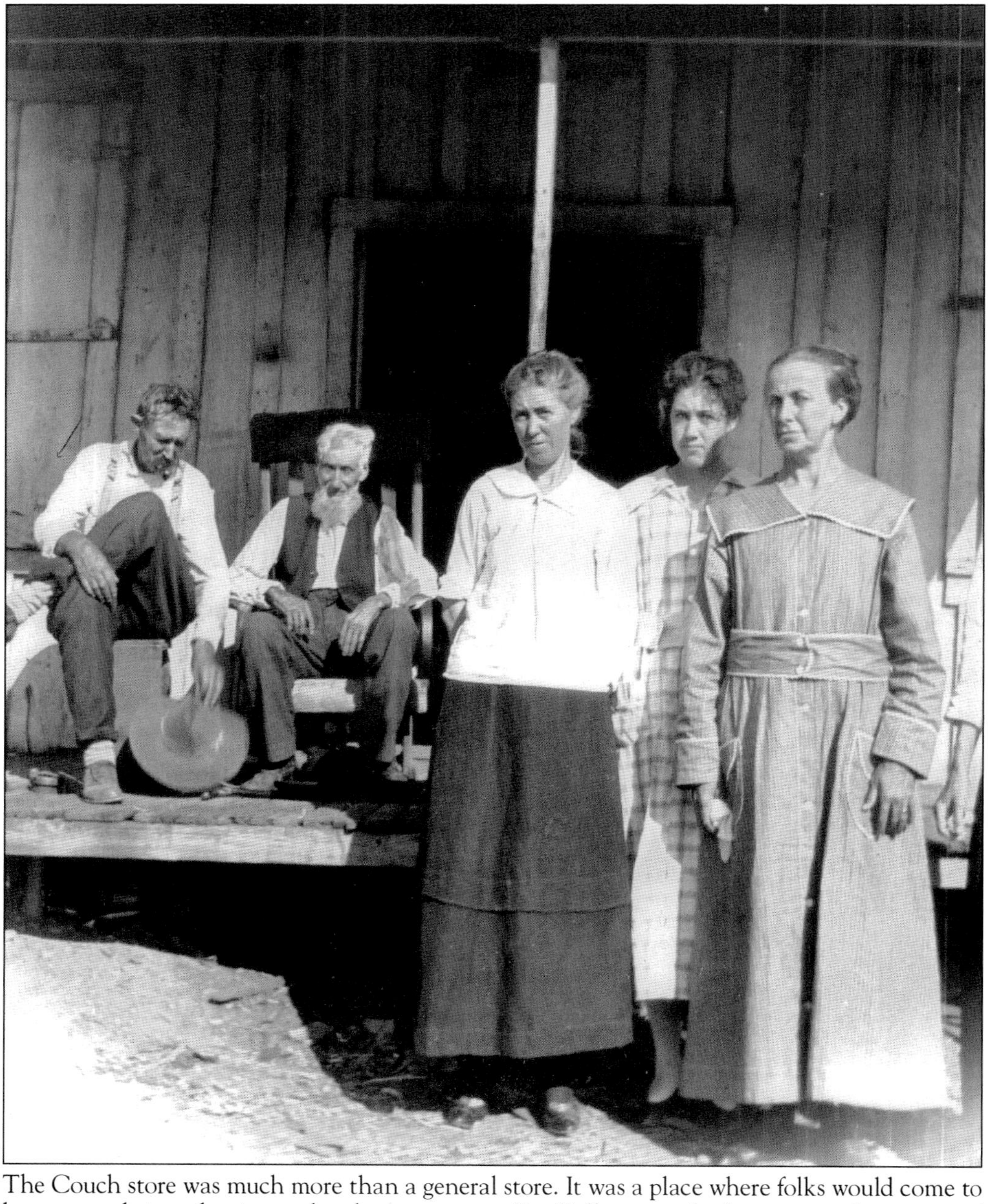

The Couch store was much more than a general store. It was a place where folks would come to have a good sit and enjoy each other's company. Dr. Colley owned a house near the corner of Bransford and Cardinal Roads, which stood vacant. So, Colley sold the house and two acres of land to George Couch for $50. After a little remodeling, the house was converted into a store. The business proved to be a great success, partly because it was the only store along Cardinal Road, which ran from Fort Worth to Grapevine. The Couch business also had a Model T, which was used for a jitney service from the store to Grapevine or Fort Worth. Shown here in front of the store are, from left to right, George Couch, Tom Sparger, Gladys Siler, Laura (Gladys's mother), and Leona Cavender. (Courtesy of Tarrant County College Heritage Room.)

Opal (Garrett) Ethridge was an Early Colleyville resident who had two major passions in her life: politics and baseball. As an adult, she attended every city council meeting; those running for municipal office would often stop by her house to seek her counsel on issues. Her love of baseball came out as she watched her son Butch, never missing a game during the 15 years he played as a youngster. The road into City Park, which leads to the city's baseball fields, is named in her honor. At right is a baby picture of Opal (left) and her sister Letha. Below is Opal's birth certificate, signed by Dr. Thaddeus Colley, Dr. Lilburn Colley's son. (Both, courtesy of Colleyville Historical Preservation Committee.)

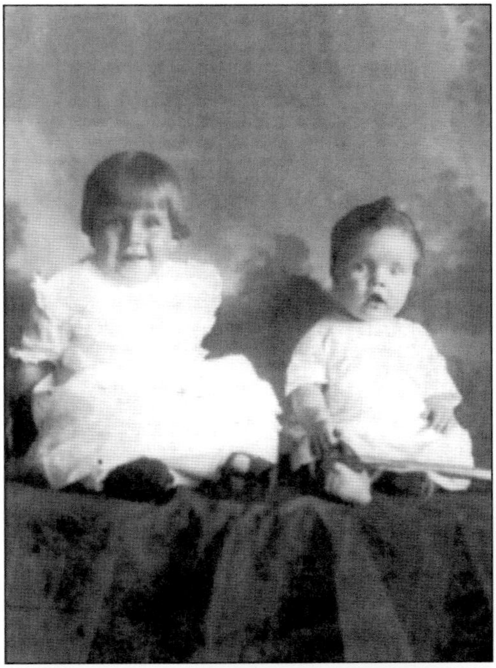

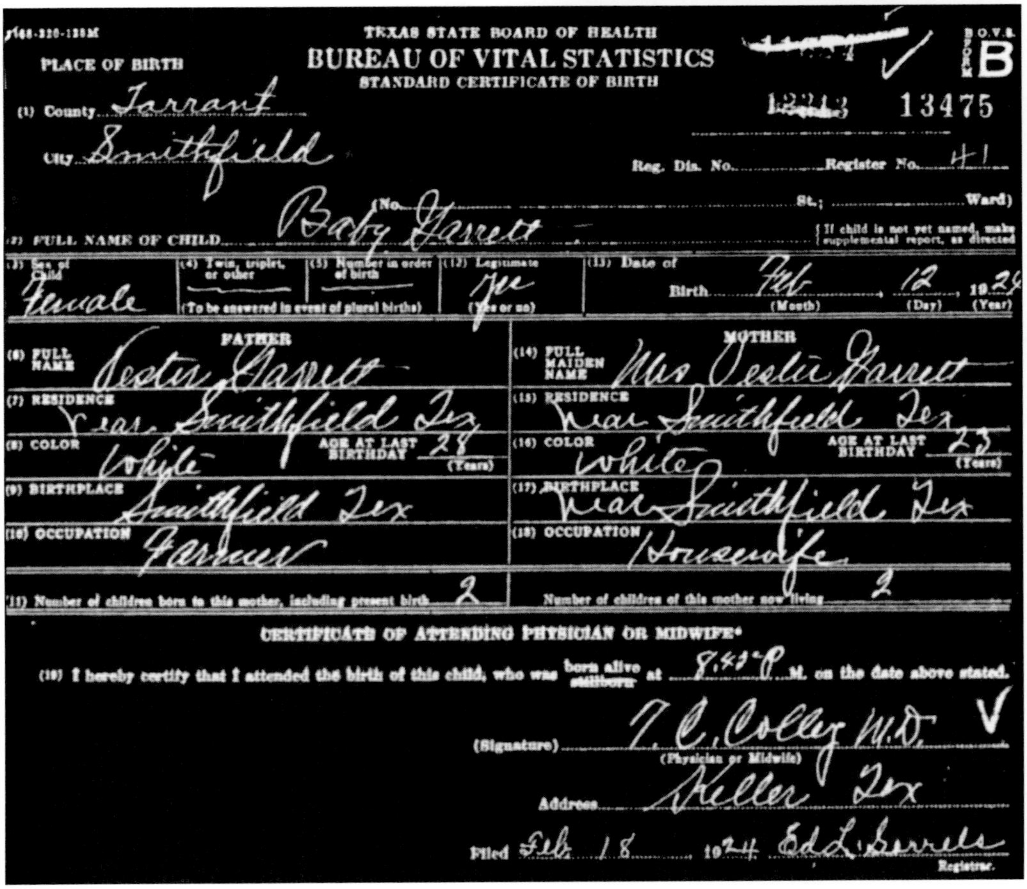

TEXAS STATE BOARD OF HEALTH
BUREAU OF VITAL STATISTICS
STANDARD CERTIFICATE OF BIRTH

PLACE OF BIRTH

FORM B

13475

(1) County Tarrant

City Smithfield

Reg. Dis. No. ______ Register No. 41

(No. ______ St.; ______ Ward)

(2) FULL NAME OF CHILD Baby Garrett (If child is not yet named, make supplemental report, as directed)

(3) Sex of Child	(4) Twin, triplet, or other	(5) Number in order of birth	(12) Legitimate	(13) Date of Birth
Female			Yes (Yes or no)	Feb 12, 1924 (Month) (Day) (Year)
	(To be answered in event of plural births)			

FATHER	MOTHER
(6) FULL NAME Vester Garrett	(14) FULL MAIDEN NAME Mrs Vester Garrett
(7) RESIDENCE Near Smithfield Tex	(15) RESIDENCE Near Smithfield Tex
(8) COLOR White AGE AT LAST BIRTHDAY 28 (Years)	(16) COLOR White AGE AT LAST BIRTHDAY 23 (Years)
(9) BIRTHPLACE Smithfield Tex	(17) BIRTHPLACE Near Smithfield Tex
(10) OCCUPATION Farmer	(18) OCCUPATION Housewife
(11) Number of children born to this mother, including present birth 2	Number of children of this mother now living 2

CERTIFICATE OF ATTENDING PHYSICIAN OR MIDWIFE*

(19) I hereby certify that I attended the birth of this child, who was born alive / stillborn at 8:45 P.M. on the date above stated.

(Signature) T. C. Colley M.D. (Physician or Midwife)

Address Keller Tex

Filed Feb. 18 1924 Ed L. Sorrells Registrar.

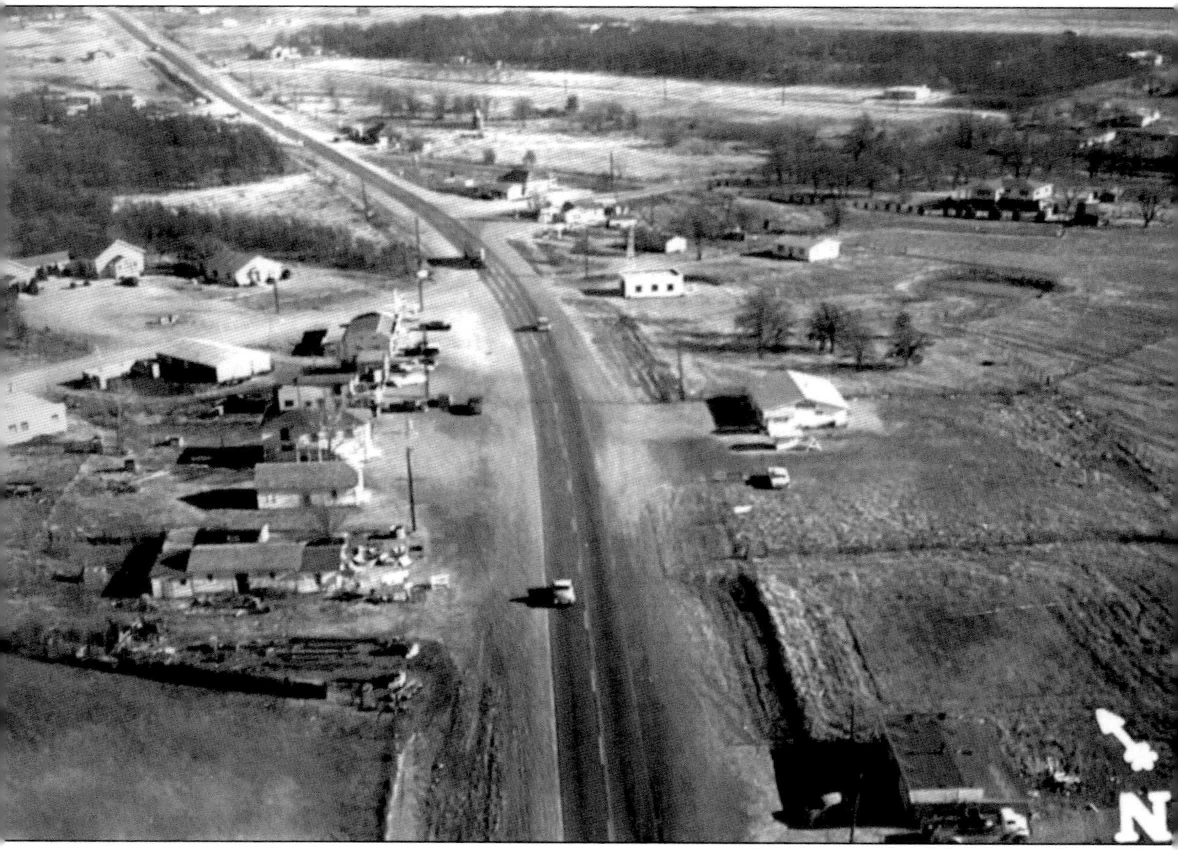

Cardinal Road, which snaked through Colleyville on its way from Fort Worth to Grapevine, was an engineering feat of its time. In 1912, it was transformed from a rutted, dirt wagon trail into a road topped with macadam, which is typically made of crushed stone compacted into layers and bound together with tar. This "macadamized" road was the first all-weather route in the area, but by 1929, it was time to improve the road again. This time, county officials decided to straighten the road as it came through Colleyville, which proved to be the death knell for Early Colleyville. Merchants who had built their stores at the intersection of Bransford and Cardinal Roads now had to move to the new intersection of Cardinal Road (present-day Glade Road) and the new highway (present-day State Highway 26, also called Colleyville Boulevard). This 1940s photograph shows "Downtown" Colleyville at the intersection of Pleasant Run Road and present-day Colleyville Boulevard. (Courtesy of Colleyville Historical Preservation Committee.)

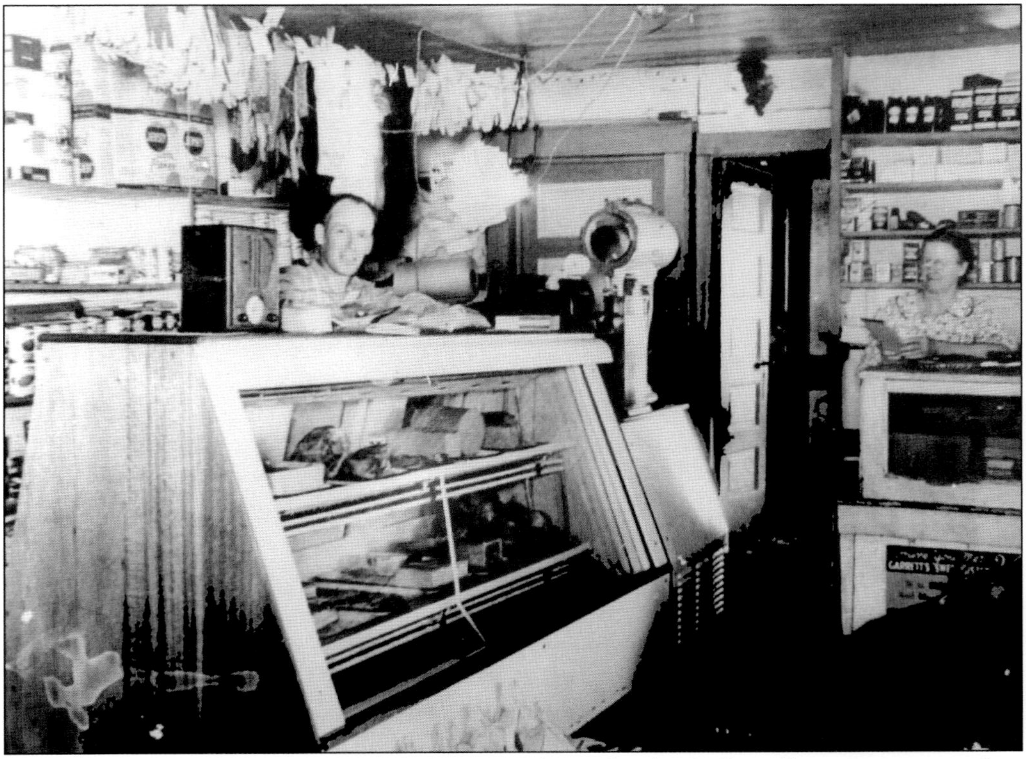

Present-day State Highway 26 quickly became a boon for the Colleyville community and its merchants. One of the early businesses was Bass Grocery. Clyde Bass (pictured) opened his store in 1934 near the corner of Glade Road and present-day State Highway 26, just to the north of present-day Red Barn Barbecue. (Courtesy of Colleyville Historical Preservation Committee.)

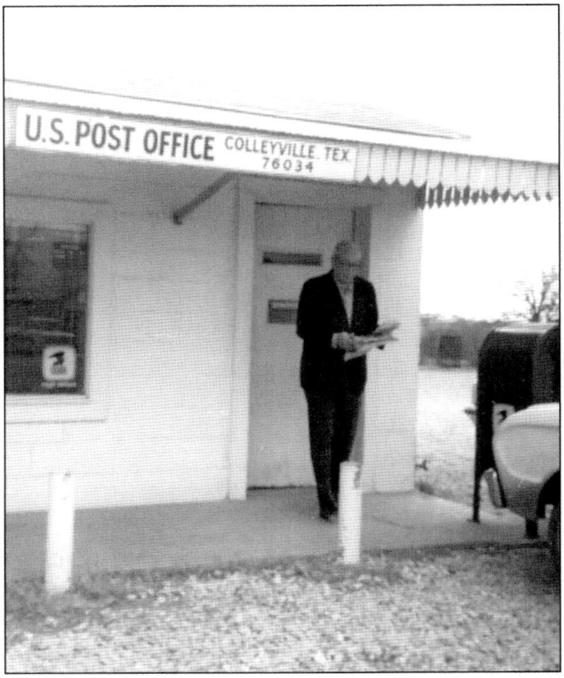

Another important service in the new Colleyville community was the post office, located inside a building at the corner of Glade Road and present-day State Highway 26. Tom Stevens only needed room on one side of the building, so he rented out the other side to Otho and Marion Bone. They ran a feed and seed store. Colleyville resident Hiram Willis is pictured here in front of the post office. (Courtesy of Colleyville Historical Preservation Committee.)

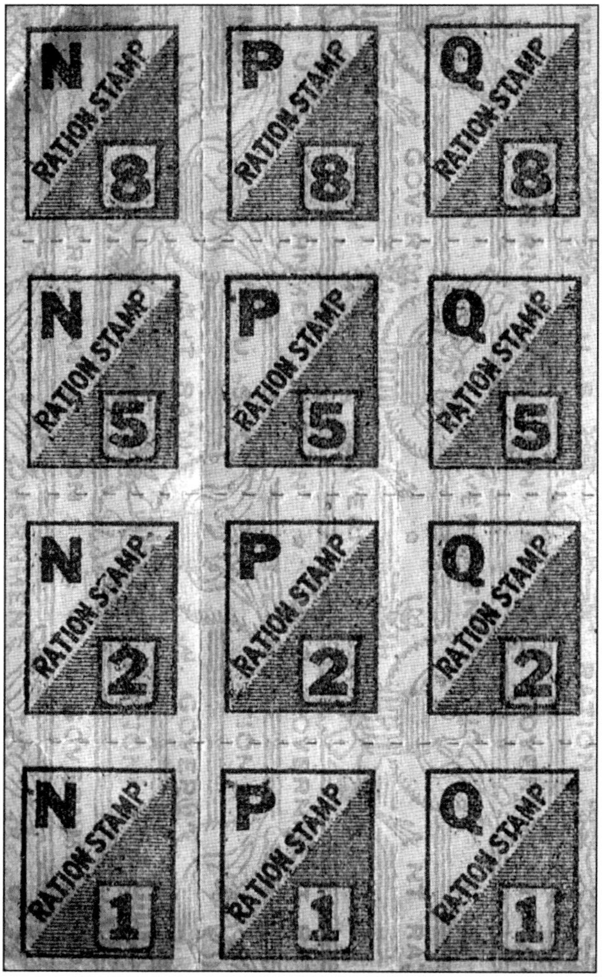

In 1943, the world was at war, and sacrifices had to be made everywhere, including Colleyville. Everything from gasoline to raw materials to food was being rationed for the war effort. The US Department of Agriculture told Americans to plant "victory gardens" if they wanted a source of fresh vegetables, and the agency issued ration stamps, like those pictured here. (Courtesy of Colleyville Historical Preservation Committee.)

Workers employed by Pres. Franklin D. Roosevelt's Works Progress Administration program also qualified for low-income housing. Several of these houses, which often included a few acres of land, a well, and a mule, were located in Colleyville along present-day Hall-Johnson Road, between Pool Road and present-day State Highway 26. (Courtesy of Colleyville Historical Preservation Committee.)

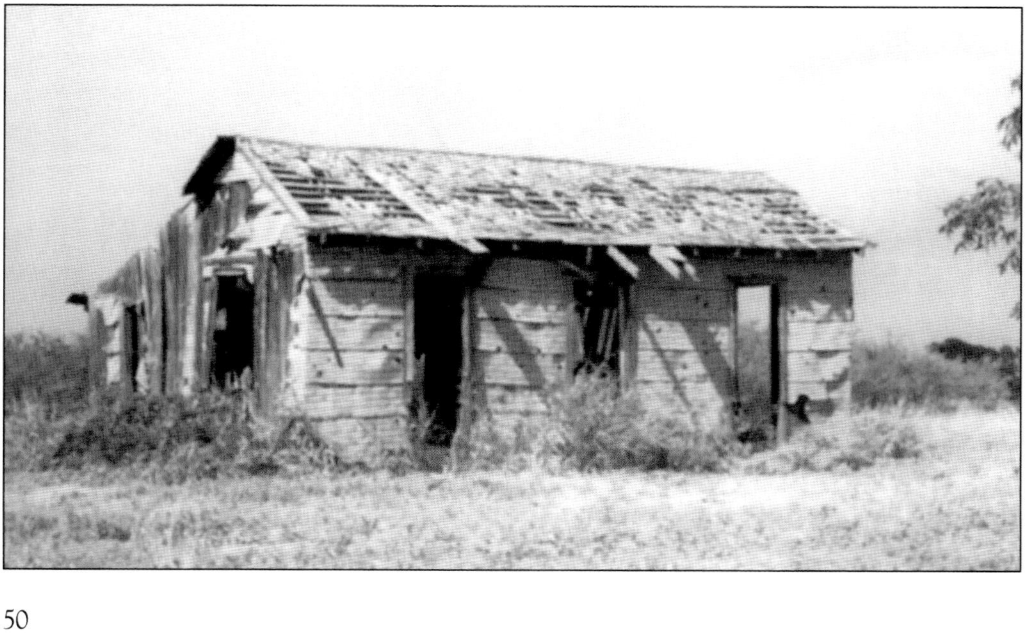

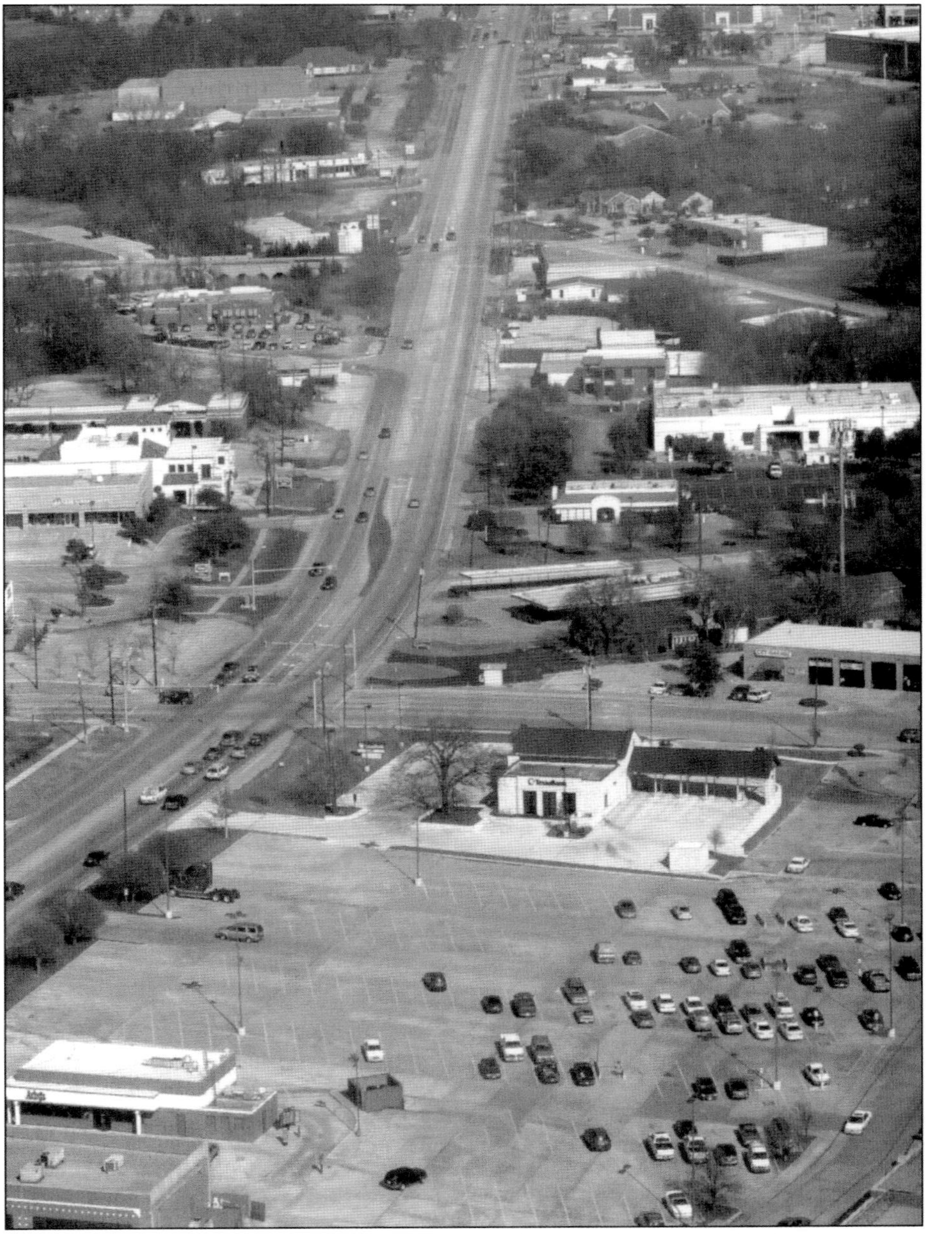

Like many other towns that have transformed from rural farming outposts to bedroom communities, Colleyville has seen its fair share of changes over the years. The straightening of Cardinal Road through Colleyville and its transformation into a state highway were perhaps the biggest factors that caused Colleyville's ascension from a parent community to a larger town. People were becoming more dependent on the automobile, and they began to see roads as the major arteries of their community. Meanwhile, the railroad, which was still vital to move freight, lost its status as the predominant mode of transportation, and the small communities that had depended upon it for so long began to suffer. Besides the rise of the automobile, political winds were also brewing in neighboring towns that would lead to the decision to unite all the parent communities as Colleyville. A portion of Colleyville that is divided by present-day State Highway 26 is shown here in 2005. (Courtesy of Colleyville Historical Preservation Committee.)

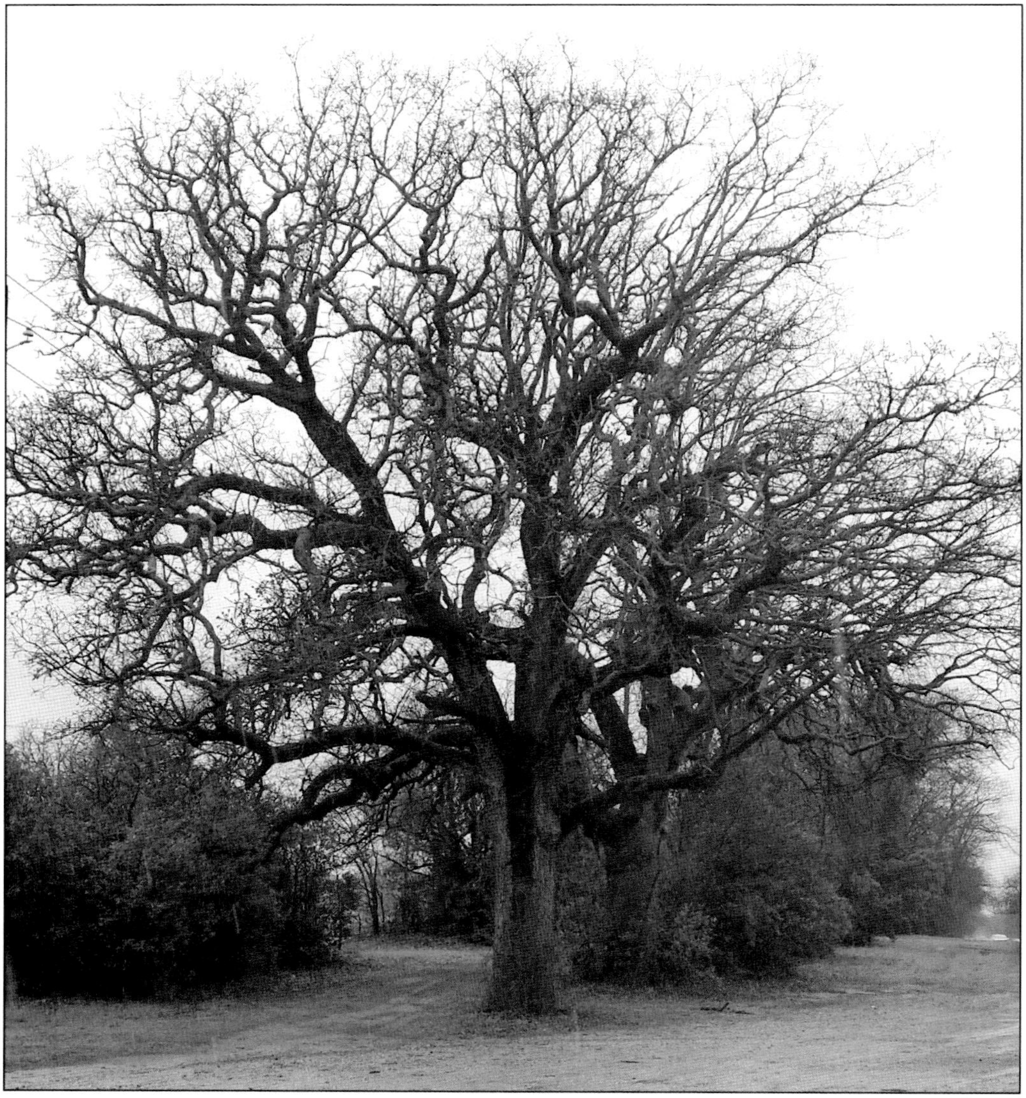

If only the trees in Texas could talk—the stories they could tell about the infancy of the Lone Star State. In the 1800s, trees were used to mete out punishments in the form of hangings and whippings, such as the Whipping Oak in Seguin where prisoners were tied to an iron ring and given lashes. Trees were also used as landmarks and as backdrops for gunfights and eerie rituals. At the Goose Island Oak, the Karankawa tribe allegedly carried out cannibalistic rituals. Before there were majestic buildings paying homage to state and local governments, political groups often met under "political trees" to conduct business. For example, land was auctioned off in 1839 to raise money to fund the building of the new state capitol under the majestic canopies of the Auctions Oaks in Austin. Political trees such as this one, located alongside the Cotton Belt line, were where politicians seeking Tarrant County offices would come to speak to local residents. (Courtesy of Colleyville Historical Preservation Committee.)

Three

A New City

Many pre-Colleyville residents did not understand what incorporation would mean for them, in terms of how it would affect their land or how they would continue to conduct business in their daily lives. The headline of a 1951 *Fort Worth Star-Telegram* article by Mac Williams summed up the opinions of many parent community residents: "Bransford, Vanishing Tarrant Town, Refuses to Relinquish Spot on Map." But, while some may have resented being a part of a "big city," they soon realized that incorporating the parent communities was a blessing that would ensure that the history and traditions of their communities would be carried into the future. Uniting as the City of Colleyville meant that none of the parent communities could be absorbed by other cities, an action that the neighboring city of Hurst had been planning at the time in order to increase the number of residents paying Hurst taxes.

Incorporation was not an easy accomplishment. New policies and laws had to be created. Services that were formerly provided by the county or by independent businesses now needed to be undertaken by the city. One of the main reasons that city leaders wanted to incorporate was to avoid paying municipal taxes, a feat they were able to carry on for nearly 20 years. To pay for essential services, city leaders used public-utility franchise money and held fundraisers. Not having to pay a municipal tax proved to be a popular feature of the city; as a result, there was a large influx of newcomers from all over Texas and beyond.

Looking at the city today, many simply see a wealthy enclave that is an ideal place to live and raise a family. But, digging a little deeper reveals that Colleyville, like many other cities that have transformed from rural farming communities to thriving municipalities, came about due to the tireless efforts of city leaders and passionate citizens who worked together to build a vision for the future while honoring their rich heritage.

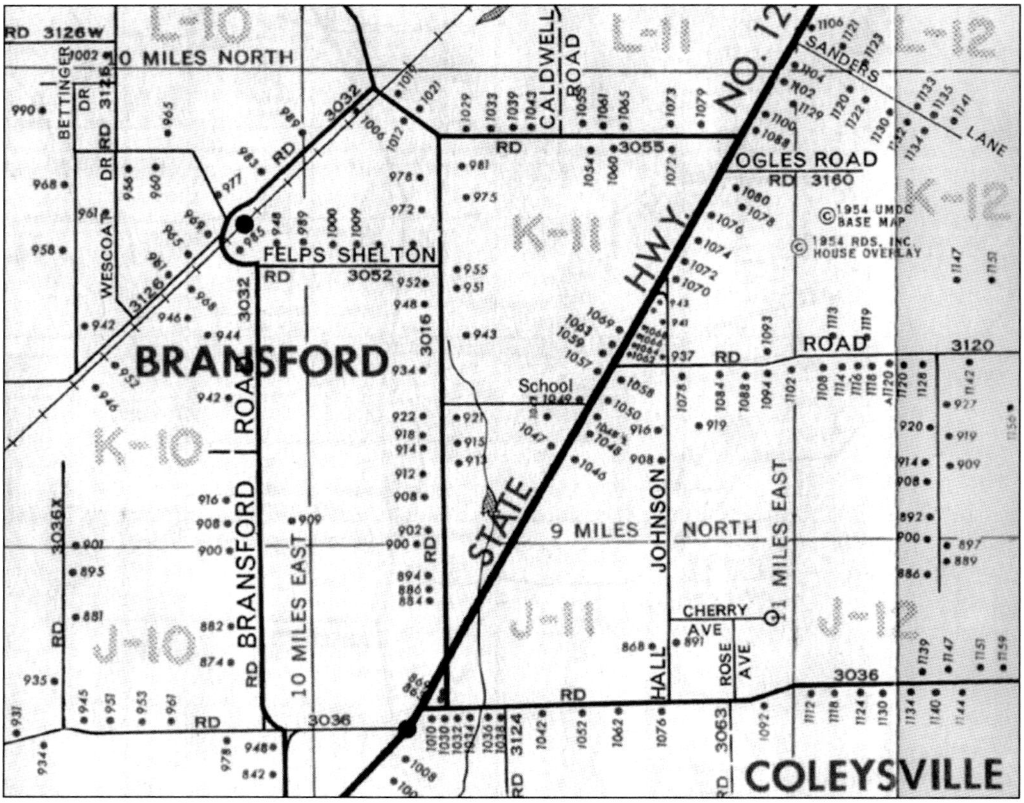

To get an idea of population sizes in the rural parts of the county, surveyors used maps such as this one to denote area population densities. This map was published in 1954, when Bransford and Colleyville (misspelled on the map) were still parent communities. Maps like this one also helped city leaders decide where to plot the initial city limits. (Courtesy of Colleyville Historical Preservation Committee.)

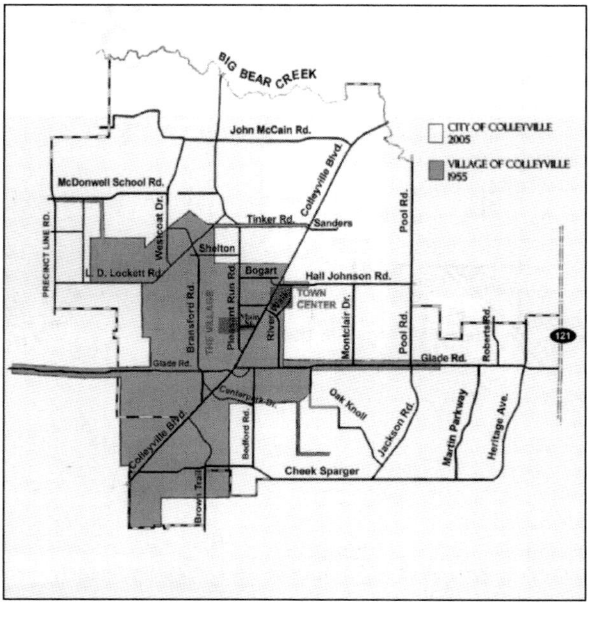

This map shows the Colleyville city limits (shaded portion) when it was first incorporated in 1956. According to Texas statutes, a minimum of 201 citizens living in a two-square-mile area was needed for incorporation. Therefore, city leaders incorporated along major thoroughfares at the time, because those areas held the highest densities. The white portion of this map shows the city limits today. (Courtesy of Colleyville Historical Preservation Committee.)

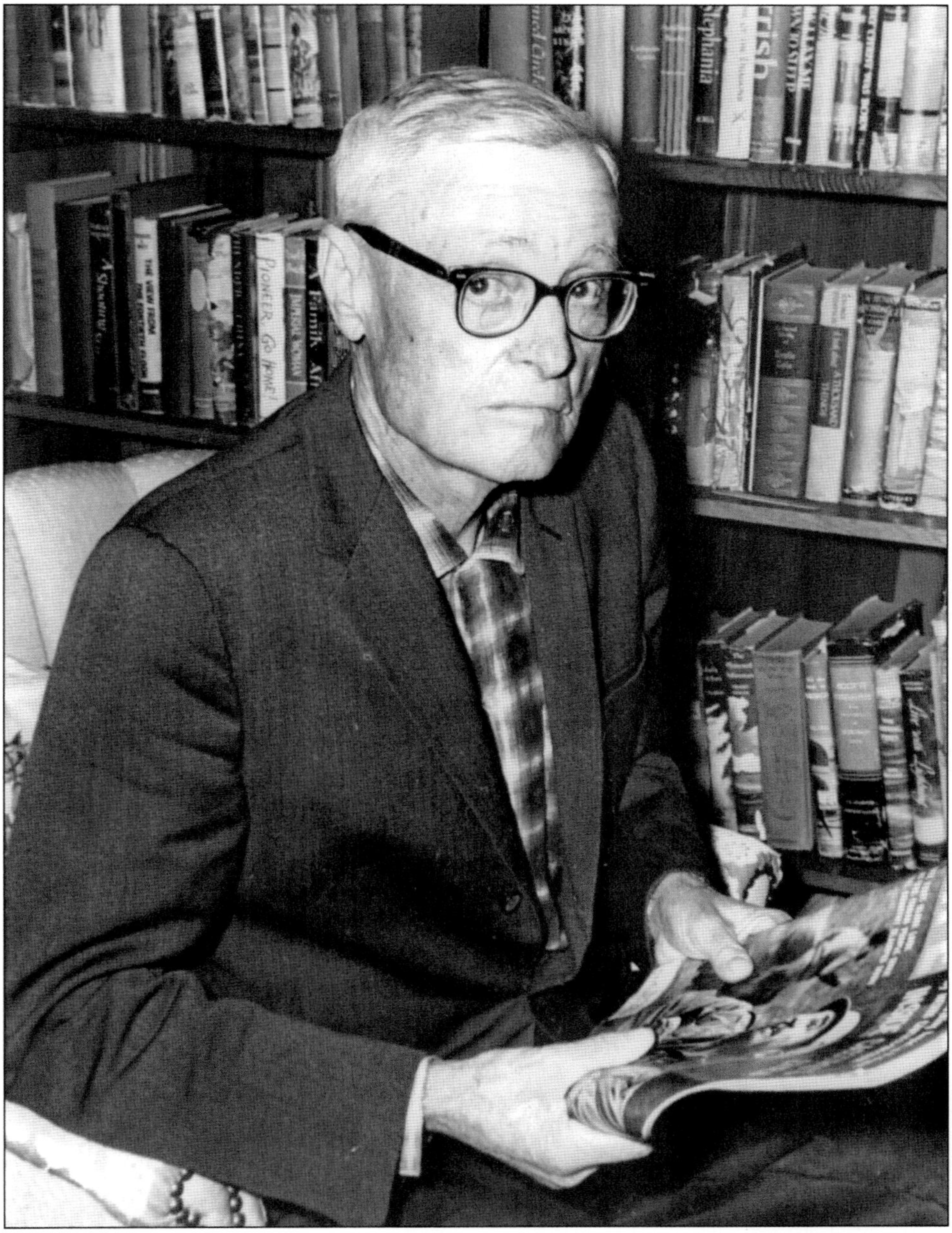

Seen here is Colleyville's first mayor, Ernest Eudaly. On January 26, 1956, Colleyville held its first election. Citizens elected a mayor, five aldermen, and a town marshal. Candidates who had garnered the highest number of votes were declared the winners and instructed to take office immediately. Henry Behrens became marshal, winning 59 votes. Harold Aldridge, L.T. Clark, Wayne Creyts, Bill Hughes, and A.B. Turner each won seats as aldermen, with 82, 64, 80, 60, and 91 votes respectively. Winning the position of mayor with 77 votes was Ernest R. "Hico" Eudaly. Colleyville collected no municipal taxes, so the first mayor and his aldermen initially conducted city business in the living room of Eudaly's personal residence, a farmhouse near the intersection of Glade Road and present-day State Highway 26. Before moving to Colleyville with his wife, Florence, Ernest worked as acting director of Texas A&M Extension Services and as an agricultural specialist for Universal Mills in Fort Worth. (Courtesy of Tarrant County College Heritage Room.)

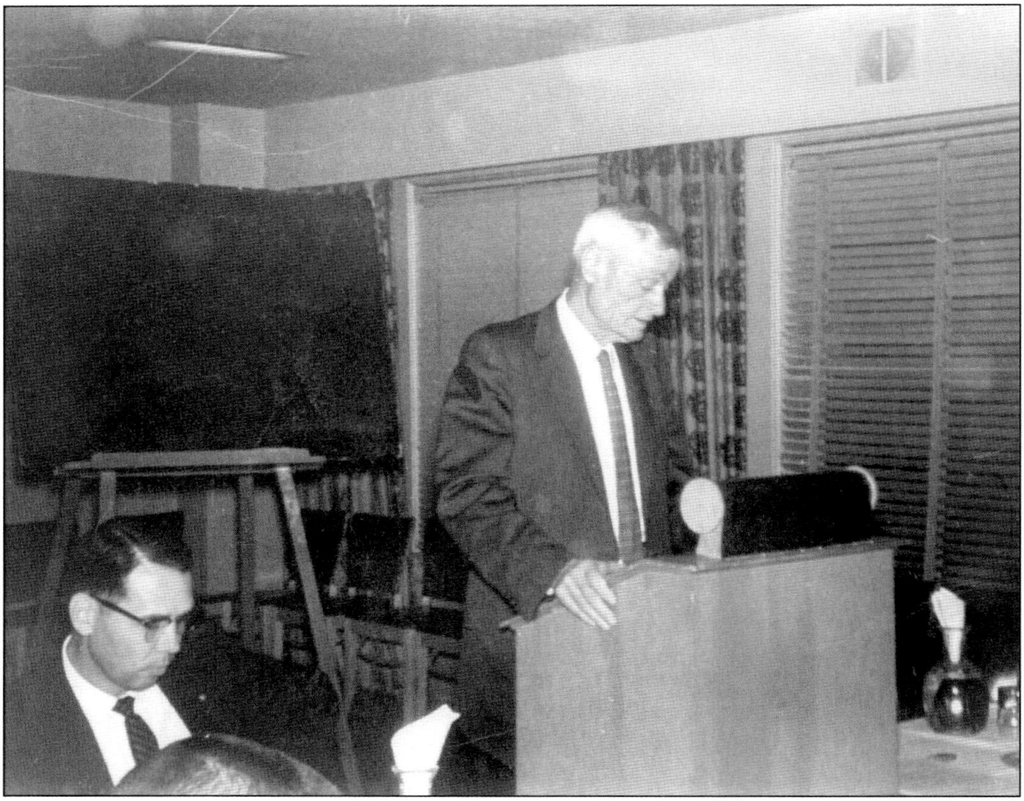

Mayor Eudaly donated part of his farmland for Colleyville's first public building, a fire hall. The hall, which still stands at the southeast corner of Glade Road and present-day State Highway 26, is presently a Compass Bank. The bank's walls are adorned with several historic images from Colleyville's past. Here, Mayor Eudaly conducts a council meeting in the fire hall. (Courtesy of Tarrant County College Heritage Room.)

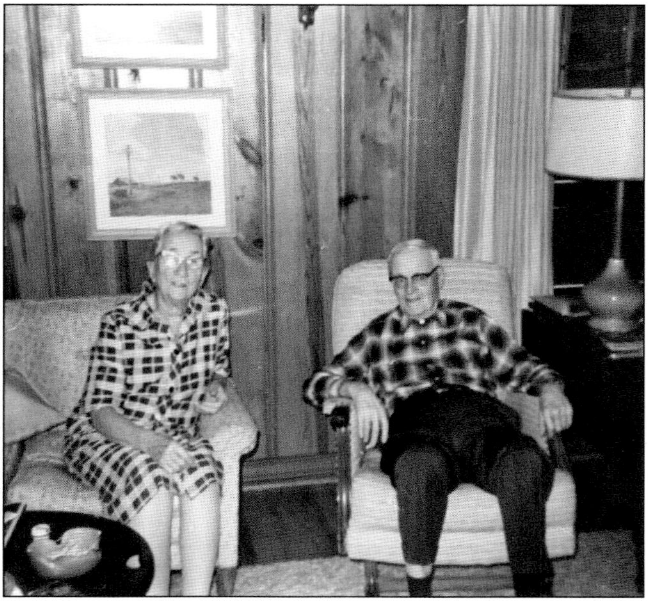

Besides donating land for the first public building, the Eudalys made other contributions to the city through gifts and service. Florence Eudaly organized one of the oldest clubs in the city, the Colleyville Garden Club, in 1961, and often hosted meetings at her residence. She celebrated her 100th birthday on July 26, 1988, which was declared "Florence Eudaly Day in Colleyville." Here, Eudaly and Florence relax at home. (Courtesy of Tarrant County College Heritage Room.)

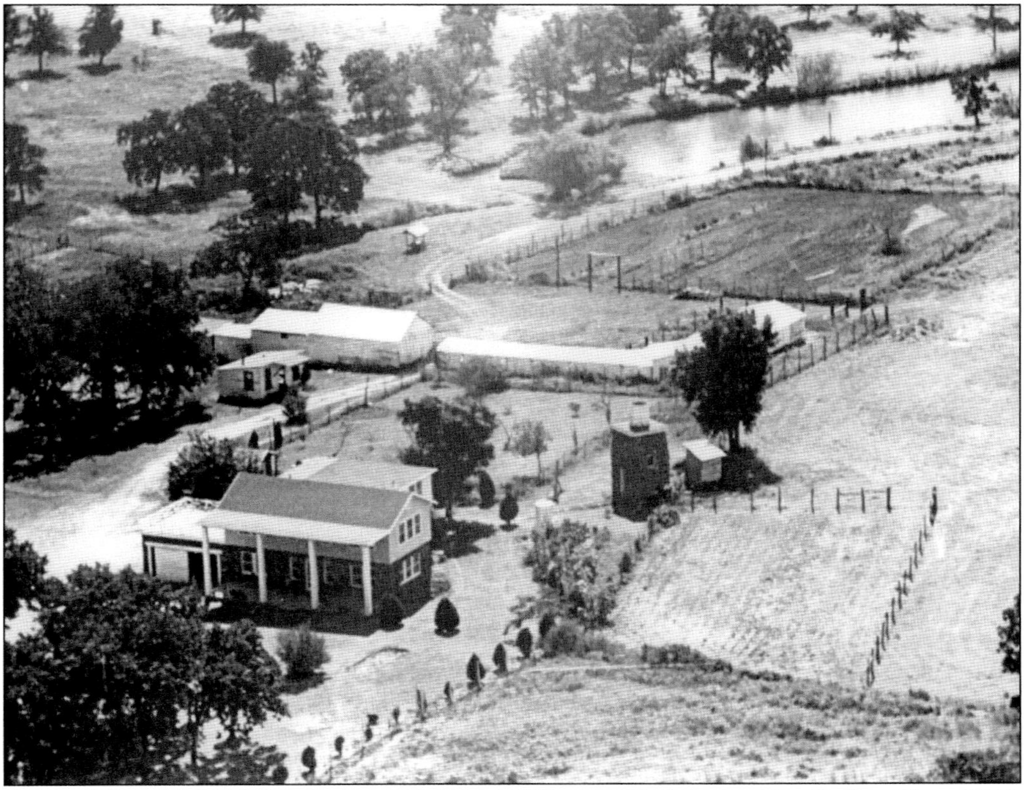

Pictured above is the Eudaly homestead. E.R. and Florence Eudaly moved to Colleyville in 1948, when it was still an unincorporated, rural community. They bought a 100-acre farm near the corner of present-day Glade Road and present-day State Highway 26, where they raised, among other things, angus cattle (below). The Eudaly farm shrank over time, as Eudaly donated a portion to the city and sold other parcels to developers. By the time of her death in 1989 at 101 years old, Florence was still living at their home, which sat on the two acres that were left of the farm. (Both, courtesy of Tarrant County College Heritage Room.)

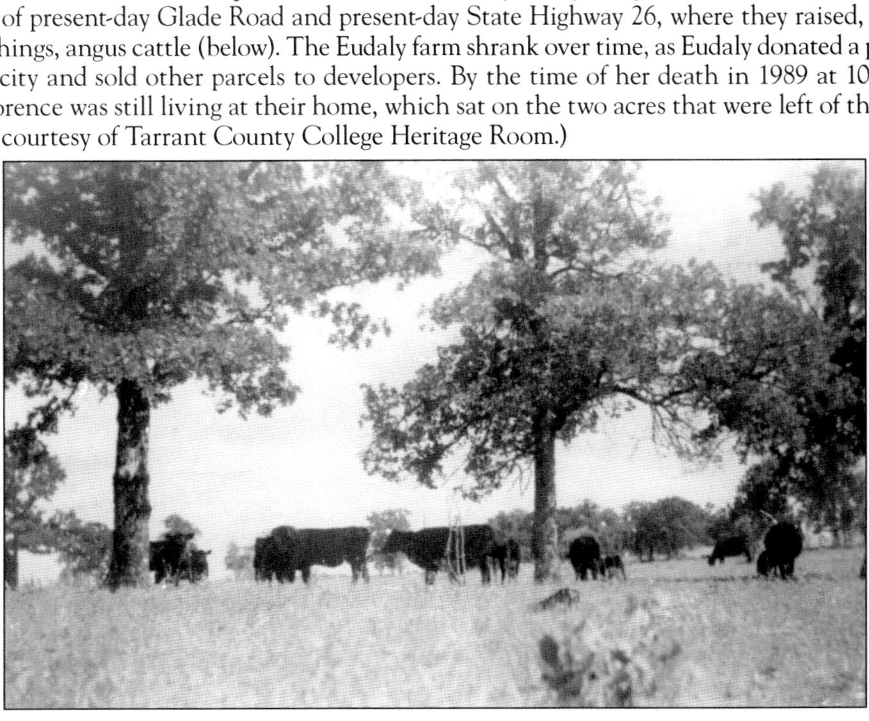

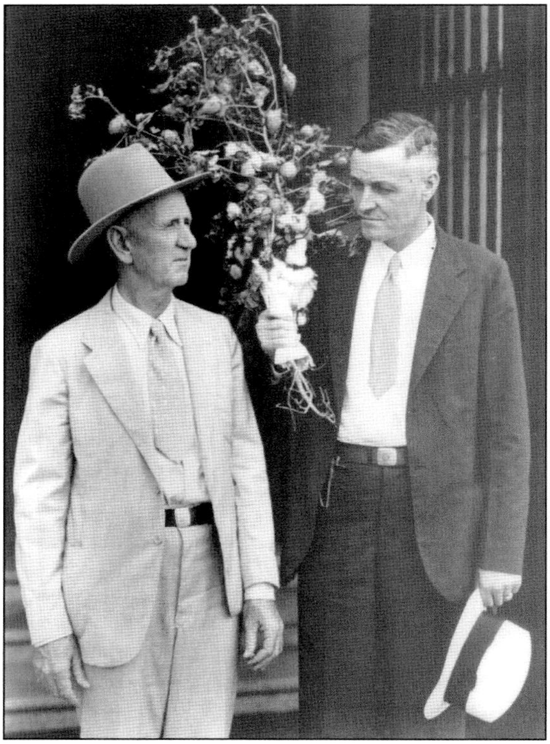

As part of Pres. Franklin Roosevelt's New Deal program, the Agricultural Adjustment Administration called on cotton farmers across the nation to destroy 10 million acres of cotton in hopes of increasing prices. At left, Mayor Eudaly holds up a cotton plant that a Colleyville farmer has plowed up. Eudaly, who administered the program, is shown below standing third from the left as President Roosevelt hands a check to a farmer who has plowed up his cotton crop. Secretary of Agriculture Henry Wallace is on the right. (Both, courtesy of Tarrant County College Heritage Room.)

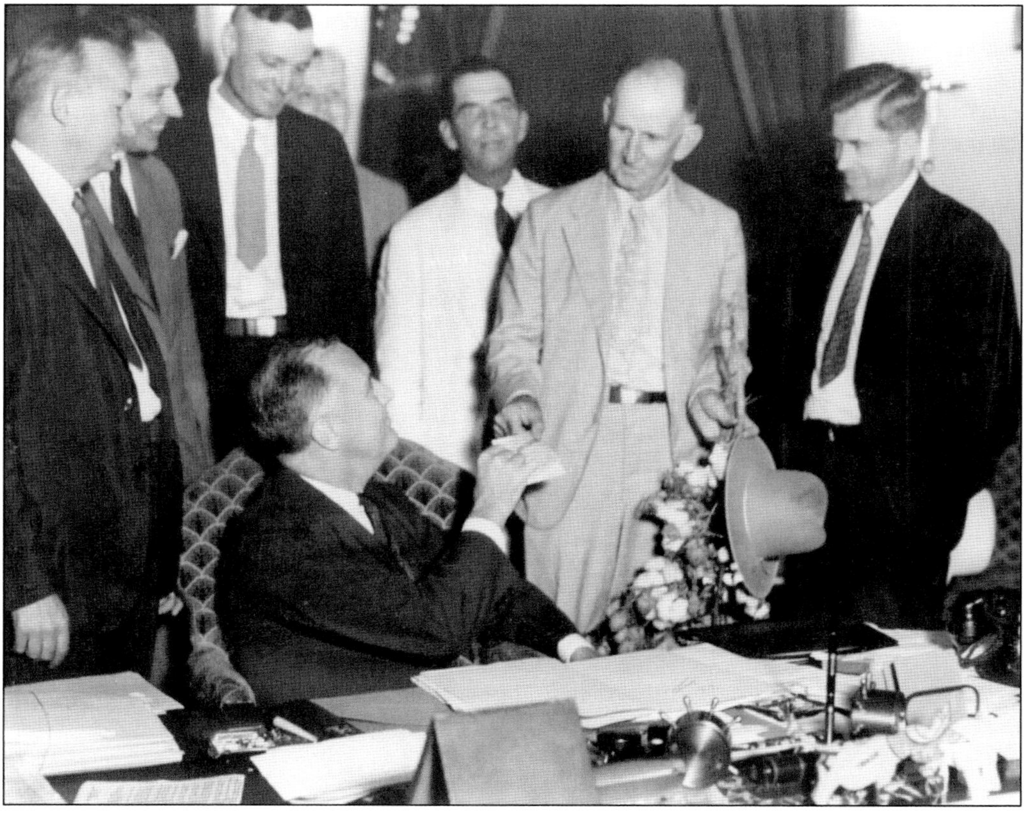

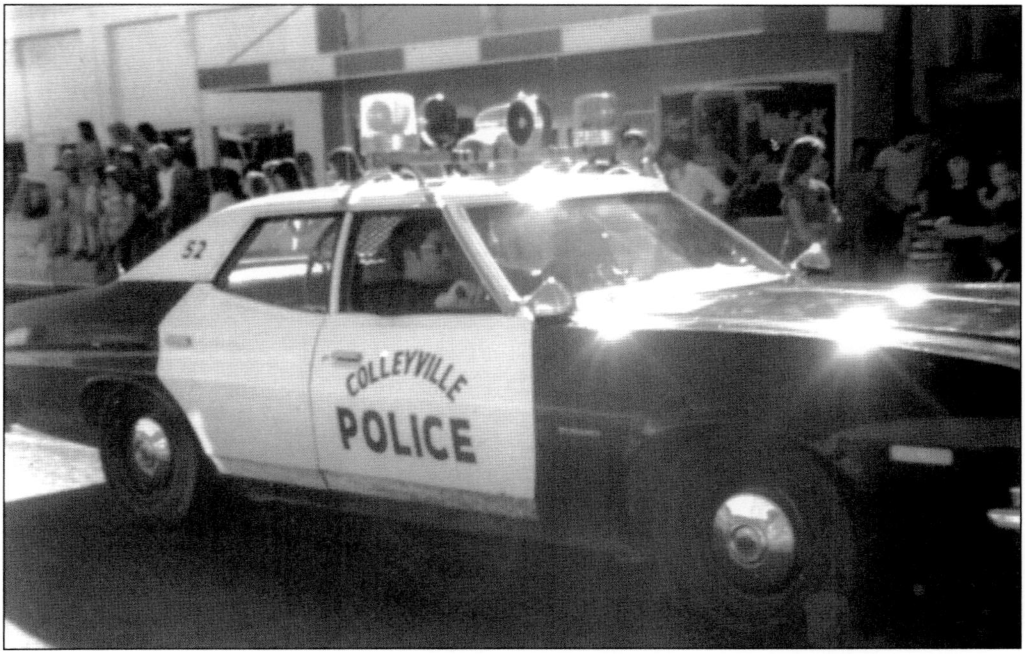

The city was incorporated in 1956, but public-safety services were not formalized until much later. While there was a town marshal appointed by the city during incorporation, prior to 1973, Tarrant County Sheriff's Department officers provided law-enforcement services. Rodney Cunningham, who worked as a Colleyville police officer from the department's inception until his death in 2013, is shown above on the passenger side of the department's 1976 Ford police unit. Prior to 1984, when a professional fire department was formed, firefighting was performed by an all-volunteer crew of residents, local businessmen, and even high school students. Because Colleyville was still very much a rural community in the middle and late 1900s, grass fires were the major problems. (Both, courtesy of Colleyville Historical Preservation Committee.)

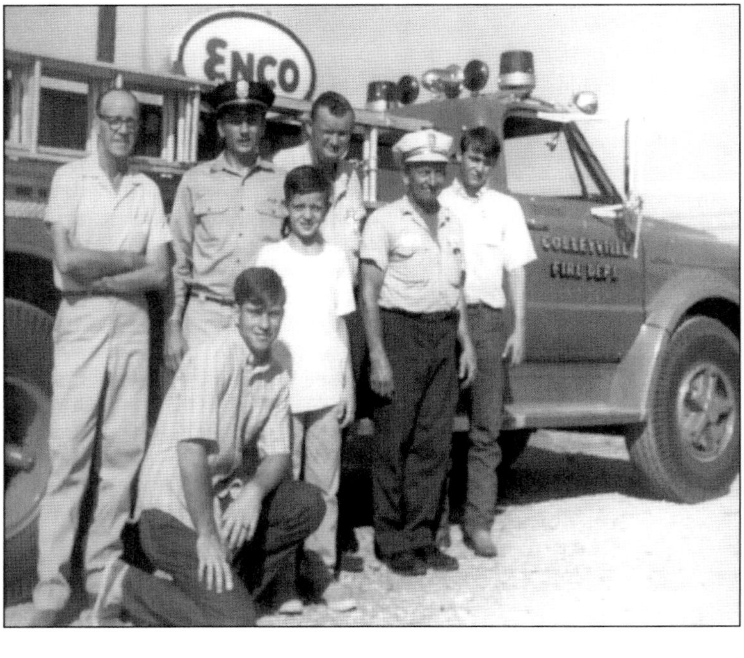

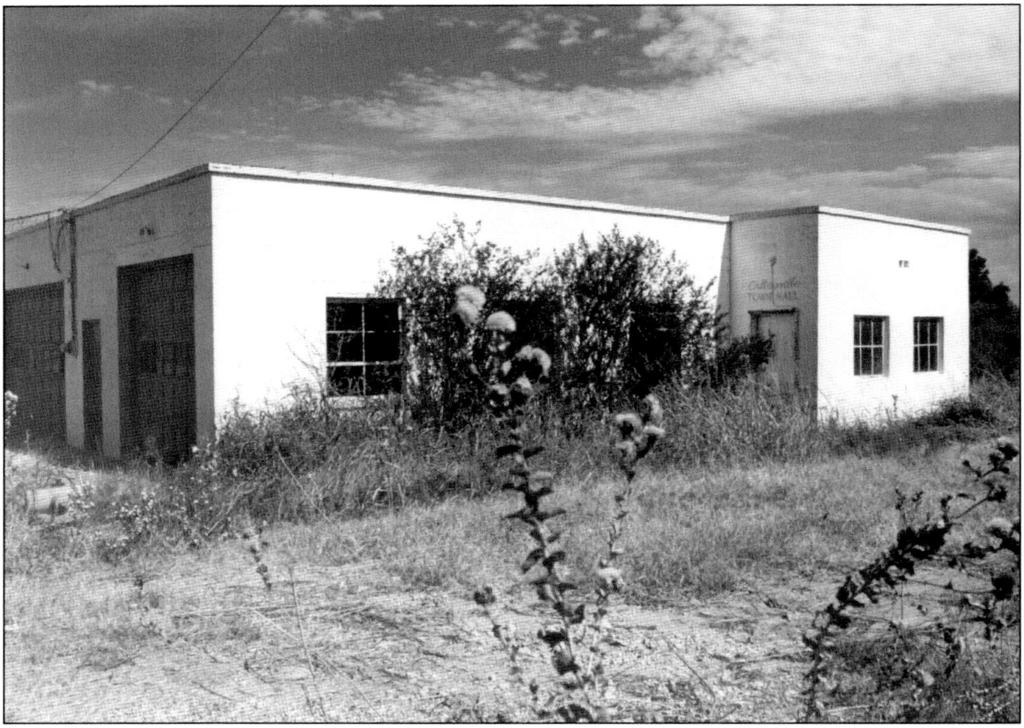

Colleyville's first city hall was also the first municipal building the city erected after it was incorporated. Before it served as a place to conduct city business and council meetings, it was a fire hall. A small room was added on the back to serve as Colleyville's town hall (above). City Hall has been housed at several locations over the years. In 1972, just two years after Colleyville started collecting property taxes, it was moved to 5201 Bransford Road, which is now occupied by the Colleyville Parks Department Maintenance Center (below). It moved two more times before settling at its current location at 100 Main Street. (Above, courtesy of Tarrant County College Heritage Room; below, courtesy of Mark Fadden.)

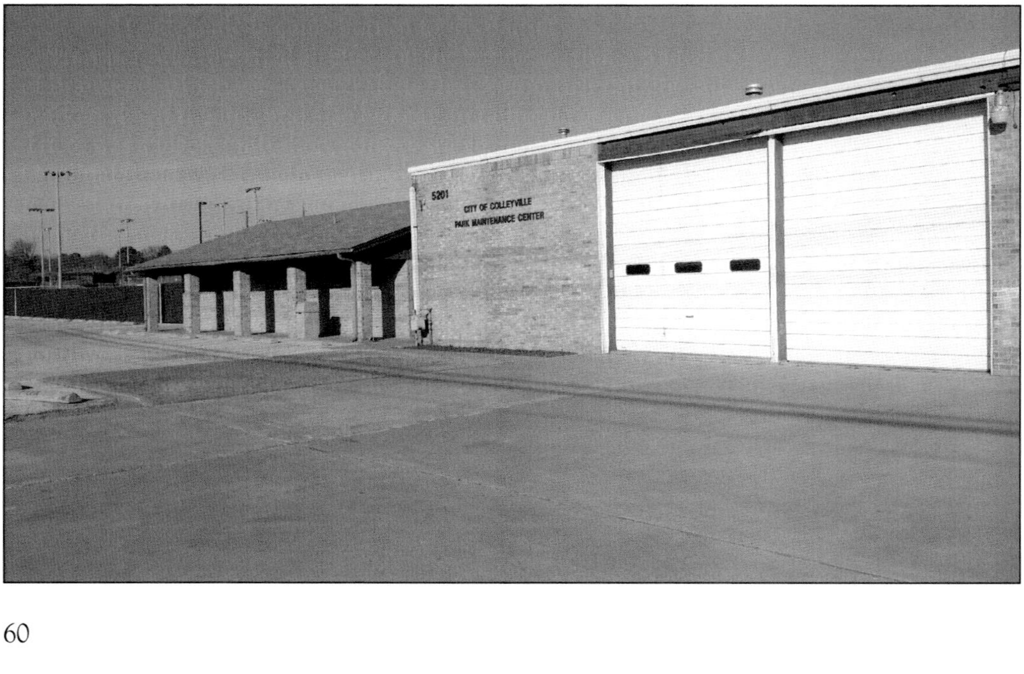

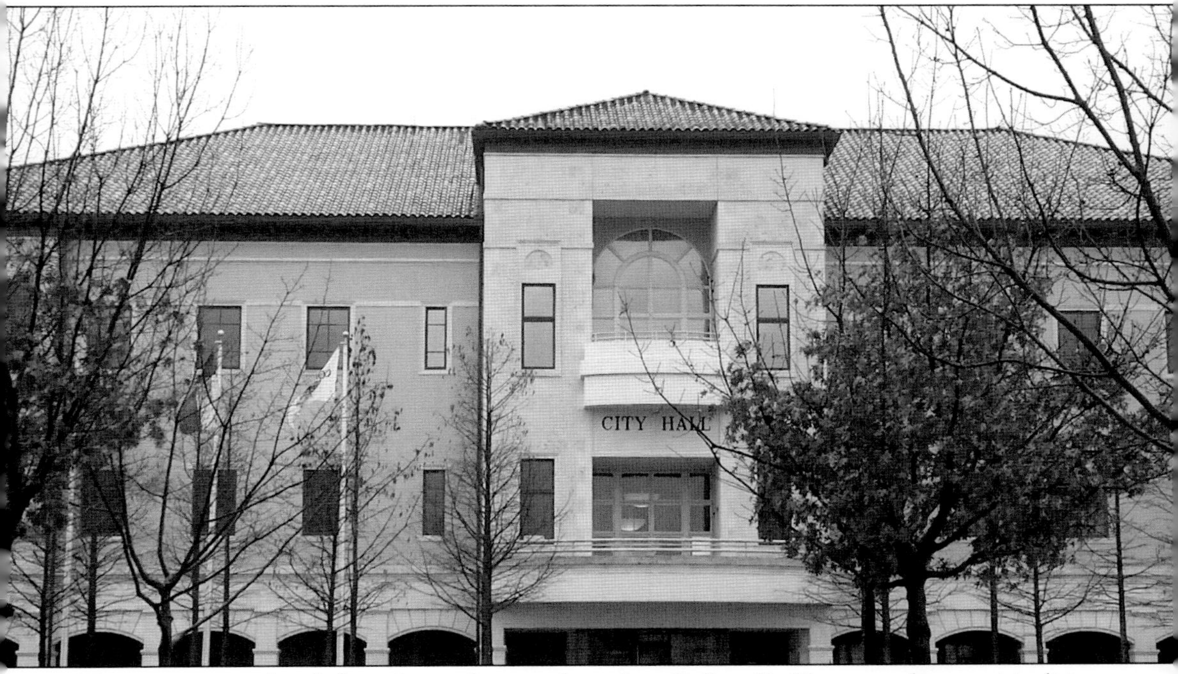

The city continued its shift in identity from rural to urban. Colleyville, like most other municipalities, has had its share of growing pains. In the 1970s and 1980s, some residents wanted growth, and others did not. Perhaps the final act in the transition from a country town to an urban community occurred in 1979, after an extensive community survey, a joint venture of the Commercial Development Committee and the Institute of Urban Affairs at the University of Texas at Arlington. The decision was made by the city council to introduce a new zoning category that allowed smaller lots than the required half-acre. This action, along with the population boom of the Metroplex around it, cast Colleyville's destiny for growth. By the time the present City Hall was built in 2003, the city's population was more than 20,000, and the average home valuation was almost $500,000. (Courtesy of Mark Fadden.)

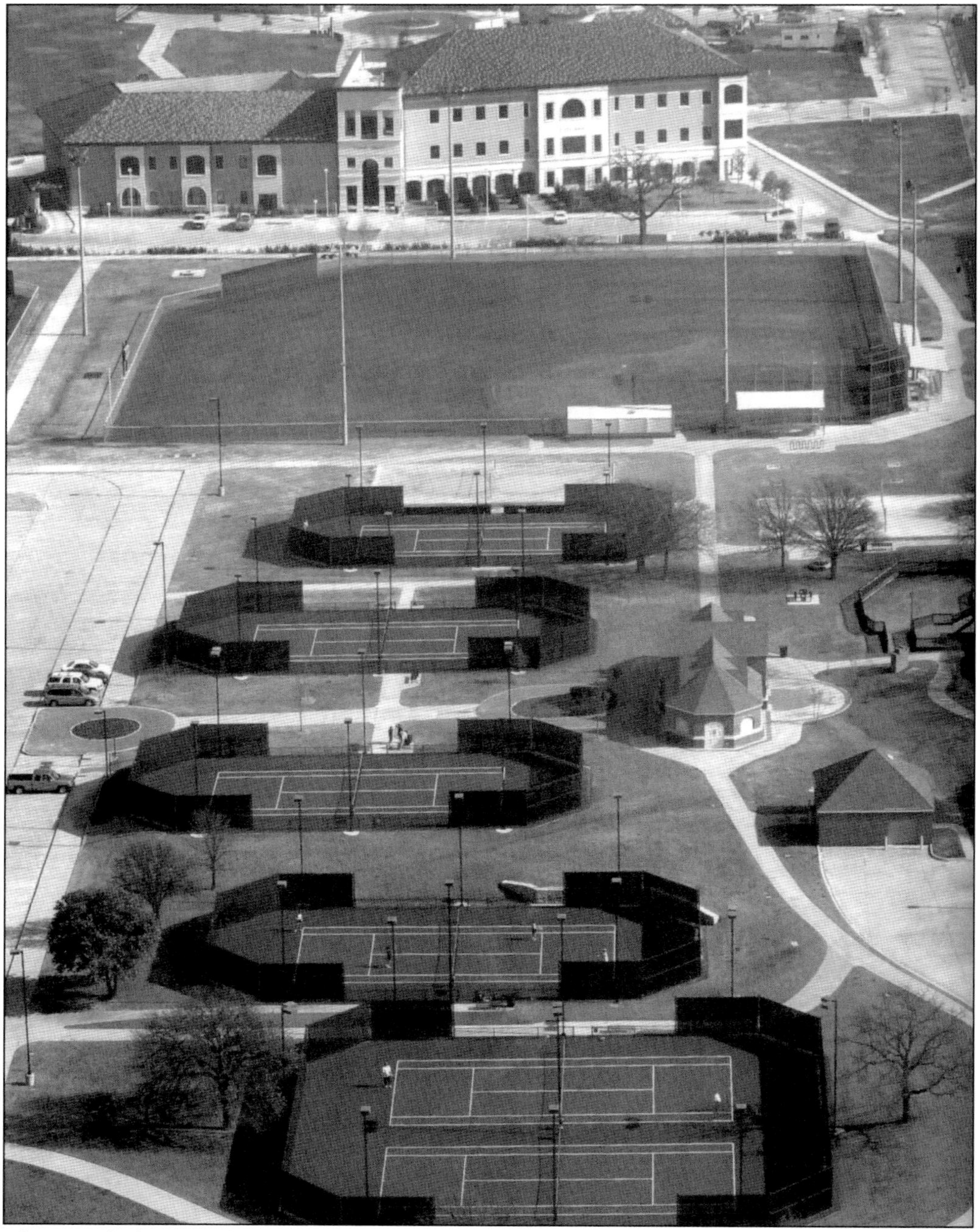

This aerial photograph captures City Park, located behind City Hall. (Courtesy of Colleyville Historical Preservation Committee.)

Four

Early Businesses

People were drawn to Texas in the late 1800s and early 1900s for many reasons. Some wanted a chance at a new life. Others wanted land they could call their own. Still others came to the Lone Star State from their homeland to avoid persecution for their actions or beliefs. Whatever the reasons for these folks to come to Texas were, there was one thing they all needed to do once they got here: make money.

Colleyville, and the parent communities before the city was incorporated, was heavily reliant upon what the land provided. Most families who lived in the Colleyville area were farmers who grew everything from vegetables and fruits to cotton as their cash crops. Some farmers branched out into the cattle business, raising beef cattle. Dairy cows also had a significant impact on the area, and Colleyville became known for its dairies.

Transportation also had an effect on the businesses that sprouted up here. The parent community of Bransford, which was located along the Cotton Belt rail line, allowed residents access to other markets down the line and also brought in railroad passengers who needed manufactured goods. There was a blacksmith shop, a livery stable, four general stores, and four doctors. When the old Cardinal Road was straightened and transformed into present-day State Highway 26, Colleyville really started to grow. The automobile made it possible for people to travel, and Colleyville's location along this major transportation artery all but cemented its prosperity. While cars became the de facto form of transportation, horsepower of the four-legged kind still had a profound influence on the city. Colleyville continued to be seen as a rural community, with riders trotting their horses along city streets. It also hosted one of the area's few horse tracks. Before it was a subdivision on the northwest side of the city just off of present-day State Highway 26, Ross Downs was a racing and training facility where many of the nation's premier racing horses came to prove themselves.

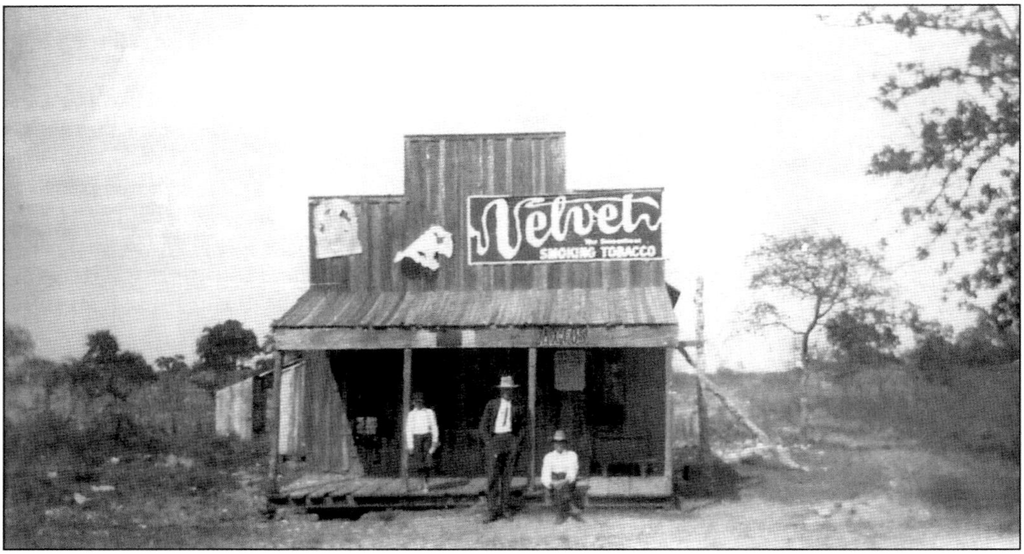

One of the first stores in the pre-Colleyville area was the Webb General Store in Bransford. Opened by John Webb in 1914, it sold essential goods like lard, coffee, and salt, and household items like brooms, soap, and matches. It also housed a public phone, which many folks used, as most residents did not have telephones in their homes. The above photograph shows the store, with a rather large advertising sign for Velvet Smoking Tobacco. Below, the extended Webb family poses in front of the store. (Both, courtesy of Colleyville Historical Preservation Committee.)

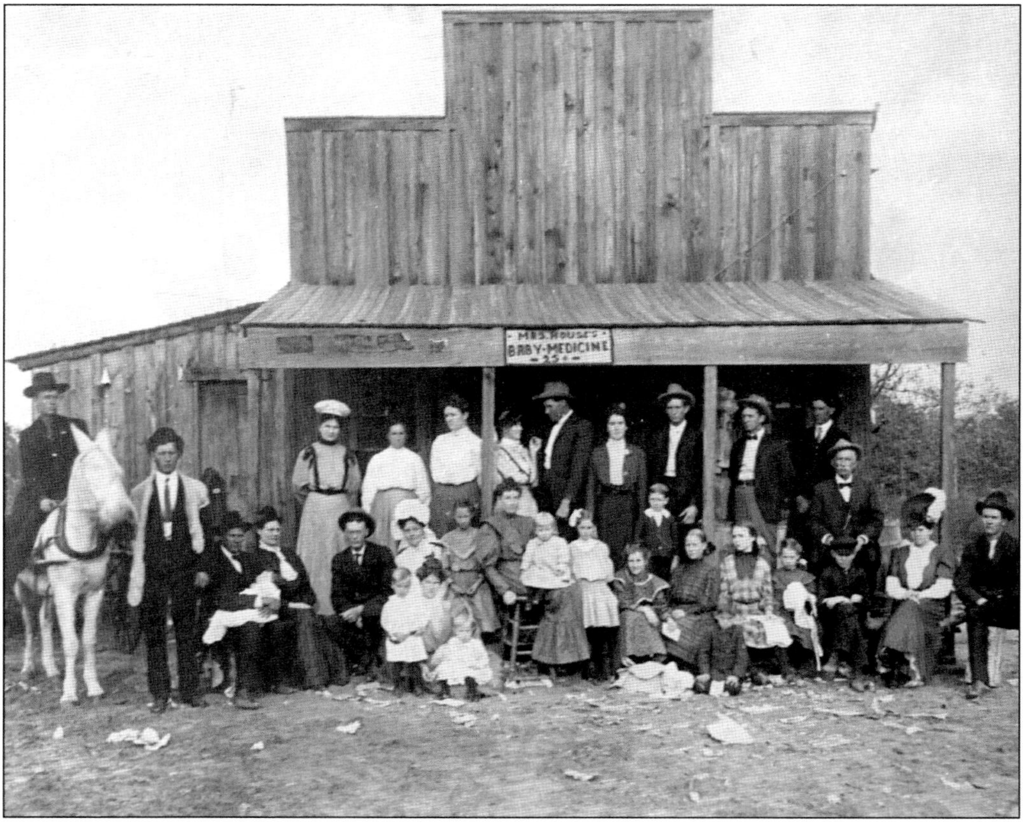

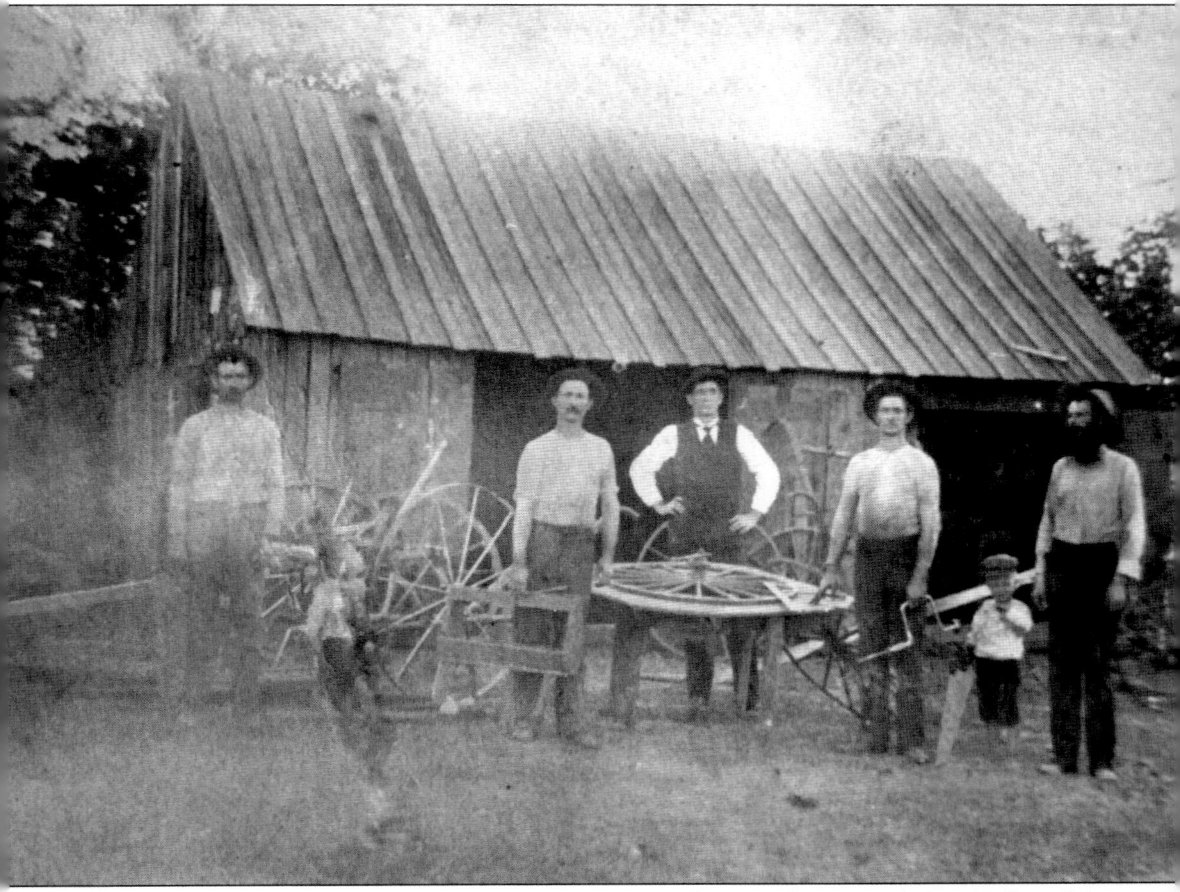

Blacksmiths were in high demand in the late 1800s, especially in rural areas, including Colleyville's parent communities. Farming was tough on both humans and machines, and blacksmiths were needed to repair equipment or make new parts altogether. They also tended to provide many more services in rural outposts such as Bransford. As blacksmiths were able to make and repair tools out of metal, possessed financial savvy to run a business, and had the patience and persistence to keep a fire going year-round, they were ideal to carry the weight of public office. They would often serve as the local magistrate or horse dealer. In most rural communities, making and repairing horseshoes was the prime job of a blacksmith. In a community close to railroad tracks, like Bransford, much of the blacksmith's work came from making repairs to train cars and the railroad itself. John Wilkinson (left of center) owned the blacksmith shop in Bransford. (Courtesy of Tarrant County College Heritage Room.)

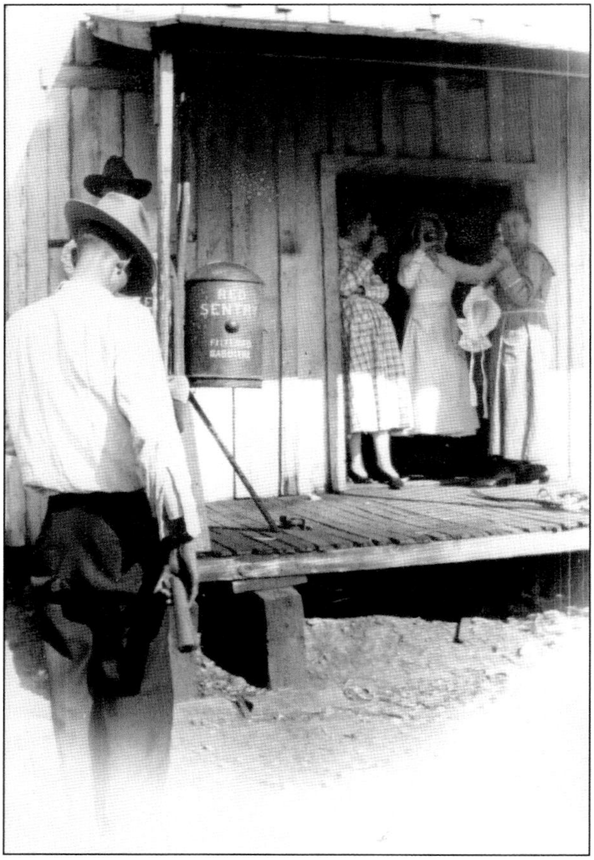

George Couch's store was another early general store in Colleyville. Like James Webb at his Bransford store, Couch carried a little bit of everything. Note the gas can affixed to the front porch. Curtis Siler (back to the camera) is shown here with three unidentified ladies. (Courtesy of Tarrant County College Heritage Room.)

Electricity was a godsend for Clyde and Nora Bass's grocery store. Once electricity was installed at their store near the corner of Glade Road and present-day State Highway 26, the Basses quickly enlarged the establishment to incorporate a meat counter, a feed store, and an icehouse. Clyde and Nora are pictured here manning the counter. (Courtesy of Colleyville Historical Preservation Committee.)

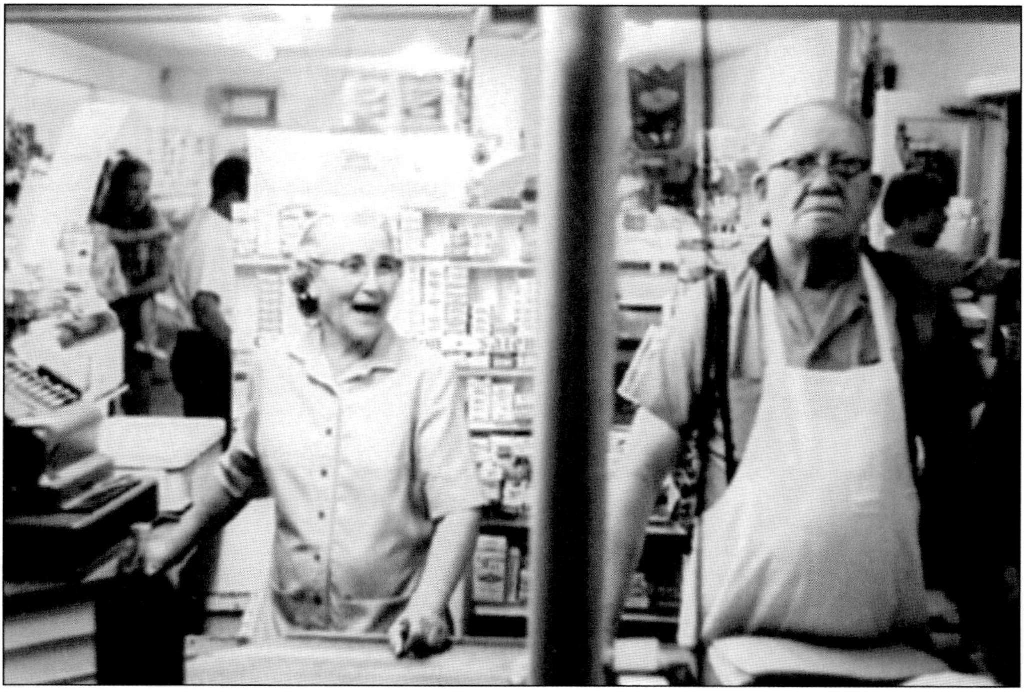

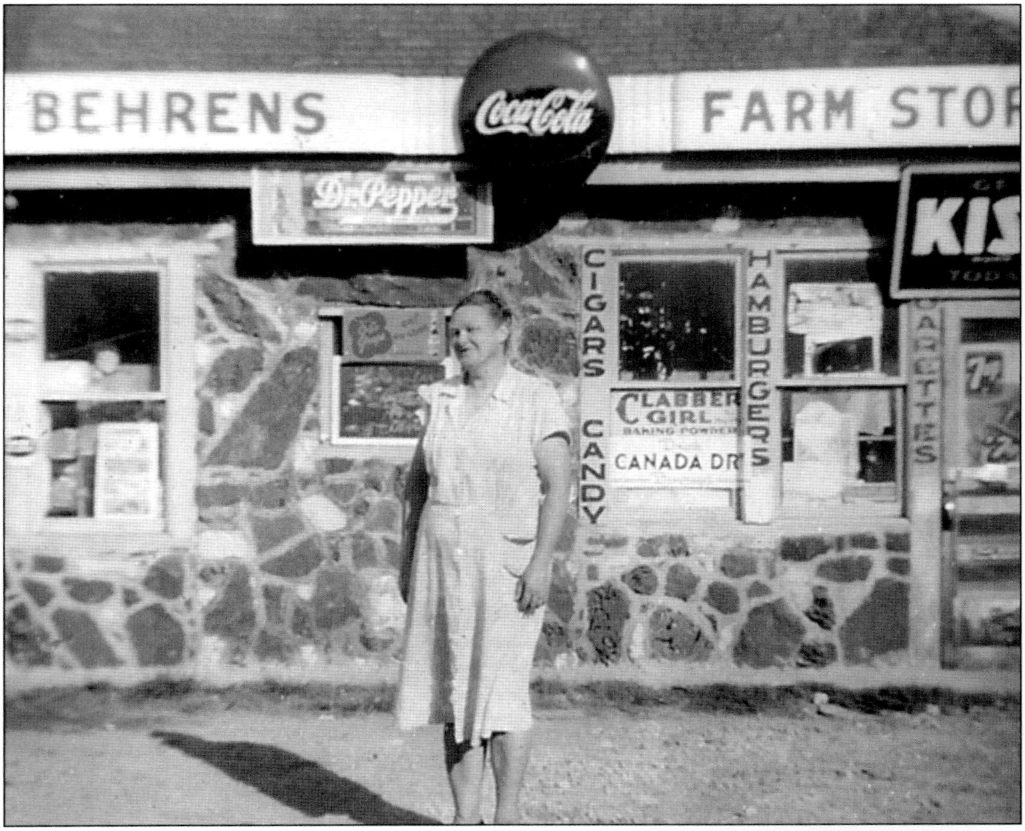

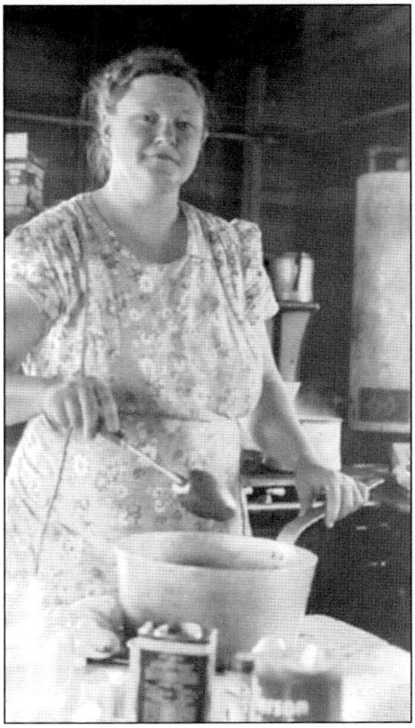

In 1944, Henry and Bessie Behrens rented a rock house and ran their farm store out of it. While Henry was in charge of selling everything from groceries and tires to bait for fishermen, Bessie ran the lunch counter. They are credited with having the first meat market in Colleyville. Above, Bessie poses in front of the store. At right, she makes her famous homemade chili. The meat for it came fresh from the in-house market in the kitchen of the Behrens Farm Store. (Both, courtesy of Colleyville Historical Preservation Committee.)

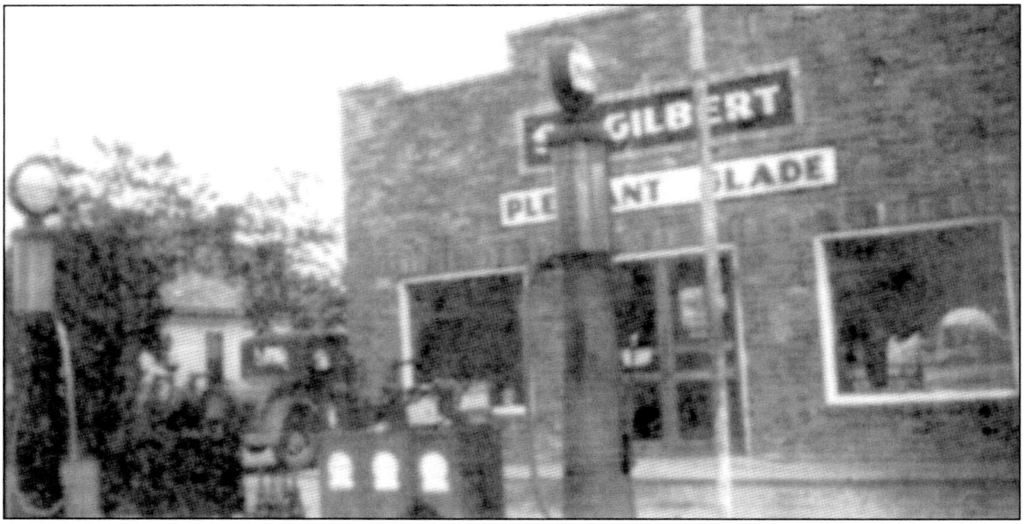

In the fall of 1923, Sidney Gilbert earned $150 picking cotton. He borrowed another $100 from his father and used the $250 to buy groceries in Fort Worth to stock a store he started in the Pleasant Glade parent community. Shown here around 1935 is the second store he opened in Pleasant Glade. (Courtesy of Colleyville Historical Preservation Committee.)

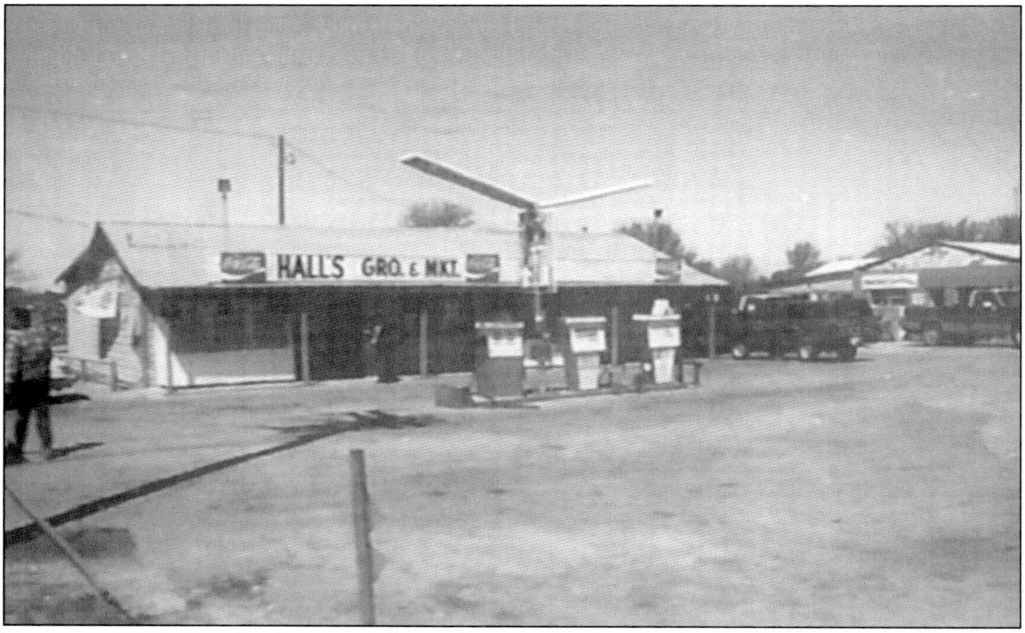

Ever since 1938, there has been a Hall's market in some form or fashion, selling essential items for the surrounding community on the corner of Glade Road and Highway 121. The original Hall's Grocery and Market sold groceries and household essentials. Today, Hall's has a convenience store, gas pumps, and a liquor store. The original building was replaced in the early 1990s by the one that stands today. (Courtesy of Colleyville Historical Preservation Committee.)

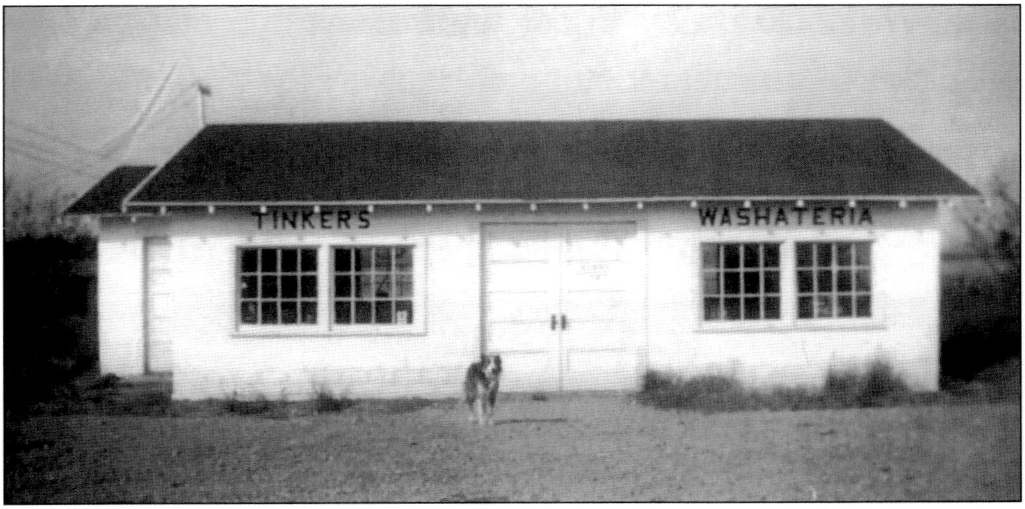

Annie and Burtrand "Buck" Tinker operated the only washateria in town (pictured), on their land next door to their house at 1204 Tinker Road. It was a popular business, as many people had too much iron in their well water for washing clothes, and the Tinkers' well water had much lower iron levels. (Courtesy of Colleyville Historical Preservation Committee.)

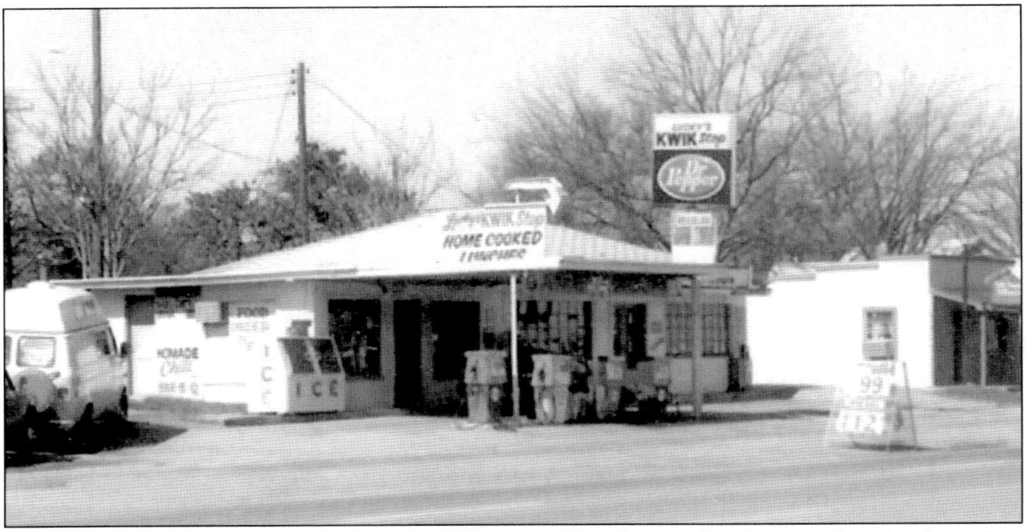

D.B. and Evelyn Couch followed in the footsteps of family member George Couch when they opened their store in 1940. Pictured here in 1986, the store sat at the intersection of Pleasant Run Road and present-day State Highway 26. Besides the Couches, others operated stores, including Lem Foster and Monnie and Luther Cantrell. In 1990, the last tenant to occupy the building was a karate school. (Courtesy of Colleyville Historical Preservation Committee.)

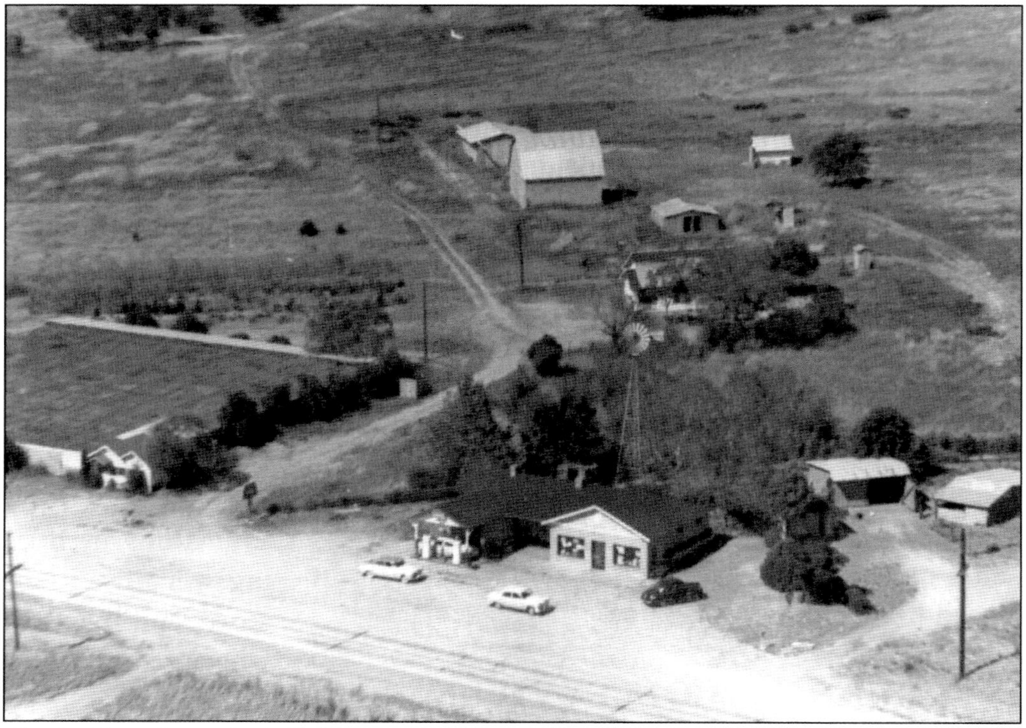

The building from which William and Lula Acuff ran their store has a unique history. Andy Felps had built it for his son, who allegedly ran a honky-tonk there. After the Acuffs opened a service station and grocery store there in 1948, a thief stole money from the register one day. This led to a 16-mile chase and the thief's eventual capture in neighboring Lewisville. (Courtesy of Colleyville Historical Preservation Committee.)

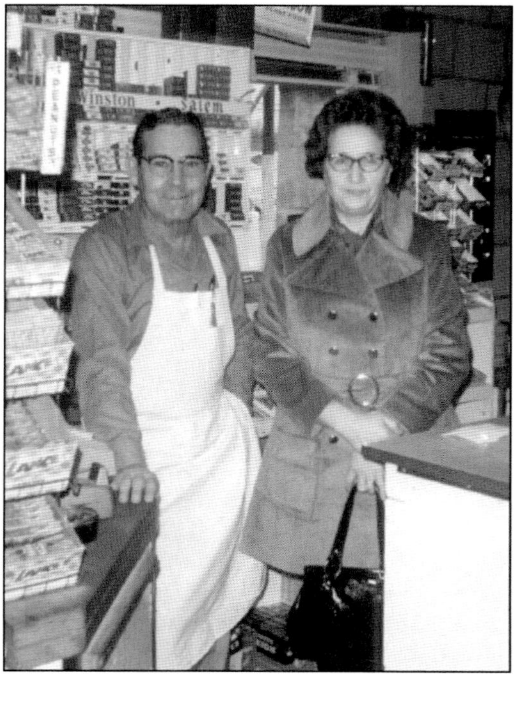

Prior to opening a store as a sole proprietor in Colleyville in the 1950s, Otho Bone was a partner in Gray & Bone Super Food Store in Fort Worth. Initially, Bone and his wife, Marion (pictured), ran their store out of the same building that housed the Colleyville Post Office. Then, Bone purchased land from Colleyville's first mayor, E.R. Eudaly, to build a new Bone Feed & Seed Store. (Courtesy of Colleyville Historical Preservation Committee.)

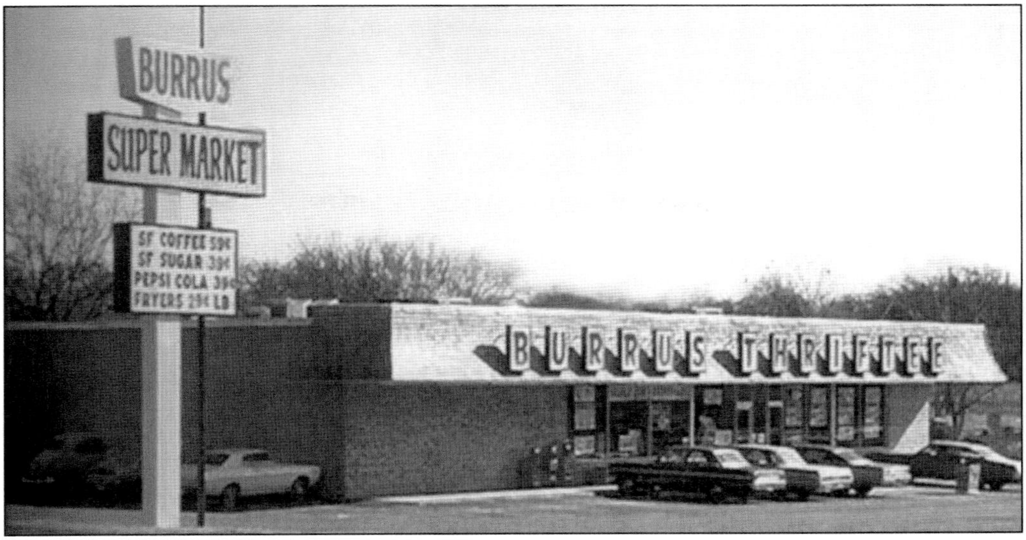

The small groceries that sprouted up along present-day State Highway 26 supplied early Colleyville residents with the necessities for everyday life. But, as time went on, the needs of residents began to change. They saw what their counterparts in Dallas and Fort Worth were getting at their stores, and they wanted the same offerings. In 1970, S.J. Burrus, who already operated a successful Burrus grocery store in Grapevine, bought four acres on present-day State Highway 26 and opened the Burrus Thriftee Super Market (above), Colleyville's first supermarket. The Burrus Deli served as the location for the "Burrus Coffee Club," where the elders of the community gathered. Pictured below are, from left to right, Alan Brimer, Opal Ethridge, Lewsi Fry, Anthony Coley, Terry Cashion, and Ed Coley. (Both, courtesy of Colleyville Historical Preservation Committee.)

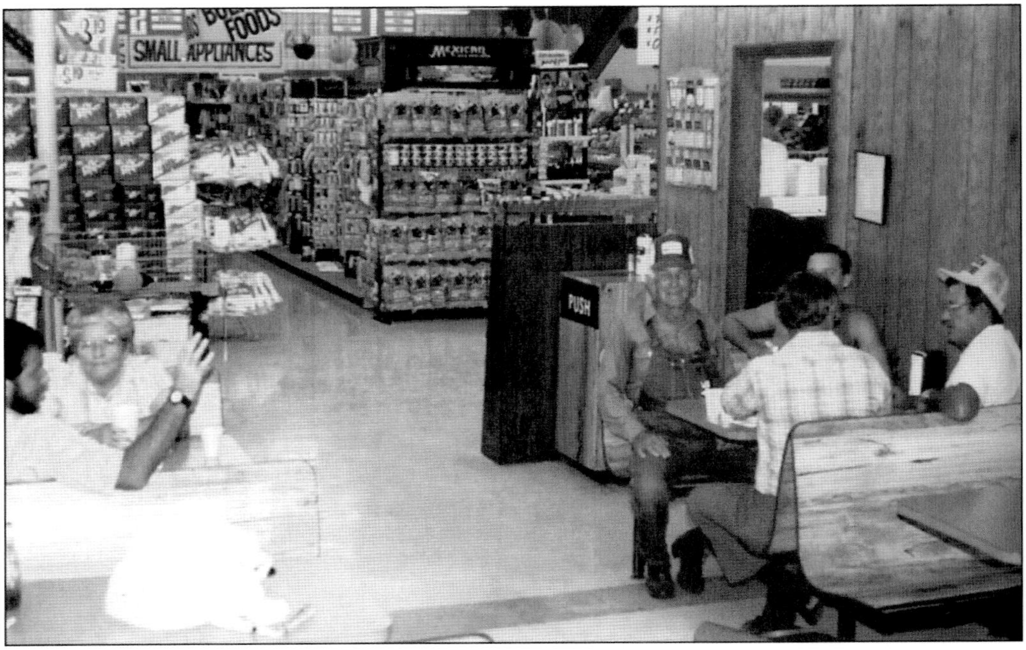

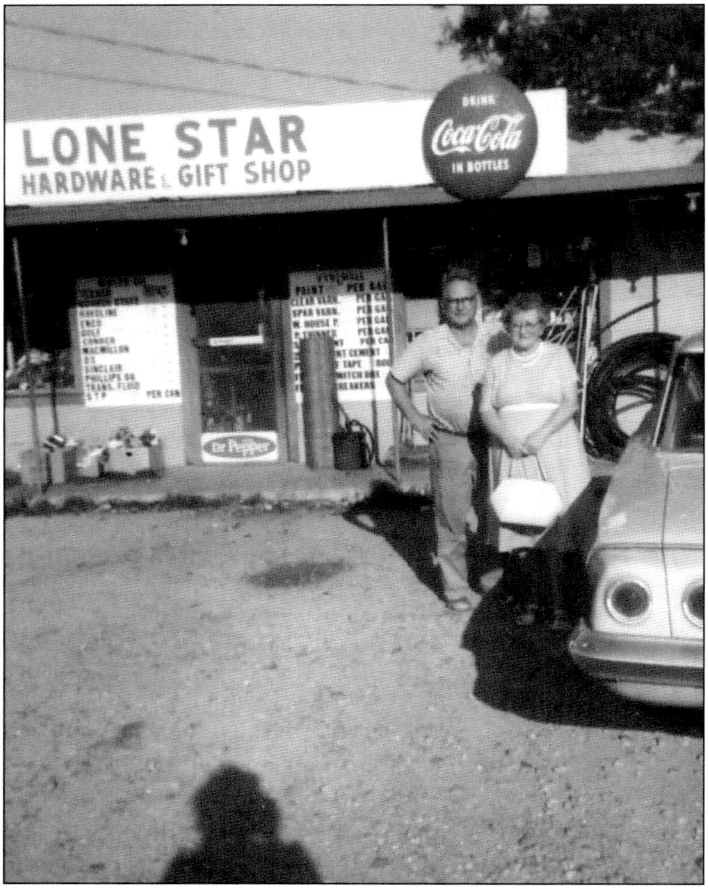

Before Colleyville was incorporated, W.R. and Sarah Livingston opened Lone Star Hardware in the heart of the community, on Glade Road and present-day State Highway 26. Transplants from Indiana, the Livingstons worked long hours at the store. Most of their business came from repeat customers, thankful to not have to make the drive to Grapevine or Fort Worth for hardware supplies. W.R., pictured at left with his wife, Sarah, also served as the first city clerk after incorporation. Davis Hardware came along a little later, in 1965. A true family-run business, wife Johnnie, husband Lester, and their kids Bea and Bob (below), all worked at the store over the years. (Both, courtesy of Colleyville Historical Preservation Committee.)

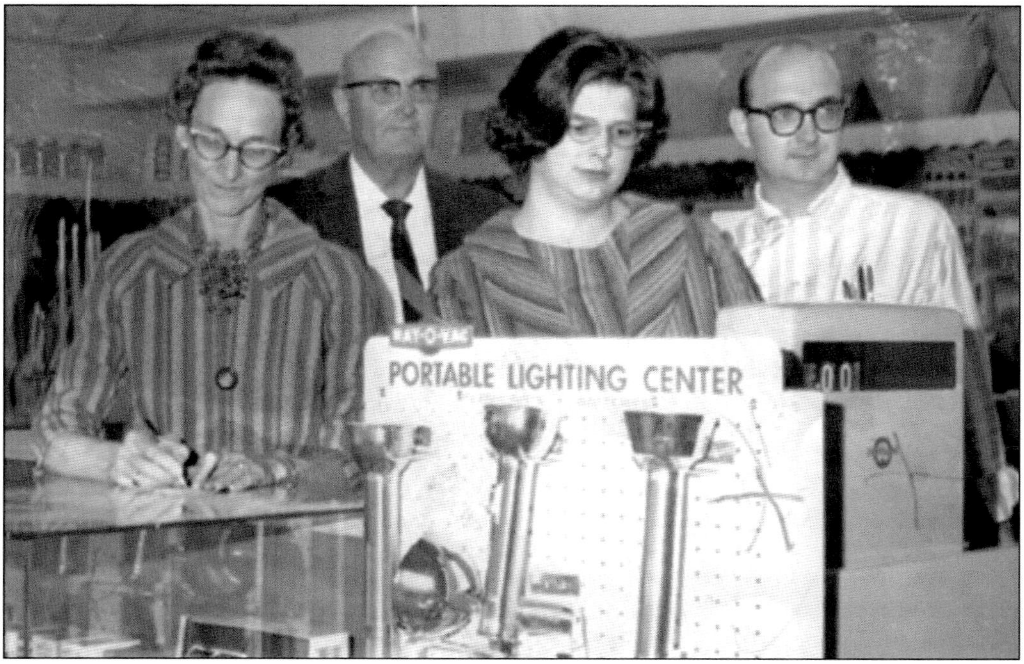

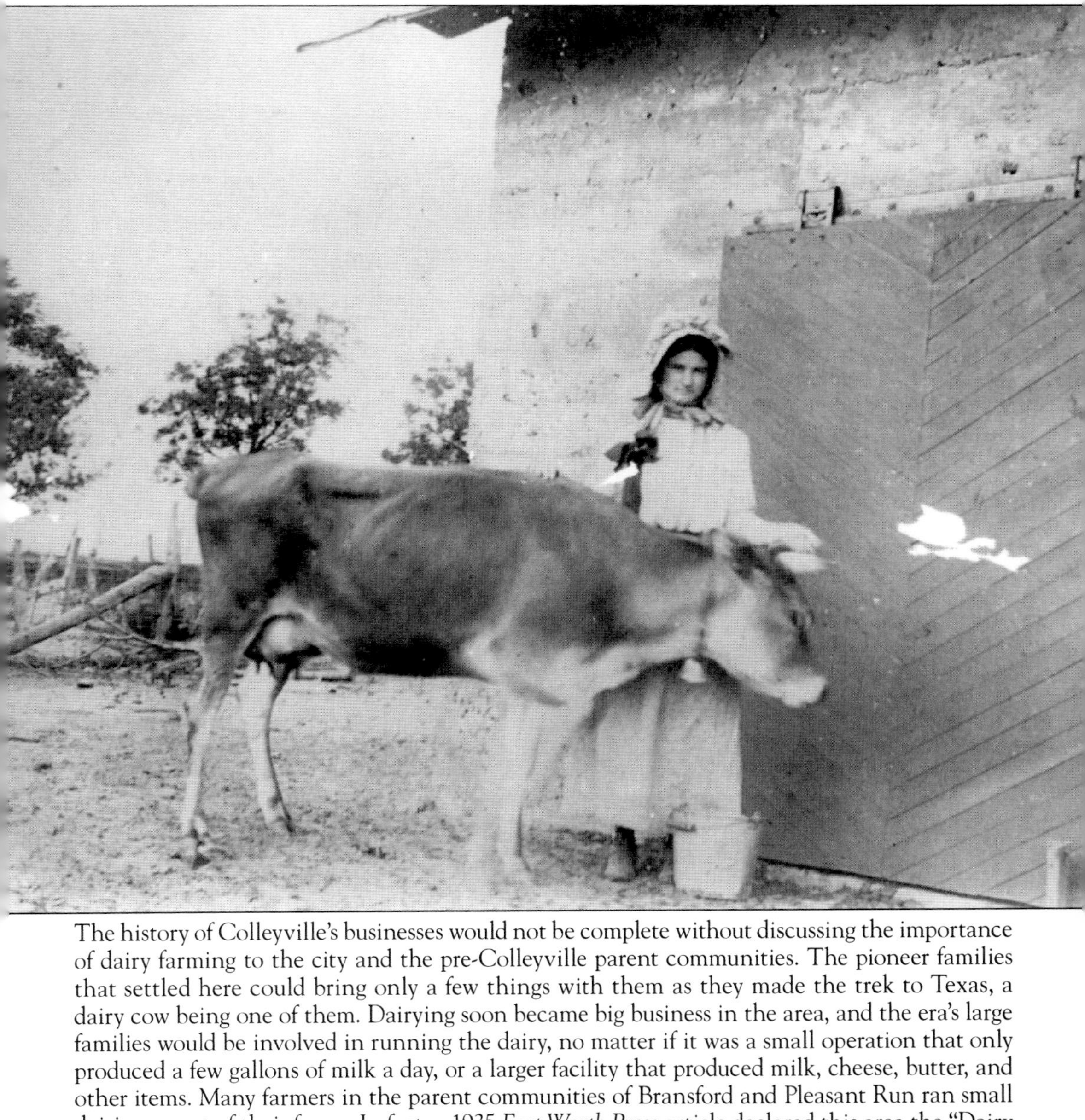

The history of Colleyville's businesses would not be complete without discussing the importance of dairy farming to the city and the pre-Colleyville parent communities. The pioneer families that settled here could bring only a few things with them as they made the trek to Texas, a dairy cow being one of them. Dairying soon became big business in the area, and the era's large families would be involved in running the dairy, no matter if it was a small operation that only produced a few gallons of milk a day, or a larger facility that produced milk, cheese, butter, and other items. Many farmers in the parent communities of Bransford and Pleasant Run ran small dairies as part of their farms. In fact, a 1935 *Fort Worth Press* article declared this area the "Dairy center of Tarrant County." Seen here around 1914, Pauline "Belle" Bidault poses with one of their cows on the family farm. (Courtesy of Tarrant County College Heritage Room.)

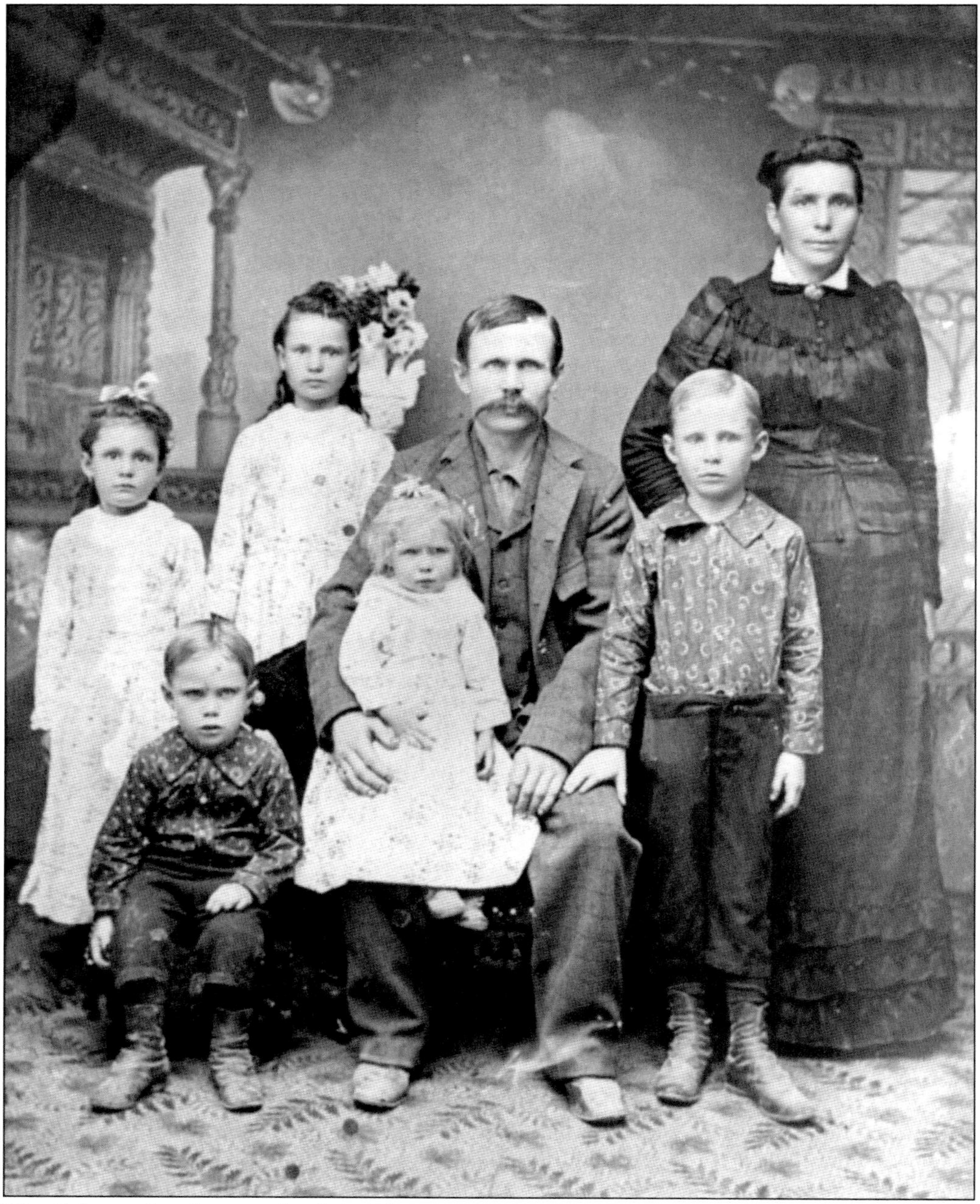

The Behrens family is credited with having the first commercial dairy business, which began operating in 1898. The dairy, which was located on the family farm just off of present-day Glade Road, sold butter, cream, and ice cream under the Behrens label. They also hauled the milk they made at the dairy to Fort Worth and sold it to Swift & Company, one of the nation's "Big Four" meatpackers of the early 1900s. The dairy operation occupied most of the family's 160-acre farm, and 60 cows were milked each day. The dairy continued operation until the 1950s, when family patriarch Henry Behrens died and his wife sold the cows to a local rancher. All the members of the Behrens family pictured here worked at the dairy at one point in time. From left to right are (first row) Ernest, Martha, and Charles; (second row) Minnie, Ella, Charles, and Minnie. (Courtesy of Tarrant County College Heritage Room.)

Dairying was not only a family operation that needed all hands on deck to be successful. The businesses were often passed down not only through the generations of the same family, but other families would often buy dairy operations when they came up for sale and continue the tradition. The McPherson Dairy was owned by the Seviek family, who operated it from 1925 to 1947. It was sold to A.G. and Mabel Benedict, who in turn sold a portion of the land to her daughter and son-in-law Barbara Jo and T.J. McPherson. The photograph at right shows Joseph Seviek with his daughter Agnes beside their Model-T Ford. Below is A.G. and Mabel Benedict with two dogs and two cars. (Both, courtesy of Colleyville Historical Preservation Committee.)

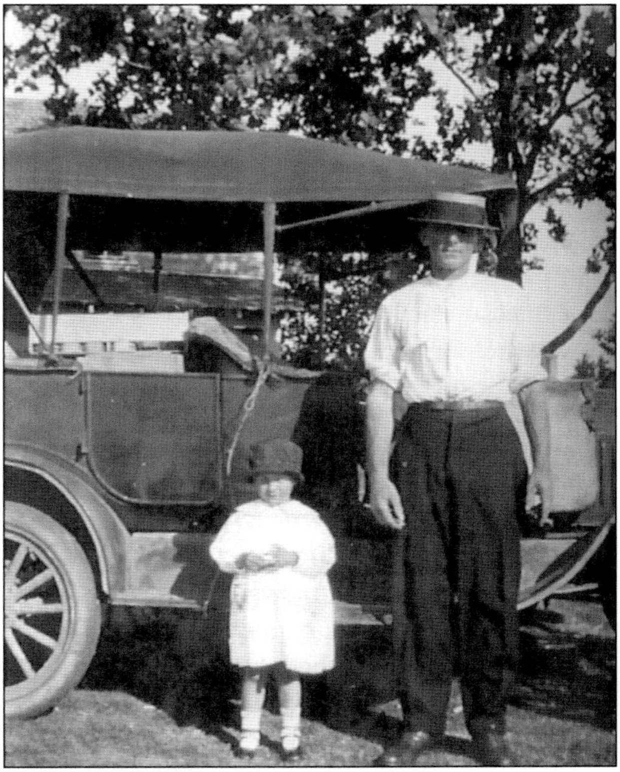

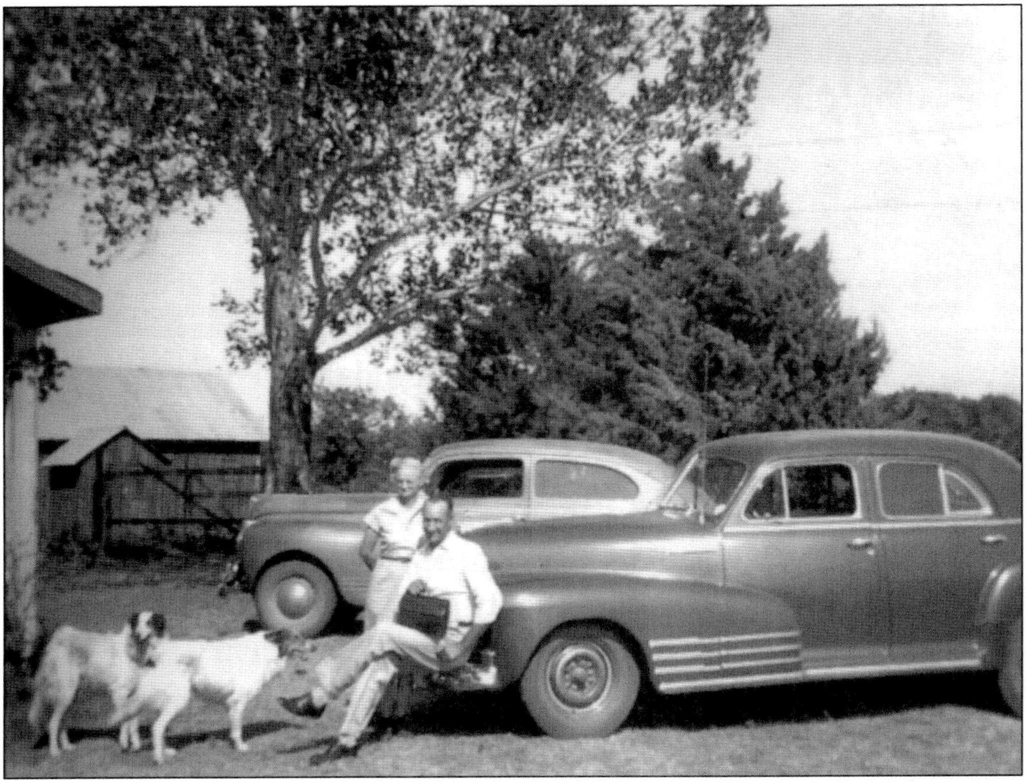

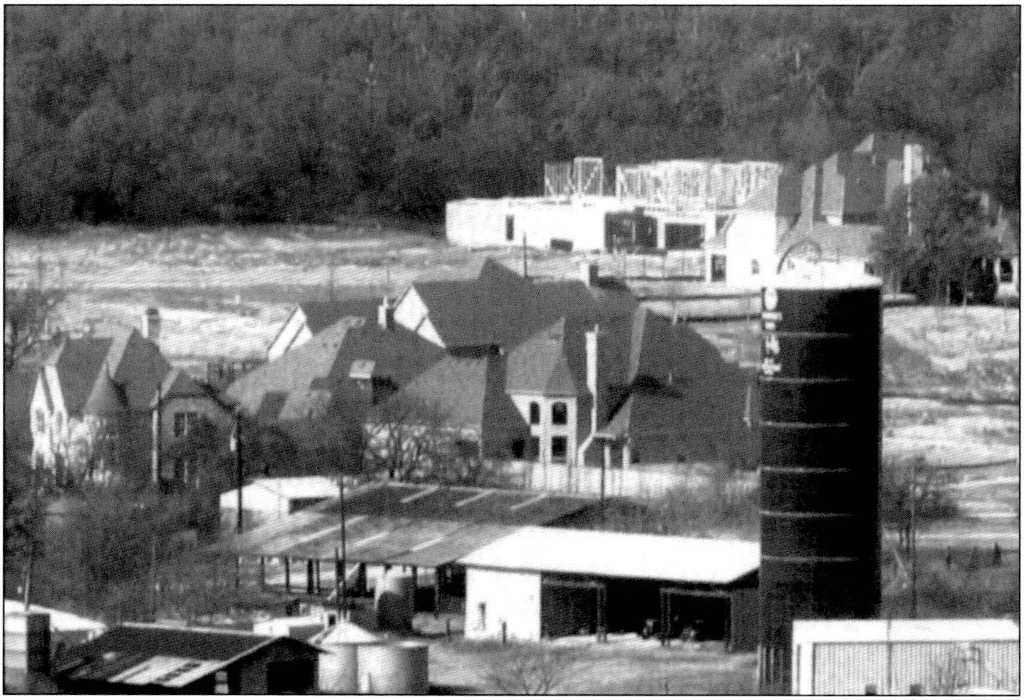

Here is a 2005 photograph of the old silo of McPherson Dairy, with new housing construction in the background. (Courtesy of Colleyville Historical Preservation Committee.)

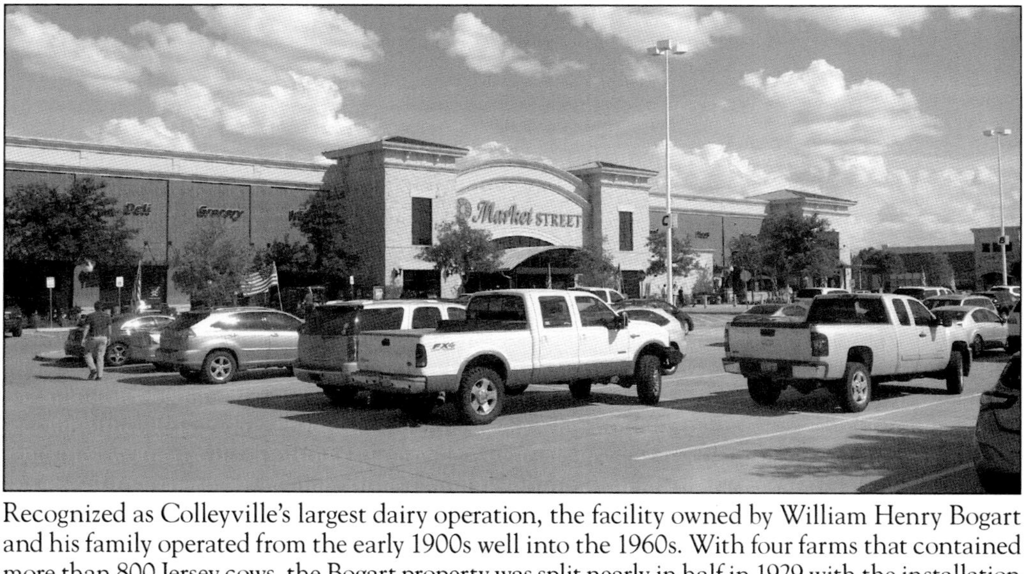

Recognized as Colleyville's largest dairy operation, the facility owned by William Henry Bogart and his family operated from the early 1900s well into the 1960s. With four farms that contained more than 800 Jersey cows, the Bogart property was split nearly in half in 1929 with the installation of present-day State Highway 26. The Bogarts also owned and operated the Golden Gate Dairy bottling plant in Fort Worth, one of the area's first grade-A bottling facilities. Their bottling plant supplied milk to Grapevine schools under the school lunch milk program from its inception until the plant closed. Market Street grocery store today occupies the site where the Bogart Dairy barn used to stand. Designated a historical site, the Bogart Dairy is indicated with a marker telling the tale of the facility and its importance to the early Colleyville economy. The marker stands at the southwest corner of the Market Street building. (Courtesy of Mark Fadden.)

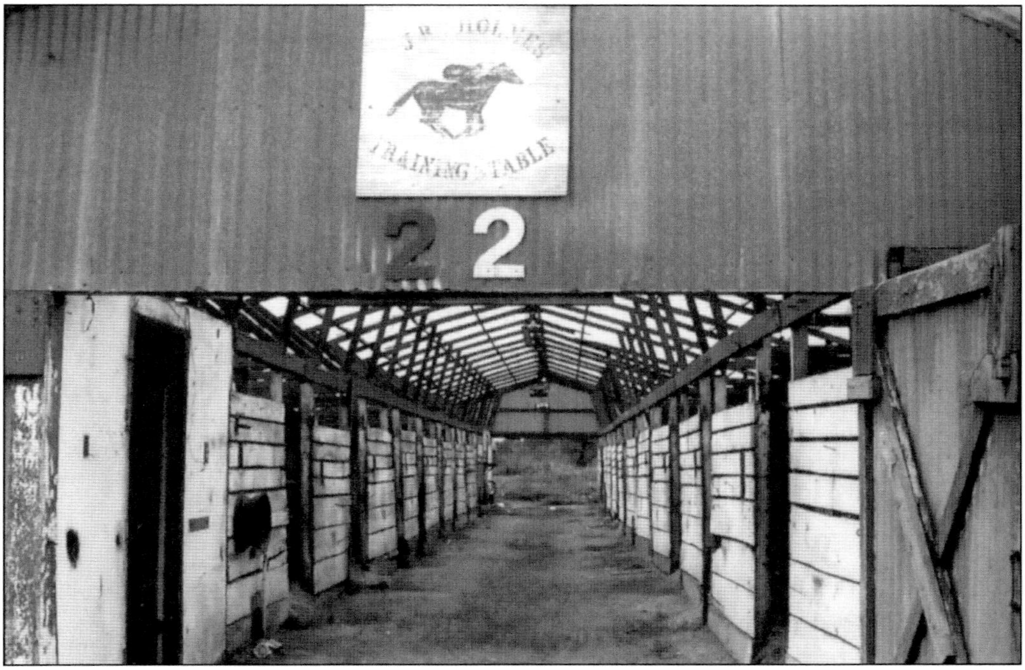

Although betting was not officially allowed at Colleyville's horse-racing track, a lot of "unofficial" betting was going on in the grandstands. Legend has it that bets would get as high as $20,000 if a race featured a local favorite. Ross Downs was a favorite track of those on the racing circuit, due to its combination of red dirt sitting on loamy soil, which not only drained quickly but was also forgiving on the horses. Several streets in the Ross Downs subdivision, including Beddo Court, McMakin Court, and Baker Court, are named after the trainers, jockeys, and others who dedicated their lives to the sport of horse racing and were a big part of keeping Ross Downs going. (Both, courtesy of Colleyville Historical Preservation Committee.)

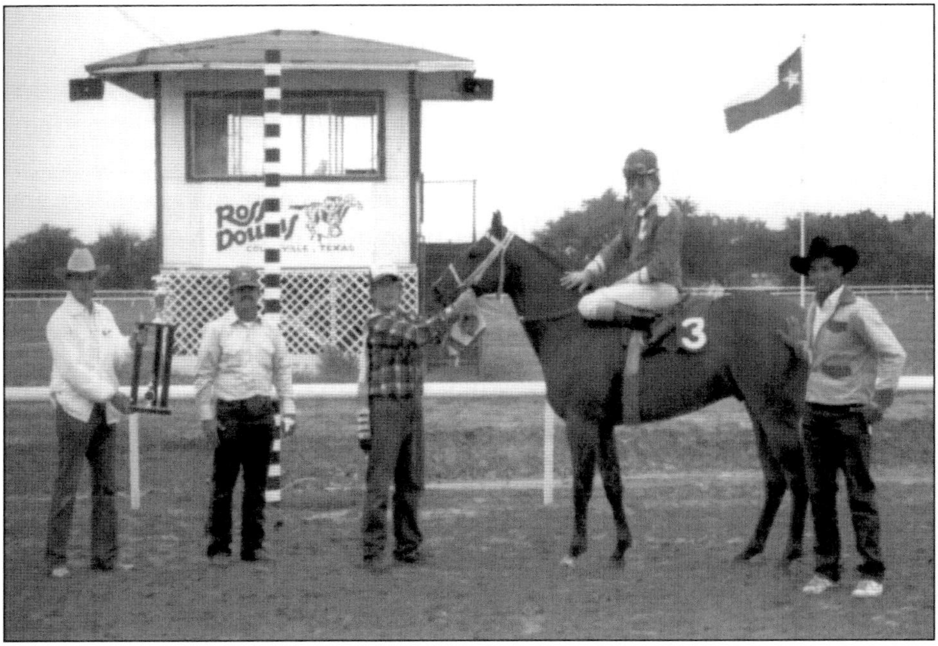

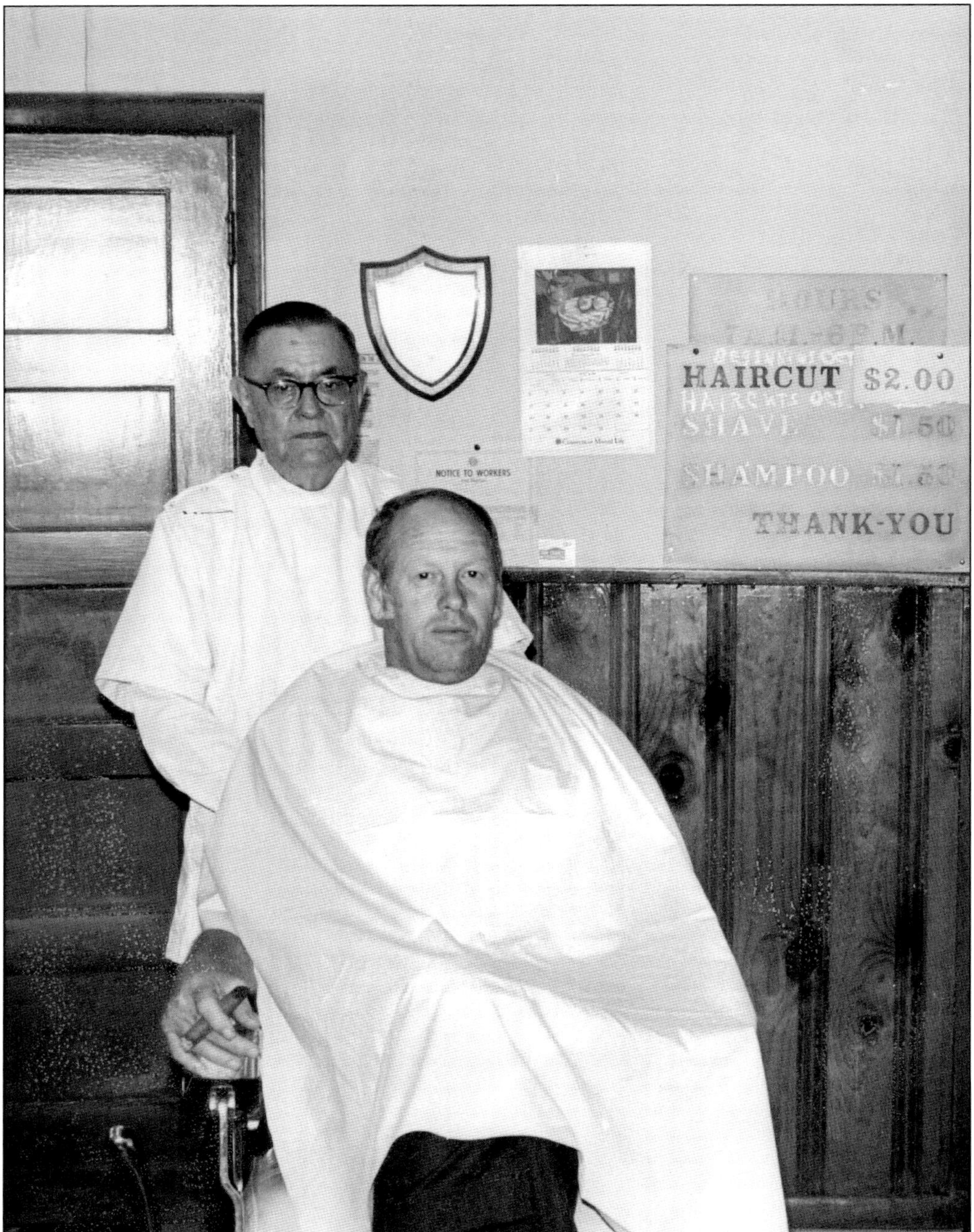

Pictured here is the interior of Clarence Cobb's barbershop. Cobb had been cutting hair in Smithfield for nearly 55 years as of 1975. He served five generations of some area families. Ford Reynolds of Colleyville is Cobb's customer here. (Courtesy of Tarrant County College Heritage Room.)

Five

Prominent Families and Influential Citizens

Cities are not made up of strangers. At its core, a city is an organization of neighbors that blends the characteristics from the land it rests upon with the people who inhabit it, giving that city its distinct personality.

Although Colleyville is surrounded by other bedroom communities similar to it in size and population, its history was shaped by the collective will of its citizens. When the opportunity arose, leaders imparted their determination to guide the city. When forces beyond the control of its citizens came into play, those prominent families and influential citizens did what they could to ensure the city and its residents would benefit as much as possible. The strength of the community's character and the never-say-die grit of its residents are why Colleyville is the premier community it is today. From the early pioneers who worked the land, to the businessmen and businesswomen who continue to provide essential services to friends and neighbors today, the spirit of togetherness, neighborliness, and determination of the city's families and citizens will help keep Colleyville moving forward.

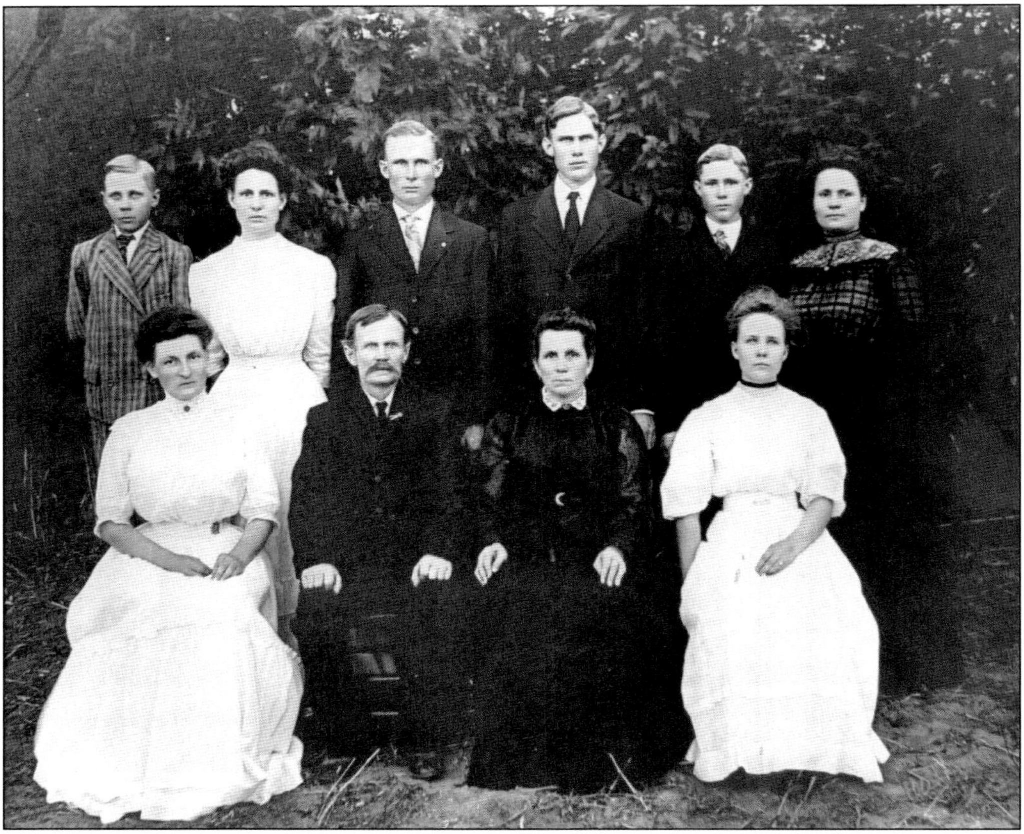

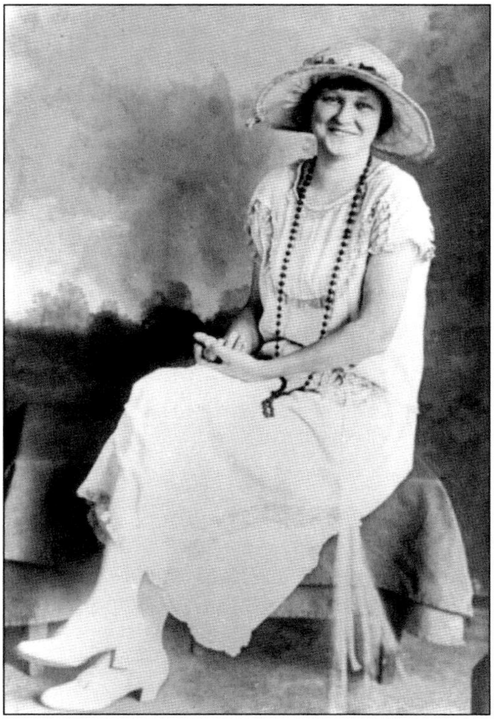

The Behrens family had the first commercial dairy in the area, and members of the family have helped run various businesses over the years, including a store on present-day State Highway 26 from 1944 to 1970. Members of the Charles Behrens family of Colleyville are, from left to right, (seated) unidentified, Charles, Minnie, and Martha; (standing) Henry, Minnie, Charles, Ernest, Bill, and Ella. (Courtesy of Tarrant County College Heritage Room.)

Along with her husband, Henry, Bessie (Allen) Behrens (pictured) was a determined, community-minded person who wanted to make sure her children had a better life. The Behrens were very involved in political and educational organizations, and were among the 27 people who signed the petition to incorporate the city. (Courtesy of Tarrant County College Heritage Room.)

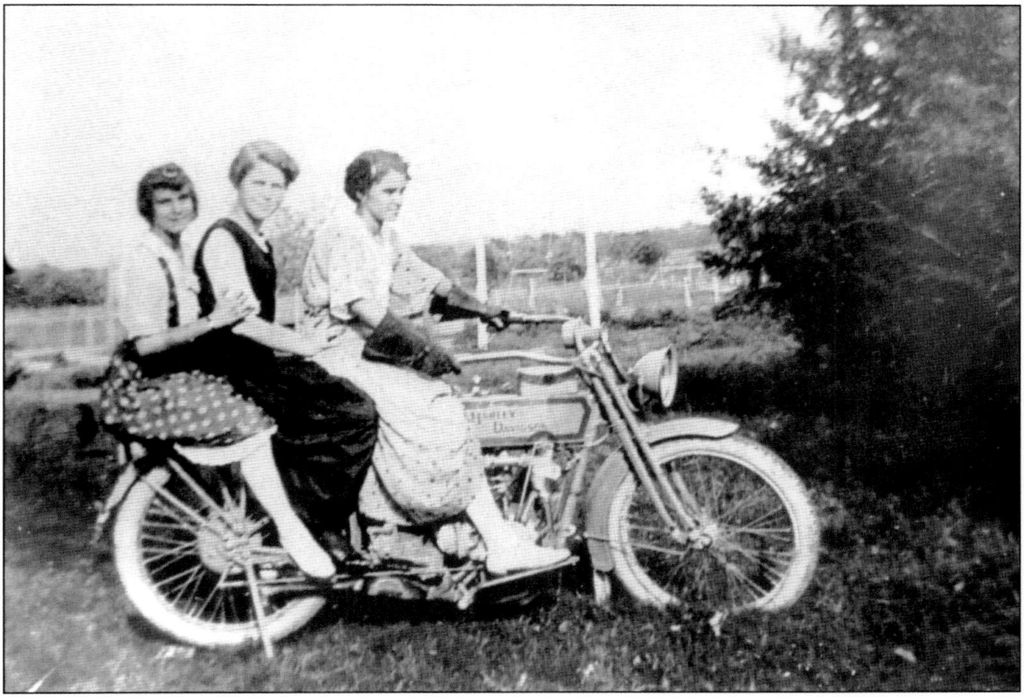

Entertaining French soldiers who came over on the weekends from training at nearby Fort Worth, the Bidaults taught their children that life is something to be enjoyed. In the above photograph, their daughters Nan (far left) and Henrietta (second from left), born in 1901 and 1899, respectively, ride with Bonnie Pate on her brother Lou's Harley Davidson motorcycle in 1919. The Bidault family made quite a lasting impression on the pre-Colleyville area, and the concrete home the family built still stands today. But it seemed the pull from their French homeland was too great. After World War I, Anthelm and Jeanne sold their property and returned to France. There, as in Texas, Anthelm became a prize-winning fruit farmer. Shown below is Jeanne with their children. (Both, courtesy of Tarrant County College Heritage Room.)

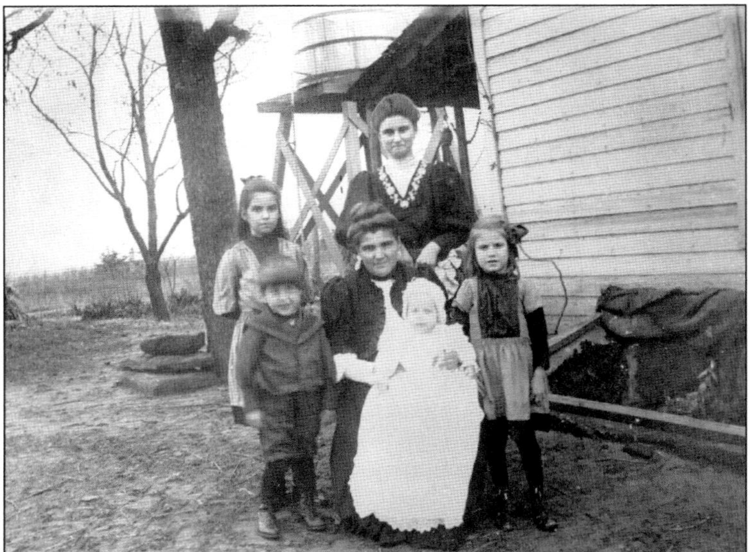

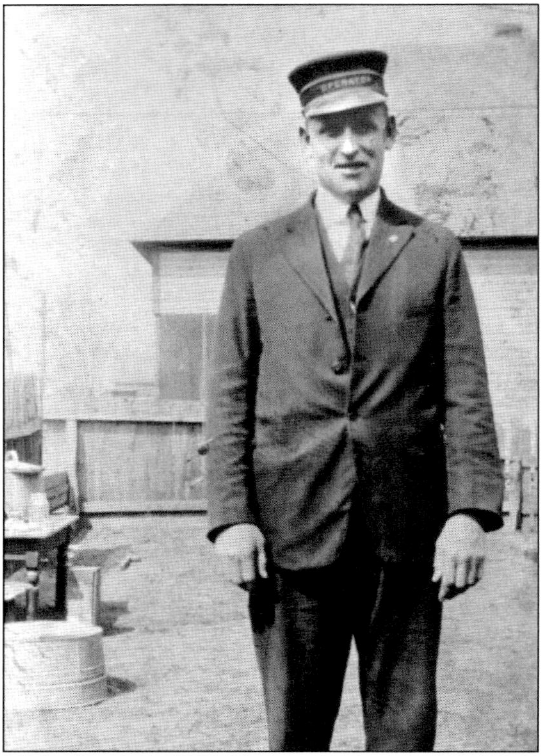

With all that Dr. Lilburn Colley did for the community for which he was named, it is easy to forget that his family members left their mark on the area as well. Colley and his wife, Martha, had four children, Ethel, Thaddeus, Darius, and Cyrus. Thaddeus, who followed in his father's footsteps to become a doctor, was often referred to as "young Dr. Colley." He moved to the nearby city of Keller, where he practiced medicine and bought a drugstore. Darius, pictured at left in his uniform, became the first conductor of the electric streetcar line in Fort Worth. For Cyrus, pictured below at left with Thaddeus, farming was in his blood. He stayed on at the family's 200-acre farm to help run it. (Both courtesy of Tarrant County College Heritage Room.)

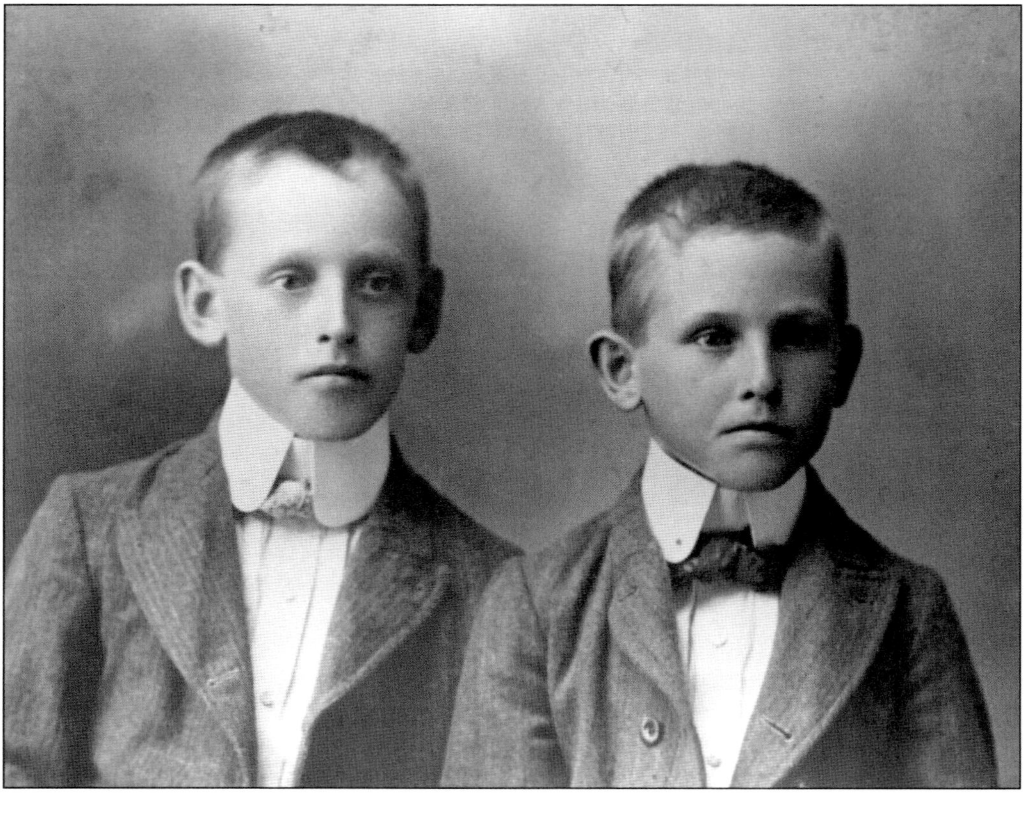

If there was ever a prominent family in a city, the McCains would be that family in Colleyville. William Dunn, an original pioneer of the area, had land in Pleasant Run, a portion of which his daughter, Sudie, and her husband, James Leonardis "Lonnie" McCain, purchased. It remains in the family today. John McCain Road, a major east-west thoroughfare through the northern part of town, is named for their son John. These two photographs show the James L. McCain family at different times. Pictured at right are, from left to right, John, Sudie, Tom (front), Charles, James, and Edd in the late 1800s. The below photograph shows the same family in the early 1900s. They are, from left to right, (seated) James and Sudie; (standing) Charles, John, Edd, Thomas, Elmer, and Eula. (Both, courtesy of Tarrant County College Heritage Room.)

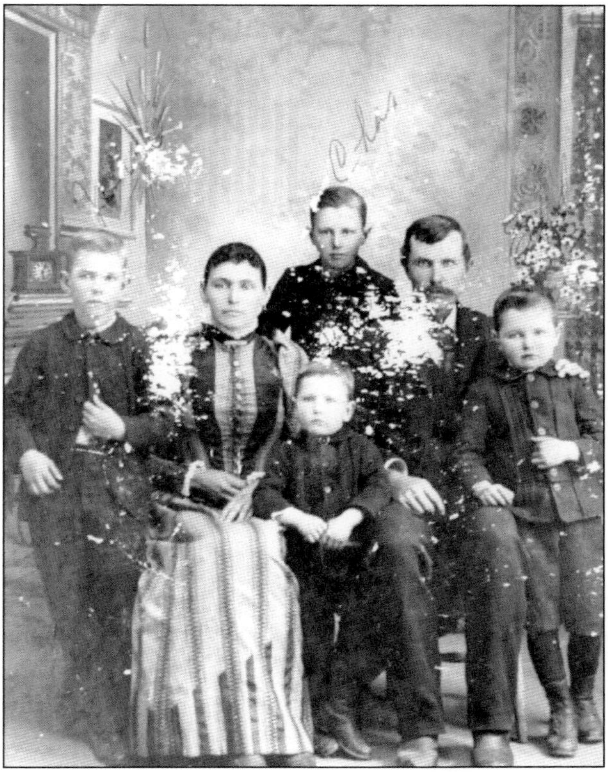

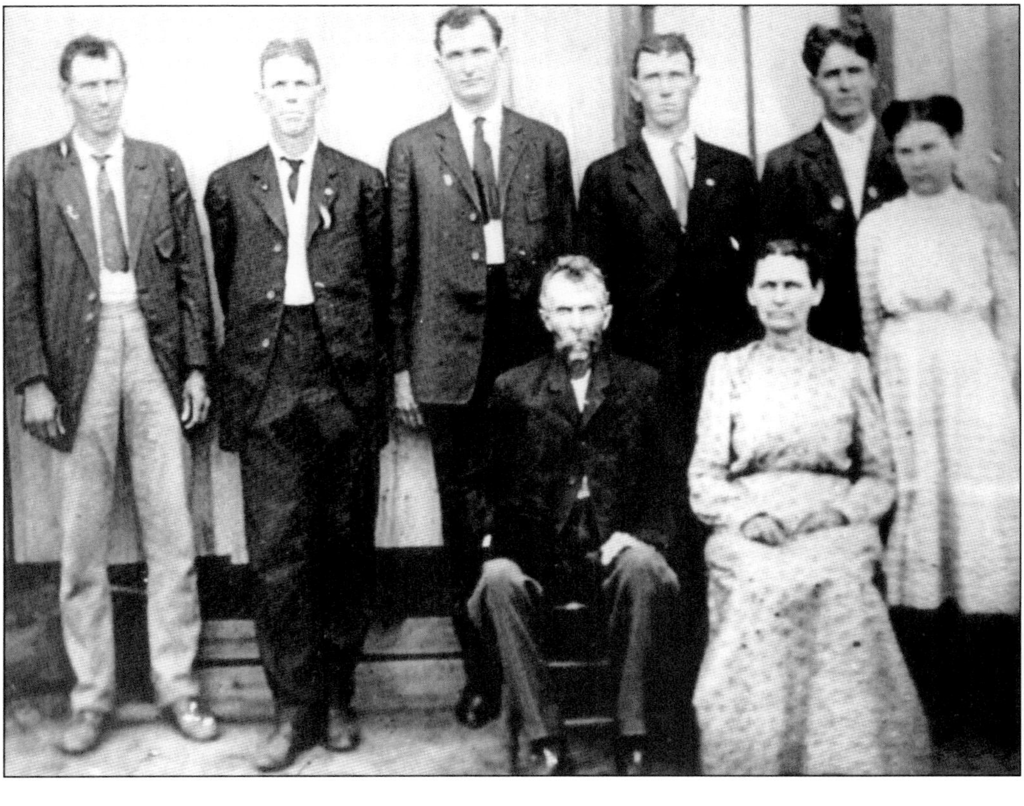

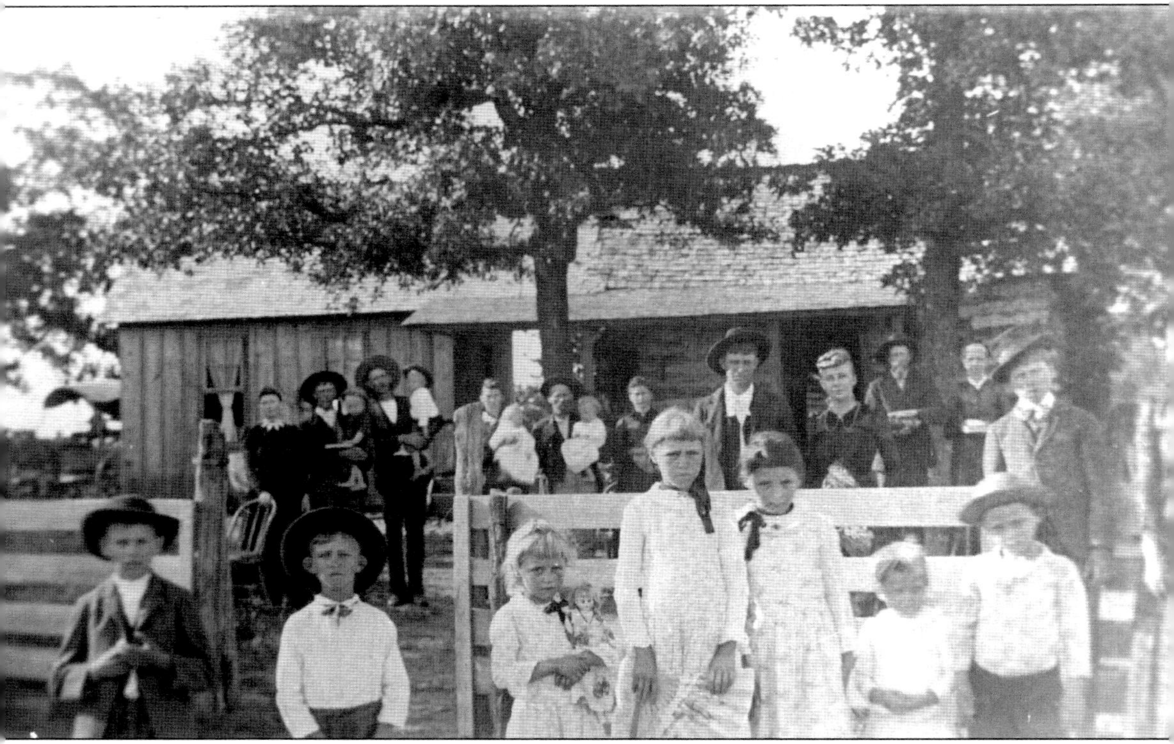

Samuel Sparger was the patriarch of a very influential family that helped both the parent community of Spring Garden and the City of Colleyville blossom. Harvey "Harv" Richard Sparger, one of Samuel Sparger's three children to settle the pre-Colleyville area, brought his family to Bedford by train in 1879. He bought several hundred acres of farmland from his brother Thomas in Spring Garden. Generations of the Sparger family grew fruits and vegetables and raised cattle, cotton, and horses on the family land. Sparger Park, named for the family, sits on a portion of the family's land along Bedford Road. This family photograph was taken in front of their original log cabin, which had a frame room addition. (Courtesy of Tarrant County College Heritage Room.)

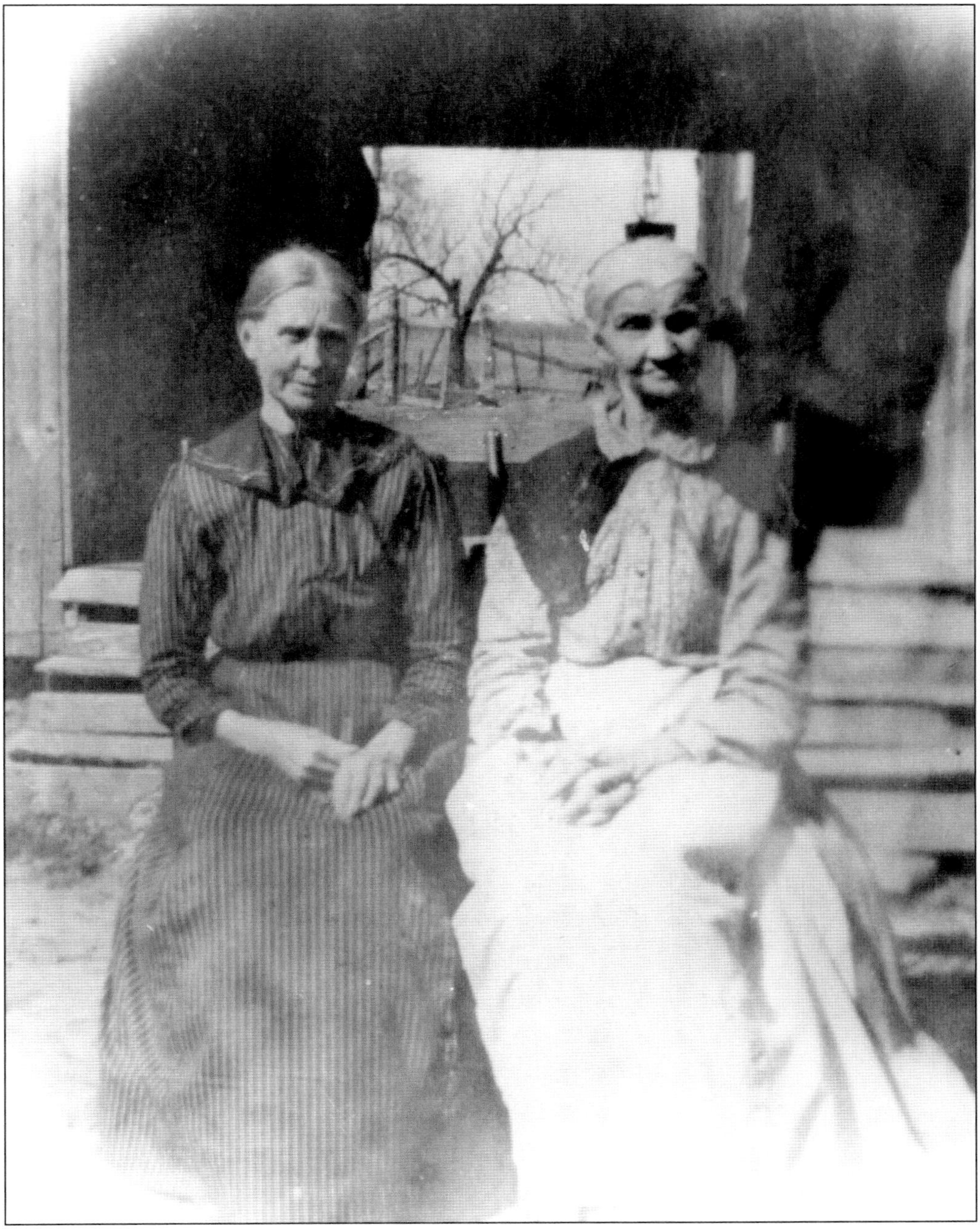

While history is mainly written about the deeds of men, women were colorful characters as well. To look at this photograph of Mary Sparger (right), with her daughter Margaret Sparger Rogers, one would not think of the courageous acts she performed to keep her family together. As the story goes, her husband, Harvey "Harv" Sparger, had been captured by Yankee soldiers during the Civil War. Mary rode a blind horse while carrying a baby to his location and stayed with him until he was let go. Their love lasted a lifetime, until Harv's death in 1914. Mary followed him shortly thereafter, dying in 1916. Both of their bodies were transported to Smithfield Cemetery in a horse-drawn carriage that is still owned by the Foust & Son Funeral Home in Grapevine. (Courtesy of Tarrant County College Heritage Room.)

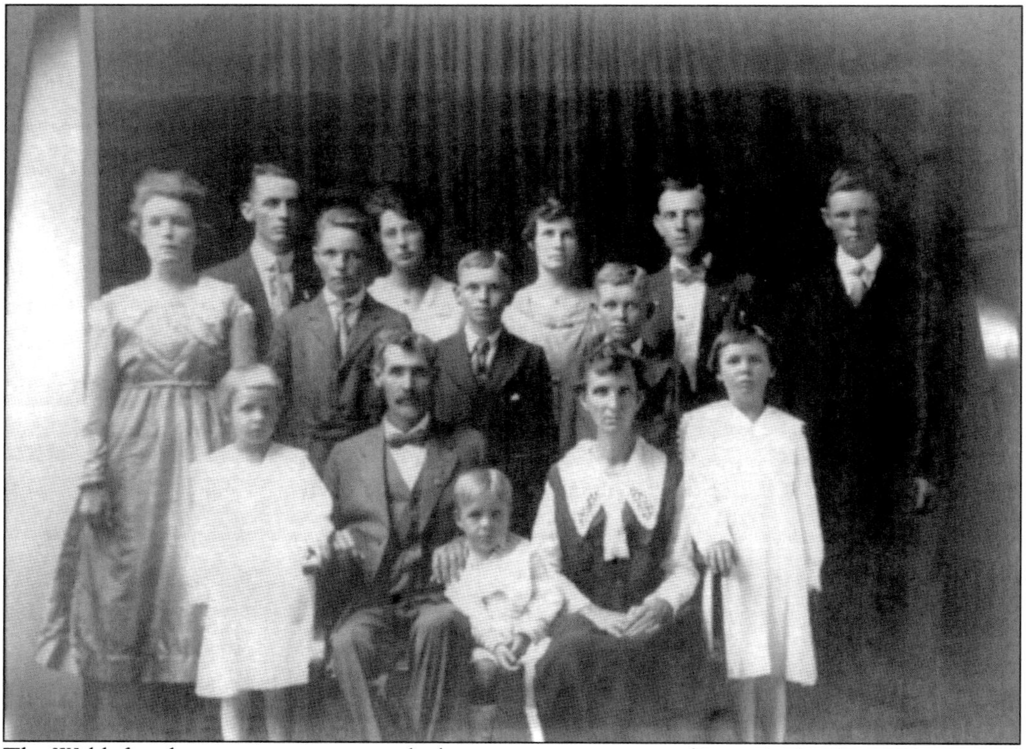

The Webb family was synonymous with the parent community of Bransford. John Rueben Webb and his wife, Orpha (Waterson) Webb, came to Bransford from Tennessee in 1895. John initially worked at the nearby gravel pit and then on the railroad before opening a general store from 1914 until 1925. For the Webbs, family and community meant everything. All of their children worked at the store. When the boys got old enough, they went to work on the railroad. While most of the Webb children moved away as they became adults, they made it back home almost every Sunday for a family dinner. The Webb family is pictured here in 1917. The family members are, from left to right, (first row) Adalene Nettie, John Rueben Webb, Winfrey Owen, Orpha Violet Waterson Webb, and Wilmer Grace; (second row) Ruby Mae, John Andrew, Stanley Eugene, and Aubrey Warren; (third row) Clarence Richard, Gladys Gabbert Webb, Sadie Webb Austin, Charlie Austin, and Kelly Howell. (Courtesy of Colleyville Historical Preservation Committee.)

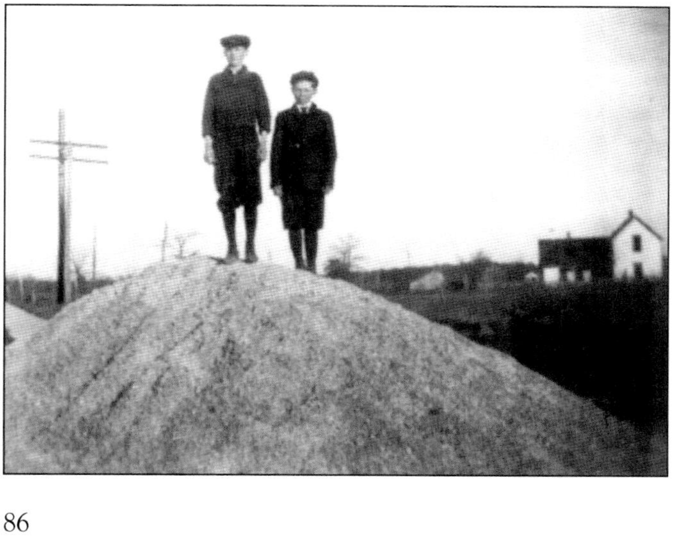

Kids will be kids, finding ways to have fun even in the simplest of ways. Stanley (left) and Aubrey Webb are shown here around 1920, playing "king of the mountain" on one of the gravel piles that was probably used for the maintenance of the railroad beds along the Cotton Belt line. Note the Webb house in the background on the right. (Courtesy of Colleyville Historical Preservation Committee.)

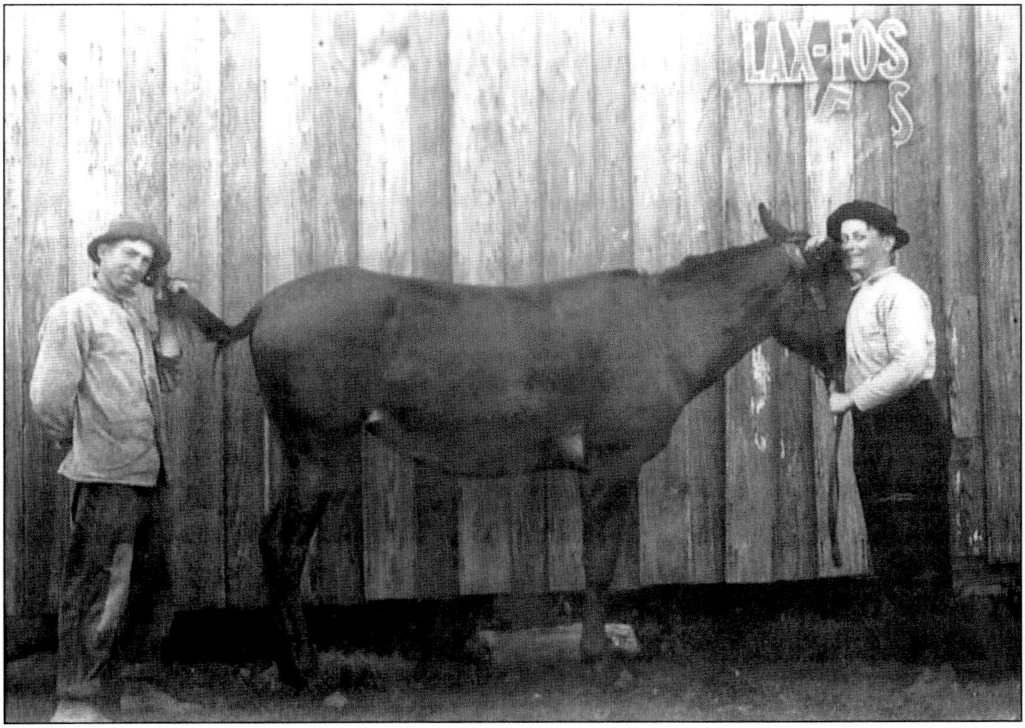

Speaking of horsing around, here we see Jasper Reynolds (left), son of two of Pleasant Run parent community's earliest settlers, Robinson Carusoe "Rob" Reynolds and Annie Reynolds, on the listening end of a "mule-call" from Clarence Webb at the Webb General Store in Bransford. This photograph was taken in 1911. (Courtesy of Colleyville Historical Preservation Committee.)

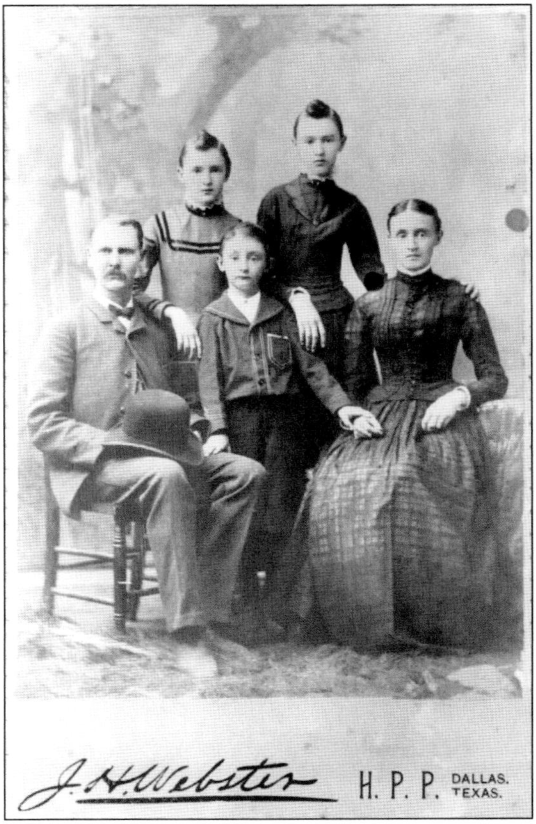

As one of area pioneer Samuel C.H. Witten's 10 children, Pinckney Lafayette Witten grew up on the Witten family farm in the parent community of Spring Garden in the mid- to late 1800s. He is pictured here as a grown man with members of his family. Shown are, from left to right, Pinckney Witten, Nancy Jeanette Witten, Ed Witten, Bella Witten, and Betty Harris Witten. (Courtesy of Tarrant County College Heritage Room.)

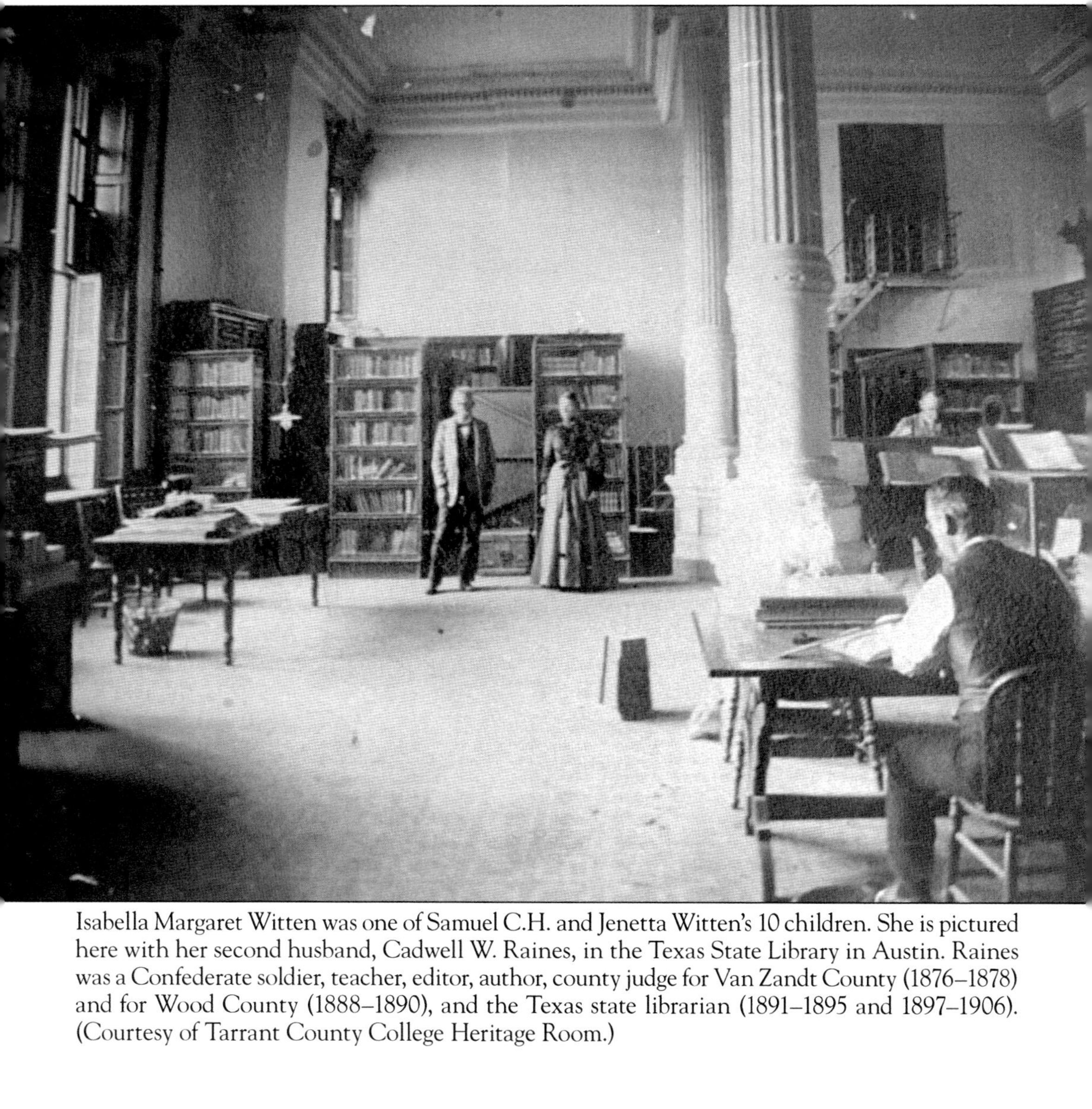

Isabella Margaret Witten was one of Samuel C.H. and Jenetta Witten's 10 children. She is pictured here with her second husband, Cadwell W. Raines, in the Texas State Library in Austin. Raines was a Confederate soldier, teacher, editor, author, county judge for Van Zandt County (1876–1878) and for Wood County (1888–1890), and the Texas state librarian (1891–1895 and 1897–1906). (Courtesy of Tarrant County College Heritage Room.)

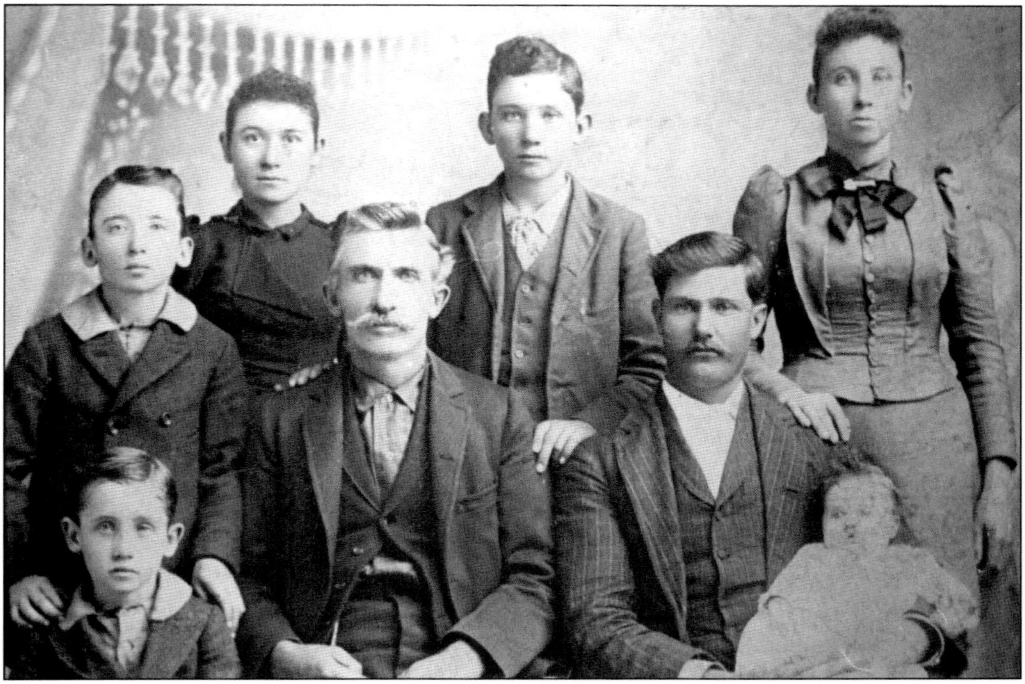

Picture here is the Cass White family. Lewis Cass White, son of area pioneers Joseph and Sarah White, married Nancy Jane Grimes on November 12, 1868. Nancy would live a relatively short life, dying at the age of 41, but it was filled with warmth from her family and doting husband and their firm faith in religion. These two photographs show how the Cass White family grew over the years. Shown above in 1895 are (first row) Arthur White (front), Lewis Cass White, and John W. Reddell (holding daughter Ada Reddell); (second row) Floyd White, Mittie Grimes, Elihu White, and Laura White Reddell. The below photograph, taken later, shows, from left to right, (on ground) Mary White, Floyd White, and Sarah White; (seated) John White, Lewis Cass White, and Lewis White; (standing) Minnie White, Elihu White, John Reddell, Laura Reddell, Arthur White, and Edna White. (Both, courtesy of Tarrant County College Heritage Room.)

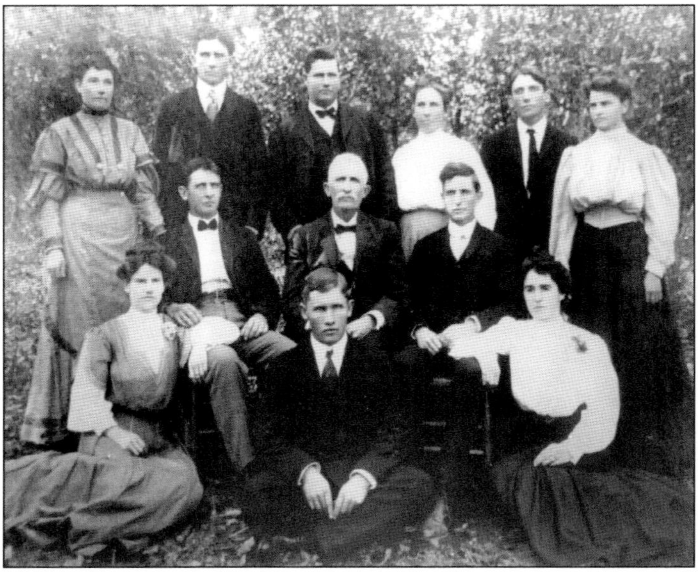

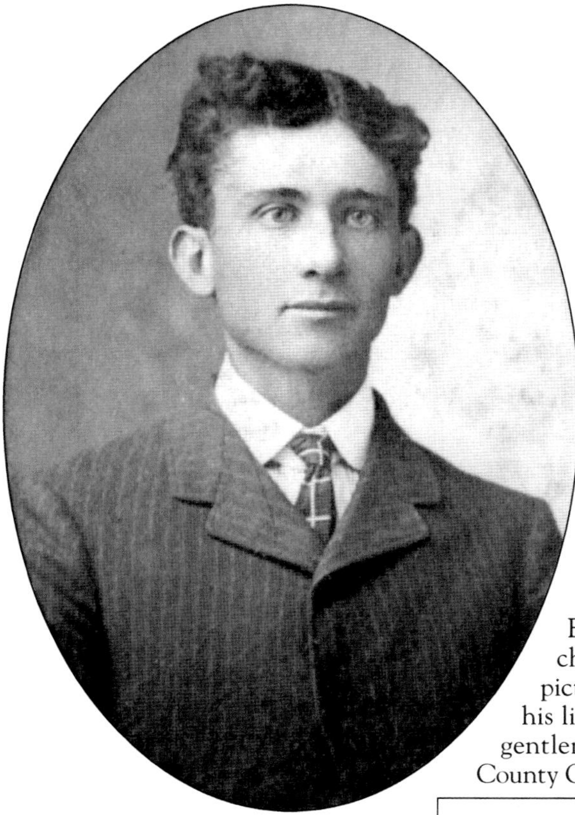

Joseph and Sarah White left a long lineage of descendants who lived in the Colleyville area at one time or another. One of their grandsons was Elihu Washburne White, who was the son of Lewis Cass White. A religious man, Cass White was very involved in the church, a tradition Elihu carried forward. Cass White was a charter member of the Pleasant Run Baptist Church and remained a faithful member for more than 50 years. Elihu White also served as a leader in the church for several decades. Elihu White is pictured here at two very different times in his life: as a young man at left and as an older gentleman below. (Both, courtesy of Tarrant County College Heritage Room.)

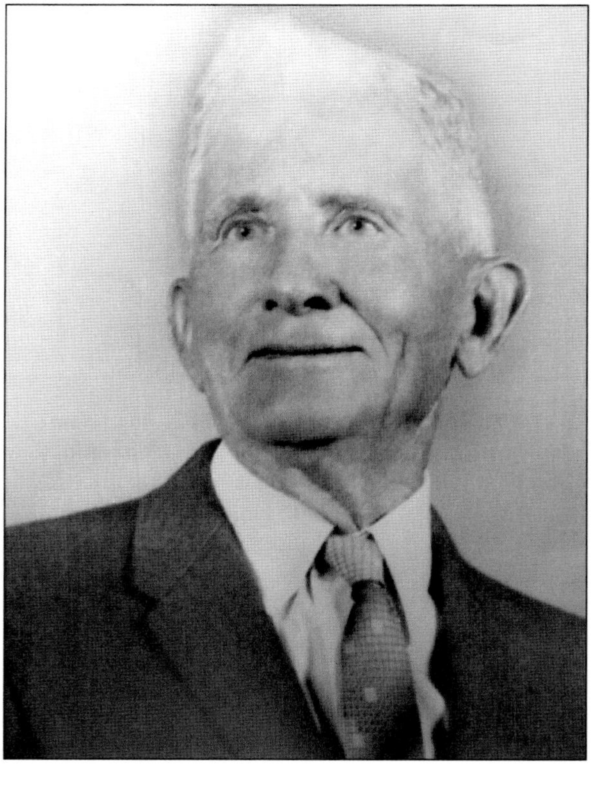

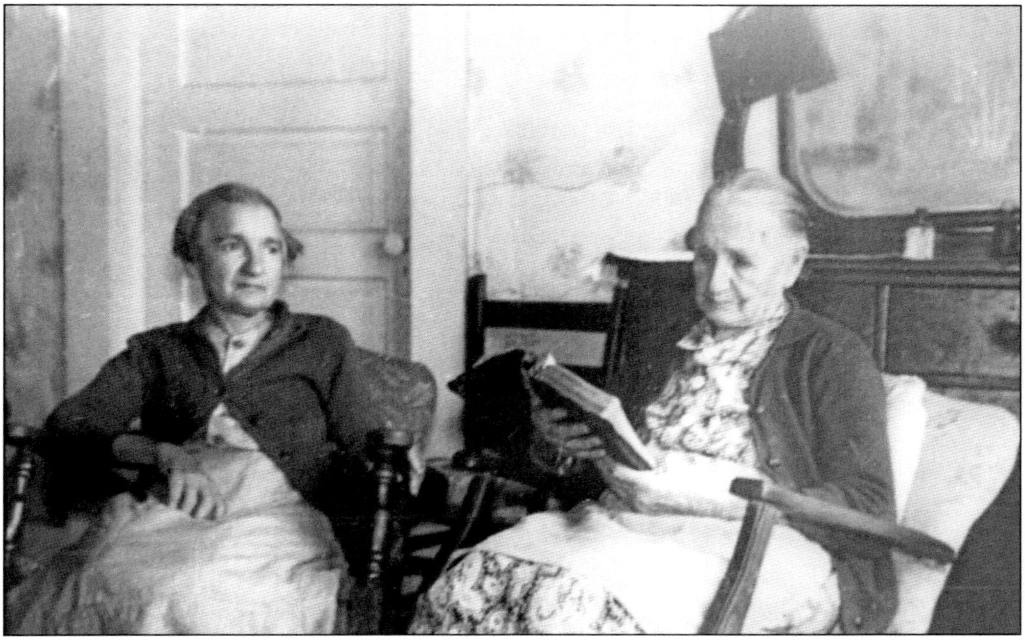

Annie and Robinson Carusoe "Rob" Reynolds were among the original settlers of the Pleasant Run parent community, moving there from Dallas County in 1902. Annie and Rob had 10 children. Ora, pictured here with her mother, Annie, was their only daughter. (Courtesy of Tarrant County College Heritage Room.)

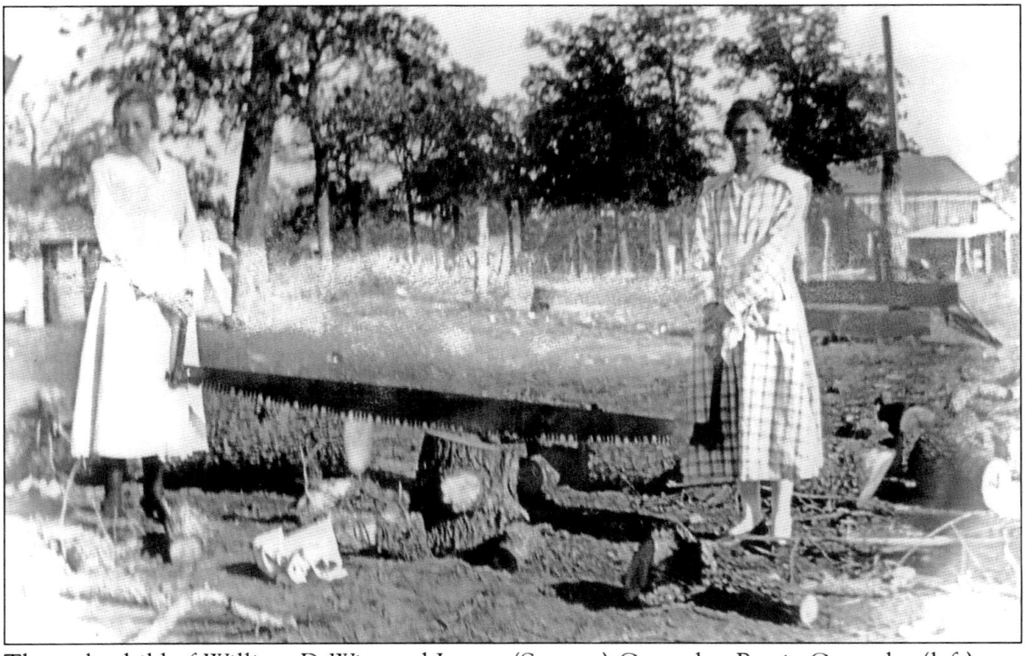

The only child of William DeWitt and Leona (Sparger) Cavender, Bessie Cavender (left) was born on November 1, 1892. The family bought a 106-acre farm in Colleyville along present-day Glade Road on Bessie's birthday in 1901. She moved away for a while, but Bessie and her husband, W.K. Simmons, missed the farm life and moved their family back to the Colleyville farm in 1933. (Courtesy of Tarrant County College Heritage Room.)

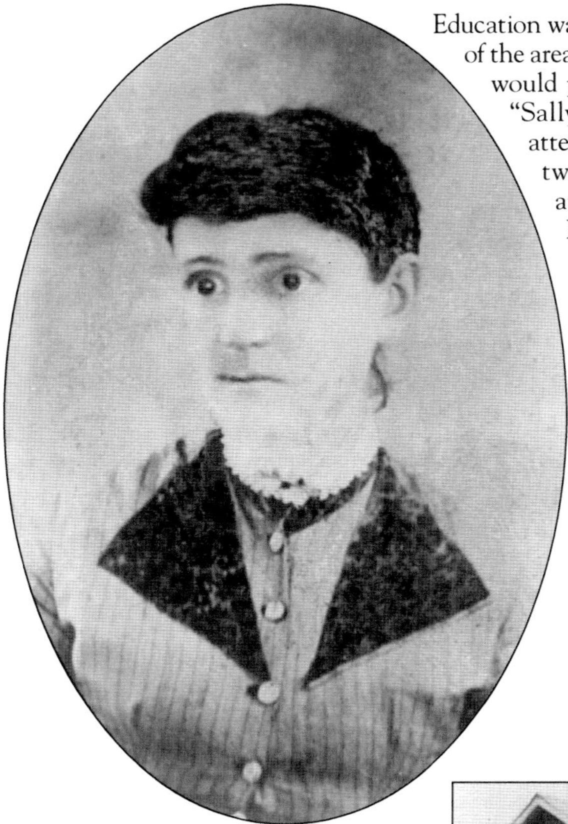

Education was something near and dear to the pioneers of the area. One of the first services that a community would provide was a school for children. Sarah "Sally" Estill was one of the first children to attend the Pleasant Glade School, one of the two schools that served the early Colleyville area. (Courtesy of Tarrant County College Heritage Room.)

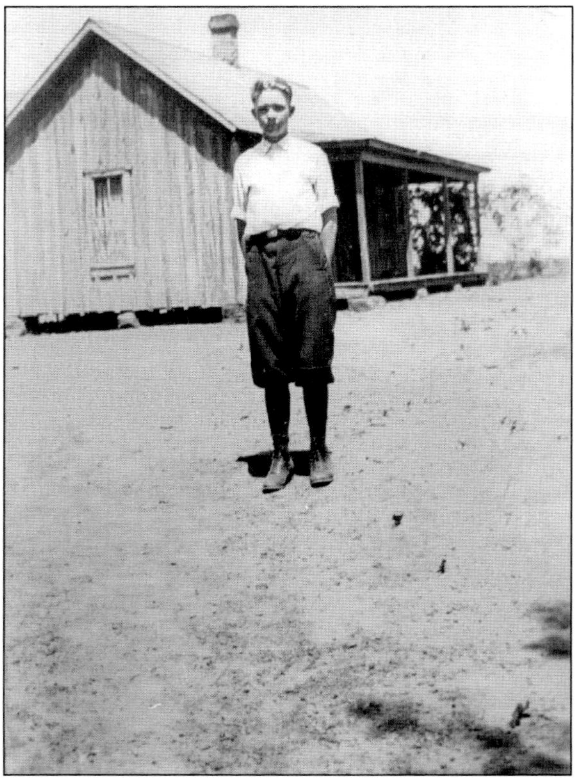

Ray Wall is a descendent of Andrew Berry "A.B." and Harriet Wall. The Walls moved to the Colleyville area in 1872 from Madison County, Arkansas. While in Arkansas, Wall served in the Confederate army, and their home was burned to the ground by Union soldiers. The family's tract of land in Colleyville stretched north from present-day John McCain Road to just south of the city's northern boundary at Big Bear Creek. (Courtesy of Tarrant County College Heritage Room.)

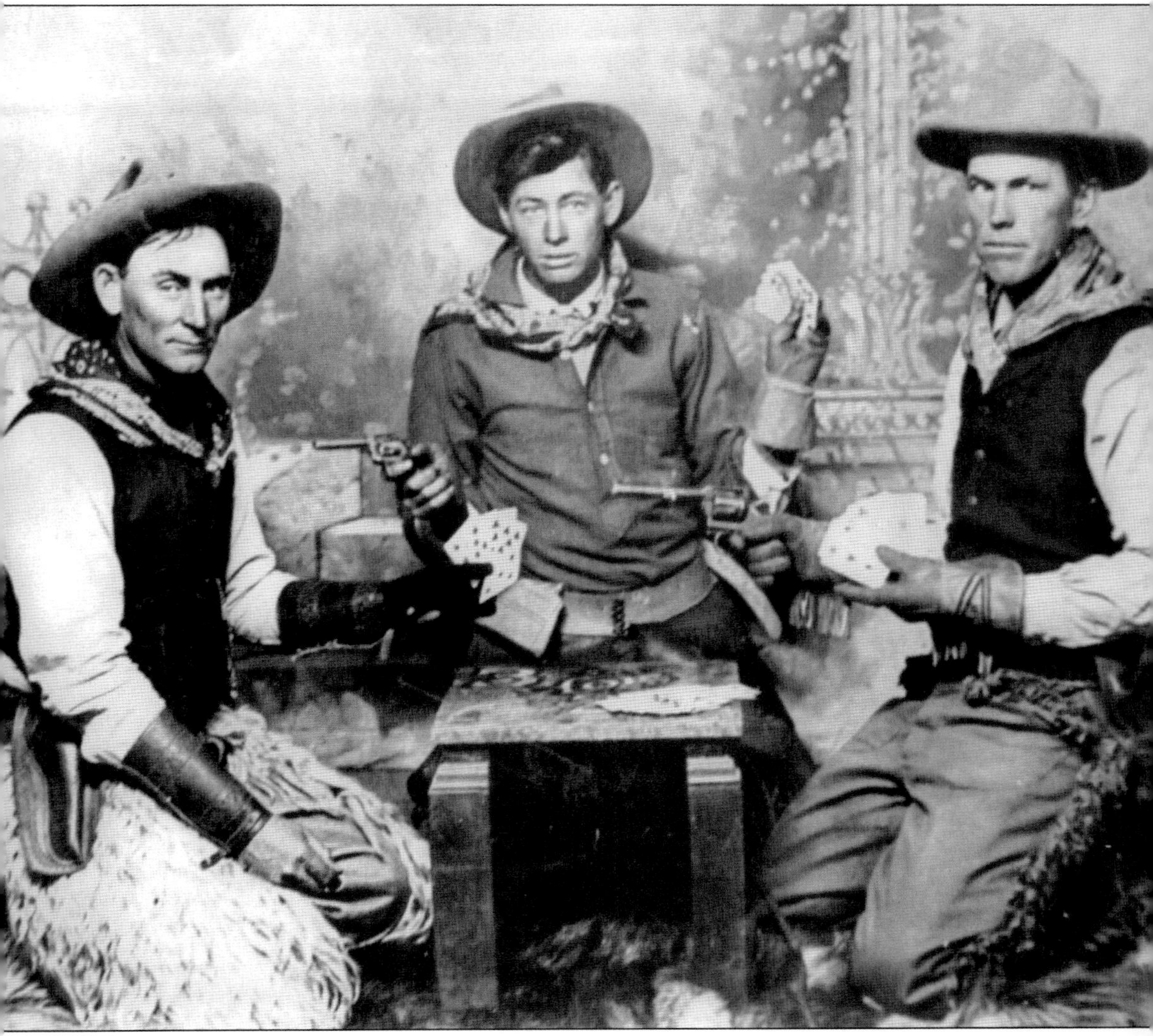

Compared to today, there were not many amusements available in rural Texas in the late 1800s and early 1900s. However, with a little imagination and creativity, folks had just as good a time as anyone could have today. Often, the most fun was had joking around with pals. The cowboys pictured here playing cards are, from left to right, W.H. Throop, John Claunch, and John McCain. At first look, they could be confused for rowdy guys. But, upon closer inspection, these were gentlemen just having a little fun for the camera. Throop was a trustee of the Woodman of the World Knights of Modern Maccabee order and donated land for the first Pleasant Run Baptist Church. McCain was not only a descendant of one of the original settlers, William Dunn, but was also the patriarch of one of the most prominent families in Colleyville. (Courtesy of Tarrant County College Heritage Room.)

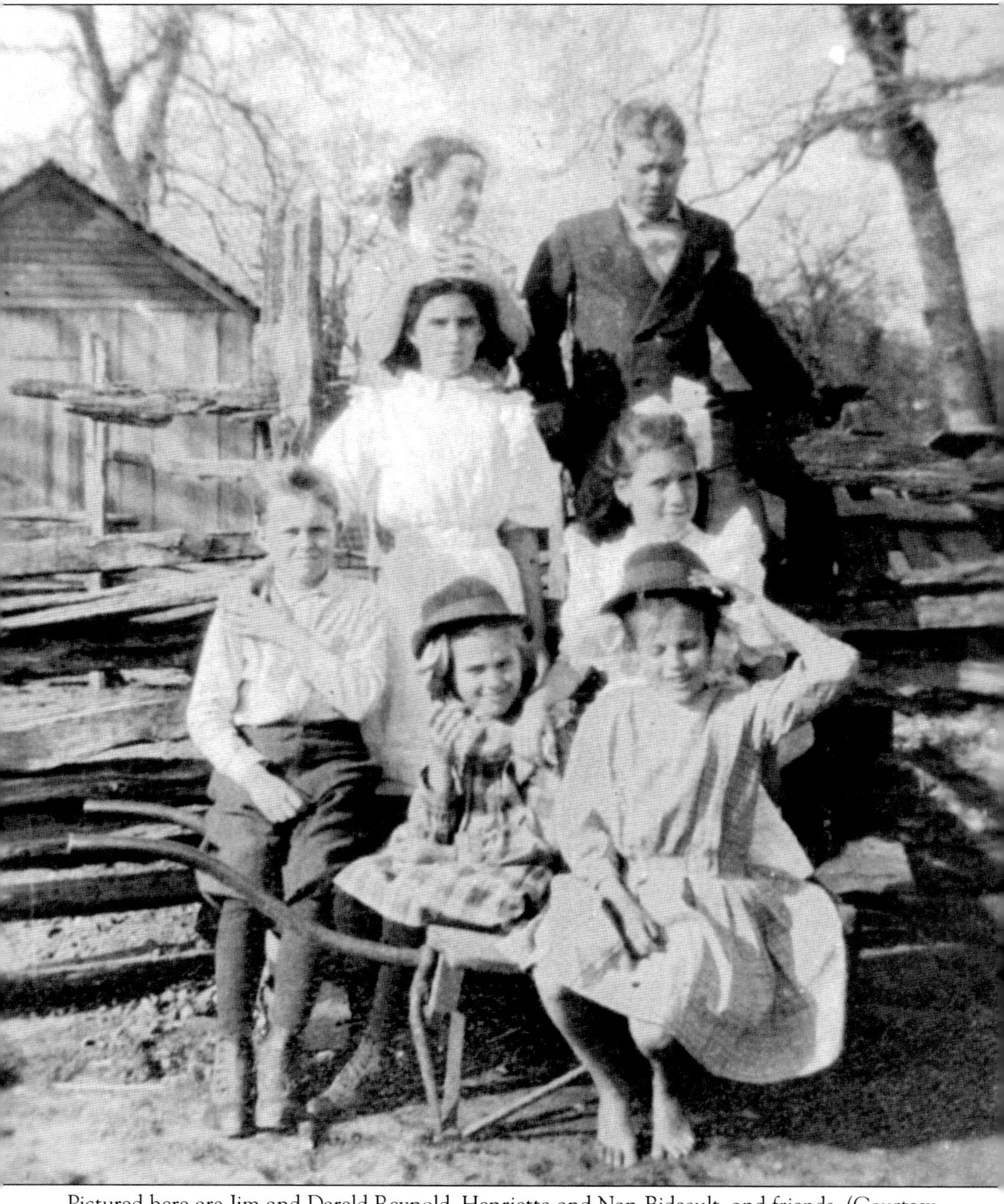

Pictured here are Jim and Dareld Reynold, Henrietta and Nan Bideault, and friends. (Courtesy of Tarrant County College Heritage Room.)

Six

Important Organizations

To see the extent to which organizations have made an impact on Colleyville, one need only take a drive down any of the major thoroughfares or neighborhood arteries to see the lasting effects of what people can do when they gather together for a common cause. By being part of groups and organizations, people who lived in Colleyville's parent communities built schools and churches and brought their rituals and customs from their homeland to the Texas prairie in the late 1800s. The earliest groups on record during this time included the Farmers Union, Independent Order of Odd Fellows (IOOF), Knights of the Modern Maccabees, and the Woodmen of the World (WOW).

As the new century dawned, groups and organizations became even more important to building a strong community. Some groups, such as the Colleyville Lions Club and the 4-H Club, had national ties and gave their Colleyville chapters lots of support. Other organizations, such as the Colleyville Garden Club and the Colleyville Fire Auxiliary, were homegrown clubs that were formed by the sheer determination of their charter members.

But, perhaps no other groups had such an influence on the Colleyville area as religious organizations. For most of the pioneering settlers, and up to many of today's residents, faith played a key role in daily life. In the pre-Colleyville period in the late 1800s and early 1900s, four churches were formed: First Baptist Church of Colleyville, First United Methodist Church of Colleyville, Pleasant Glade Baptist Church, and Pleasant Run Baptist Church. Today, there are more than 20 religious organizations that call Colleyville home. These groups, along with other social and fraternal organizations, continue to prop up the foundation of the community through their good works.

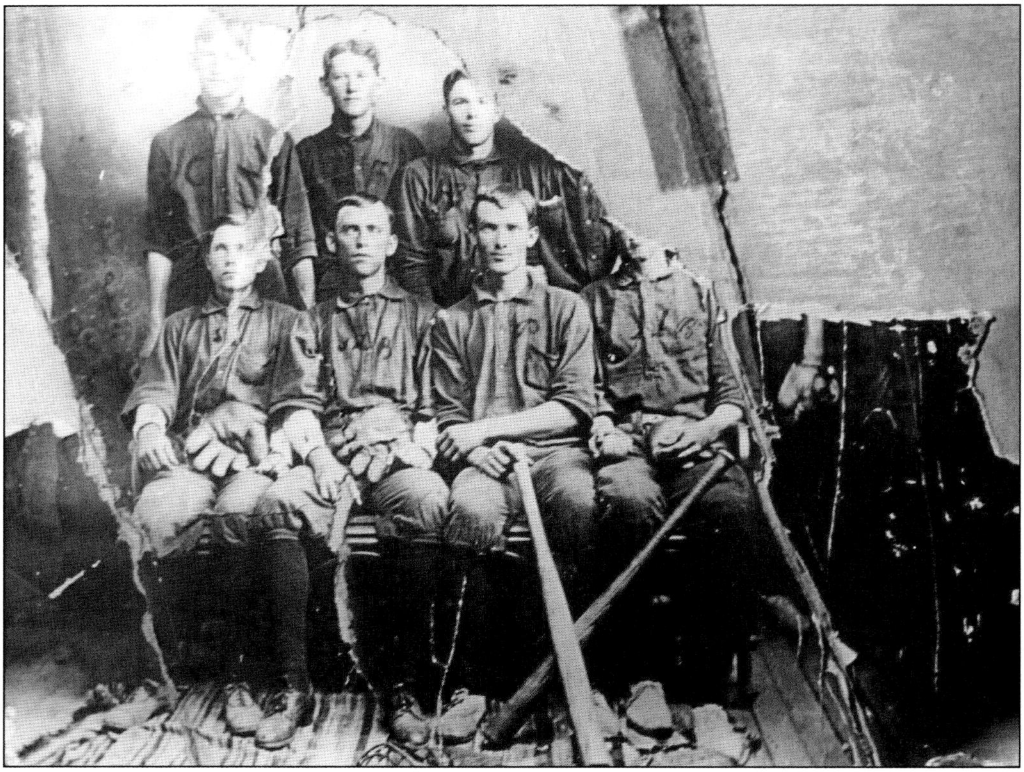

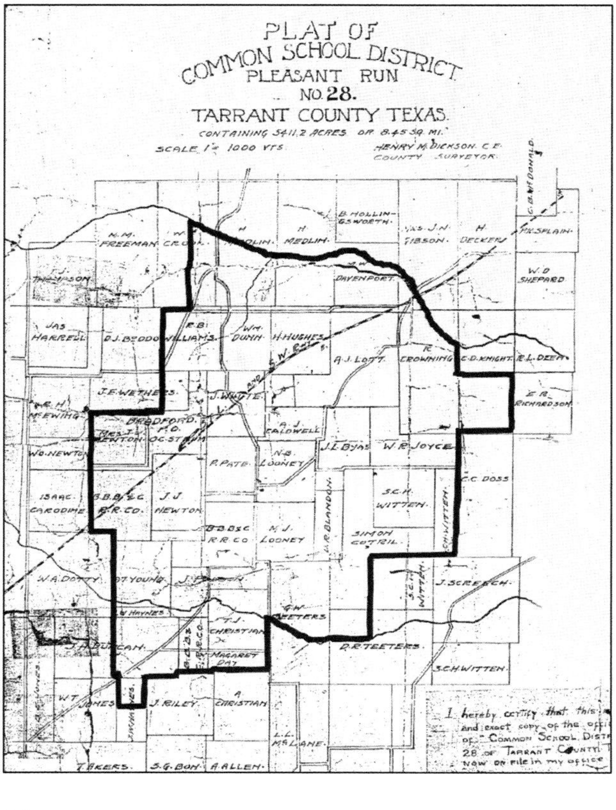

The Pleasant Glade School was one of two schools that served the pre-Colleyville parent communities. Sports were a big part of both schools, but they often did not have enough players to form a team. As seen in this photograph of the Pleasant Run–Pleasant Glade baseball team, the two schools often had to merge players to form one team. (Courtesy of Tarrant County College Heritage Room.)

The Pleasant Run School opened its doors in 1870. Beginning as a tuition school, children would attend three months out of the year at a cost of $1.50 a month. It was transformed into a public school and served children for 92 years. Shown here are the boundaries of the Pleasant Run Common School District. (Courtesy of Colleyville Historical Preservation Committee.)

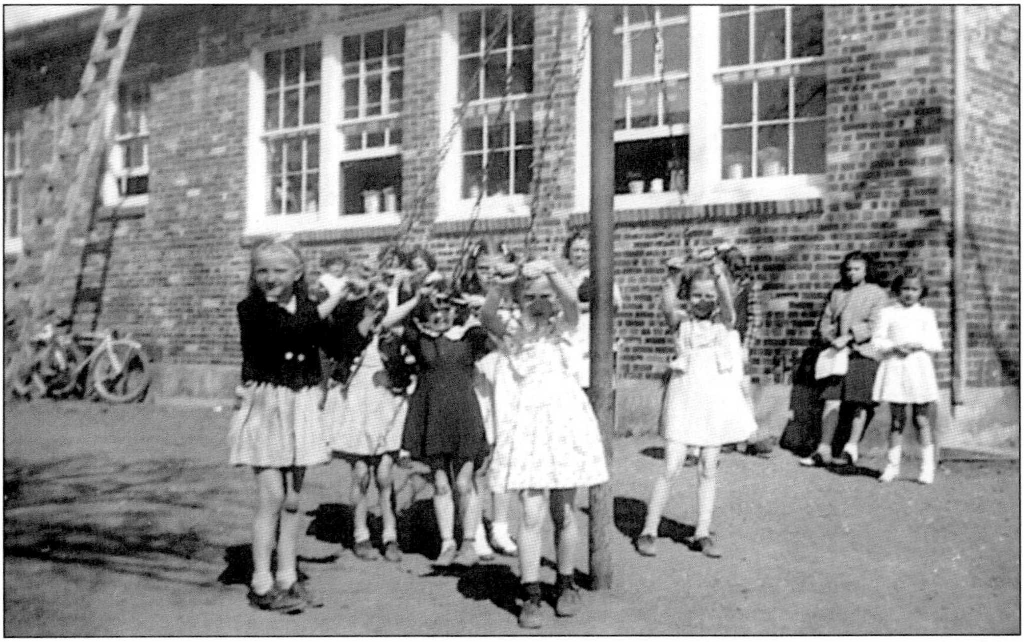

Playgrounds are synonymous with schools, and Pleasant Run was no different. However, much of the playground equipment at the Pleasant Run School was homemade, including the "Johnny-stride" (pictured). This would inevitably cause an accident, sending kids home banged up. (Courtesy of Colleyville Historical Preservation Committee.)

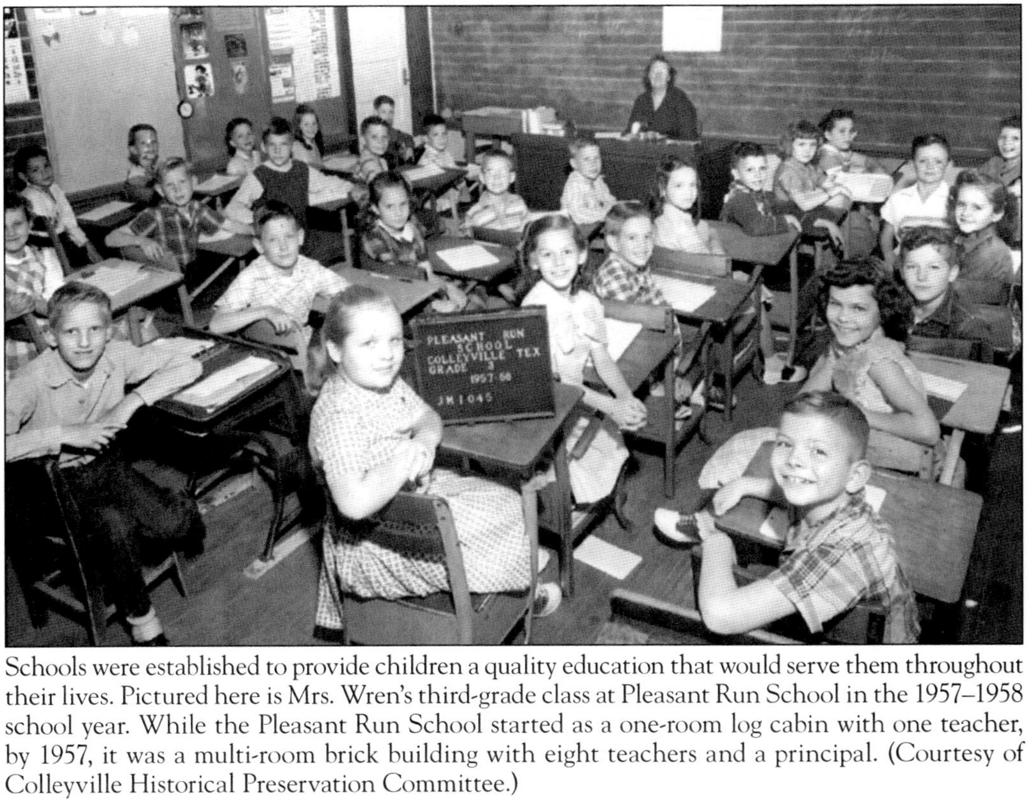

Schools were established to provide children a quality education that would serve them throughout their lives. Pictured here is Mrs. Wren's third-grade class at Pleasant Run School in the 1957–1958 school year. While the Pleasant Run School started as a one-room log cabin with one teacher, by 1957, it was a multi-room brick building with eight teachers and a principal. (Courtesy of Colleyville Historical Preservation Committee.)

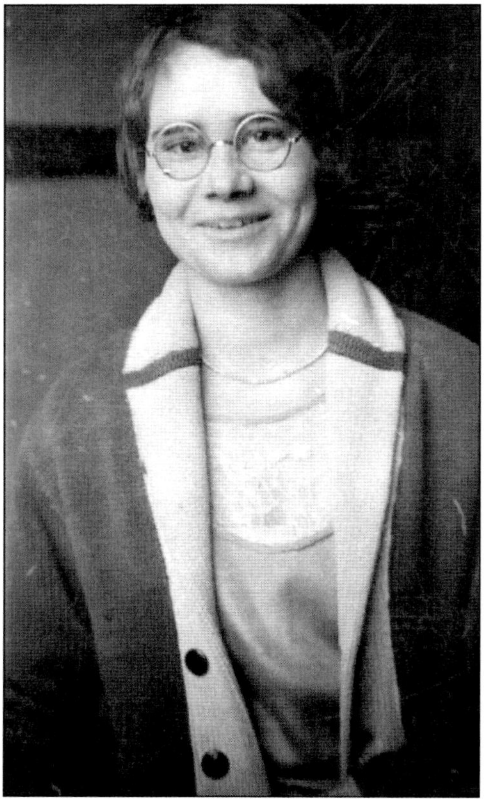

Teachers are what make a school. At schools in rural areas in the early 1900s, teachers did much more than provide lessons. The kids often stayed after school was over and played until the sun went down, with the teachers keeping watch over them. Some of these smaller schools had a hard time paying teachers' salaries. Teachers often had to wait until area farmers sold their harvests in the summer to get paid. Wilma Sargent (left) and Ruth Ragsdale Knox (below) served as teachers at the Pleasant Run School in the early 1900s. (Both, courtesy of Tarrant County College Heritage Room.)

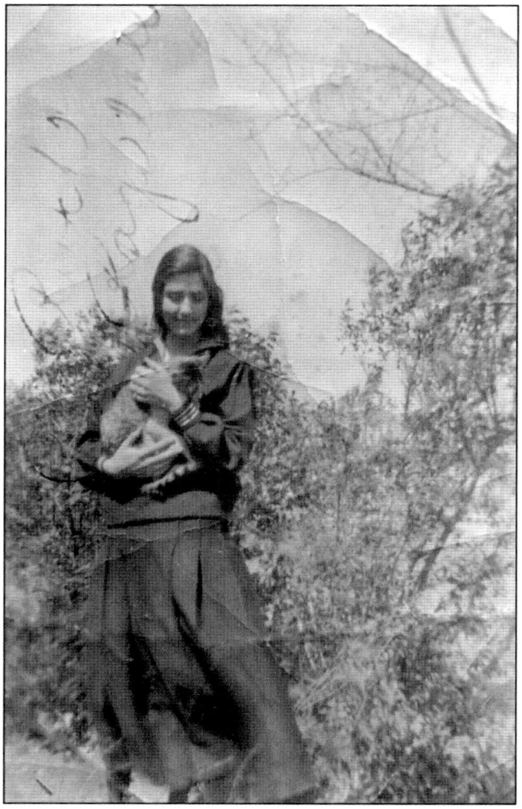

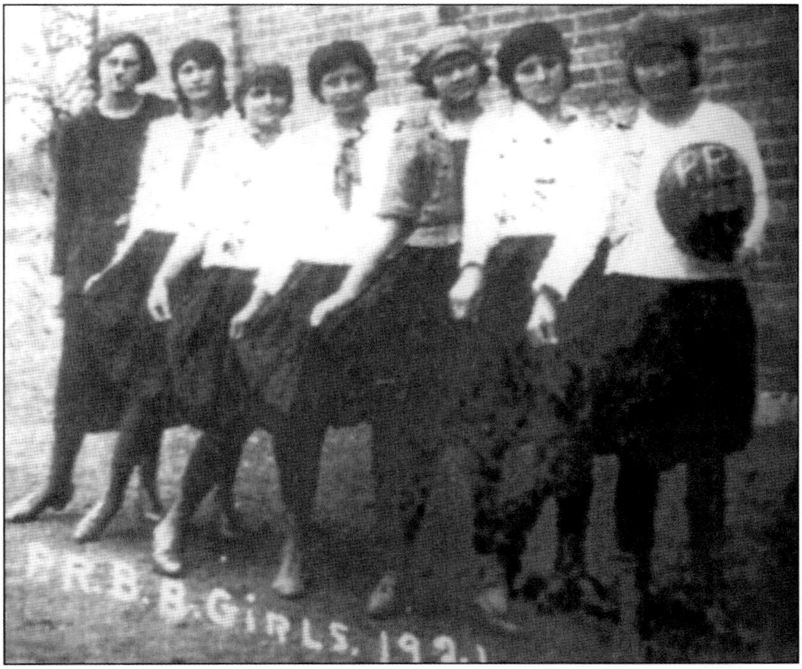

The Pleasant Run School offered both boys and girls an opportunity to play team sports. The school had an old metal gym where the teams played. The girls had a dressing room; the boys had to climb a ladder to the loft, where they would change into their uniforms. Pictured above are members of the girls' basketball team of 1921. They are, from left to right, Florence Reynolds, Joe McCain, Bertha Buckner, Altie Mae Brumlow, Mildred Averett, Ollie Mae Hammock, and Zona Pirkle. The boys' basketball team of 1932 is shown below. Posing are, from left to right, (first row) Harold Reynolds Marvin Daniel, and Claude Reynolds; (second row) William Floyce Crow, John Harold Calvin Crow, Joe Reynolds, and J.W. Daniel. (Both, courtesy of Colleyville Historical Preservation Committee.)

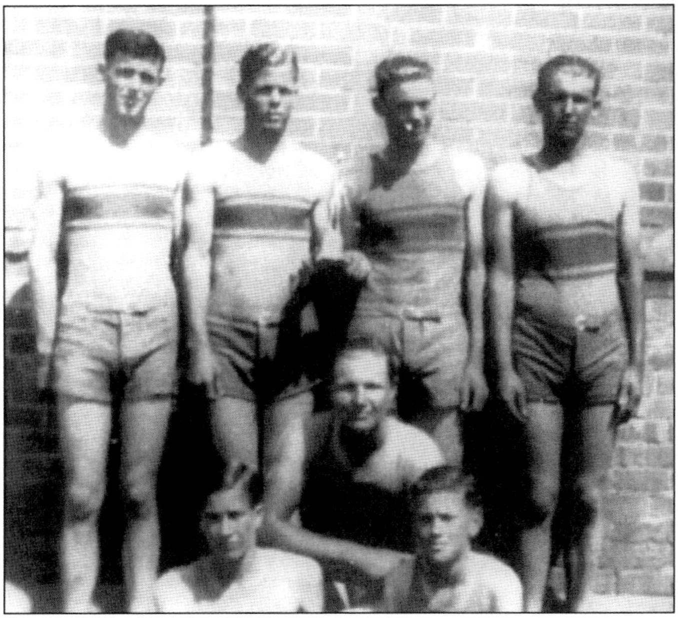

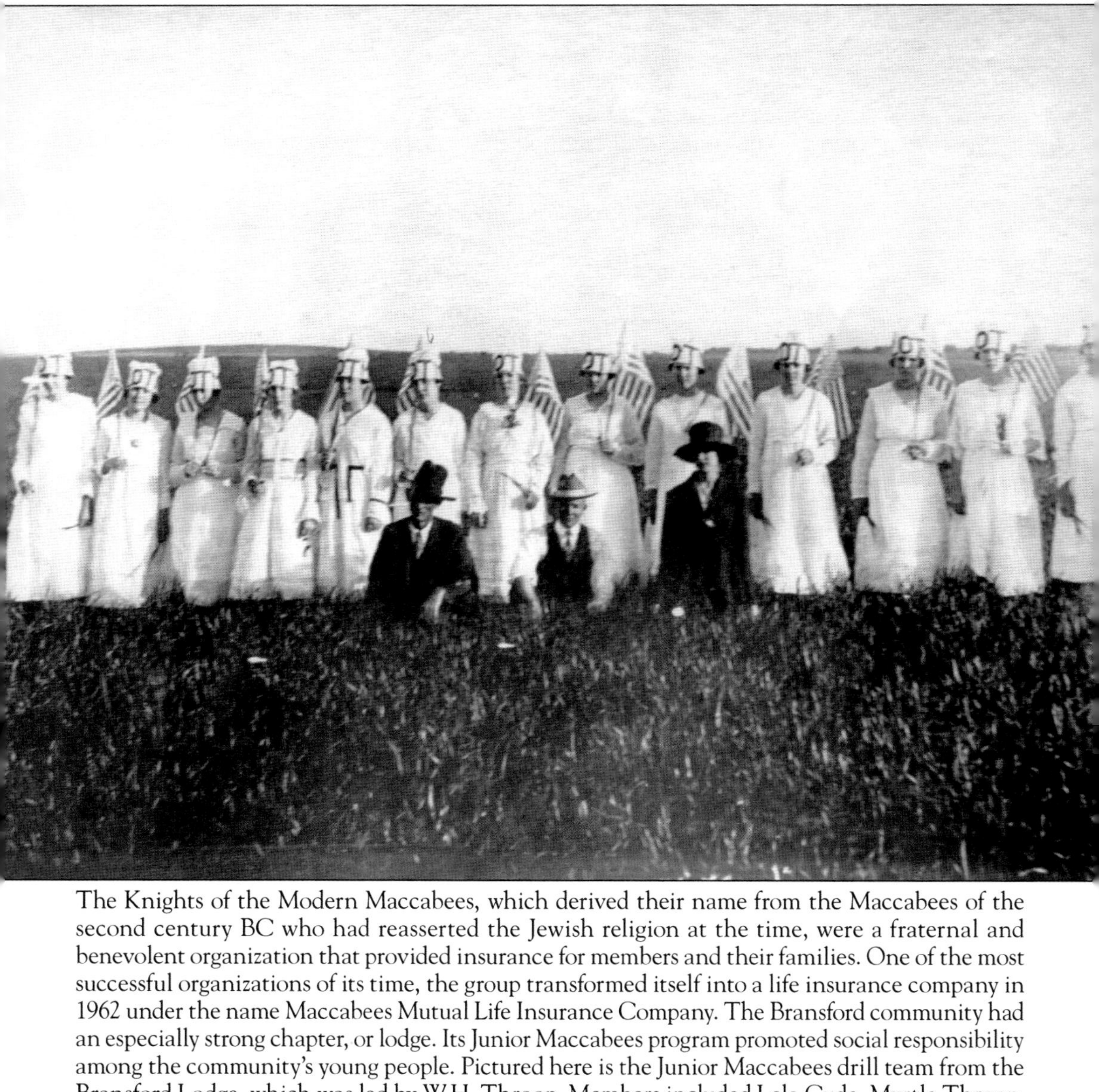

The Knights of the Modern Maccabees, which derived their name from the Maccabees of the second century BC who had reasserted the Jewish religion at the time, were a fraternal and benevolent organization that provided insurance for members and their families. One of the most successful organizations of its time, the group transformed itself into a life insurance company in 1962 under the name Maccabees Mutual Life Insurance Company. The Bransford community had an especially strong chapter, or lodge. Its Junior Maccabees program promoted social responsibility among the community's young people. Pictured here is the Junior Maccabees drill team from the Bransford Lodge, which was led by W.H. Throop. Members included Lela Cude, Myrtle Throop, Ruby Webb, Cleo and Clara McCain, and Willie Cox. Pictured in front are, from left to right, W.H. Throop, Jim Reynolds, and Gladys Gabbert, who served as the pianist. (Courtesy of Tarrant County College Heritage Room.)

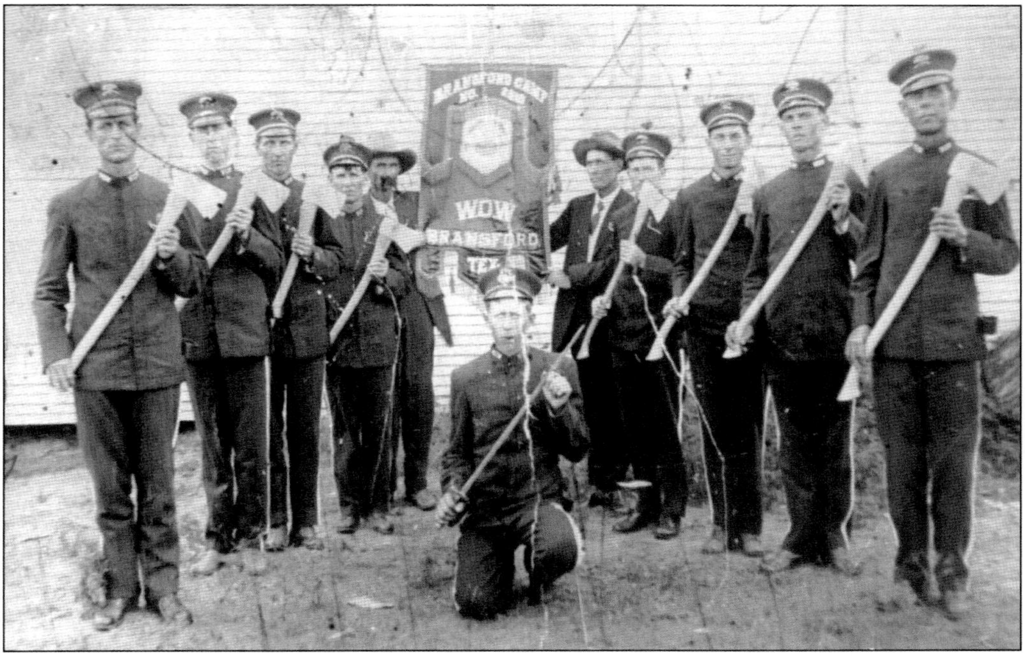

The Woodmen of the World (WOW) was another organization that evolved into an insurance company in the modern age. Formed in 1890, WOW also had strong roots in Bransford. Along with Farmers Union, Independent Order of Odd Fellows (IOOF), and Knights of the Modern Maccabees, WOW built and used the Bransford Lodge building to hold its meetings and ceremonies. When the city was incorporated, the lodge building was moved to the heart of Colleyville, near the intersection of present-day State Highway 26 and Glade Road. Above, WOW members stand in front of the lodge. Below, WOW members gather to recognize graduates in front of the Bransford hall. (Both, courtesy of Tarrant County College Heritage Room.)

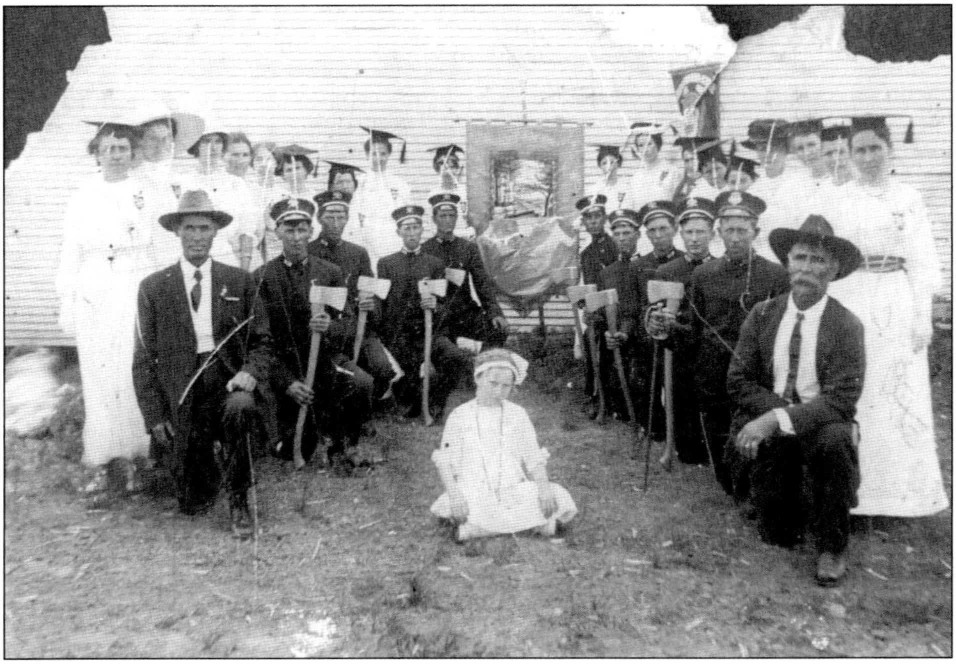

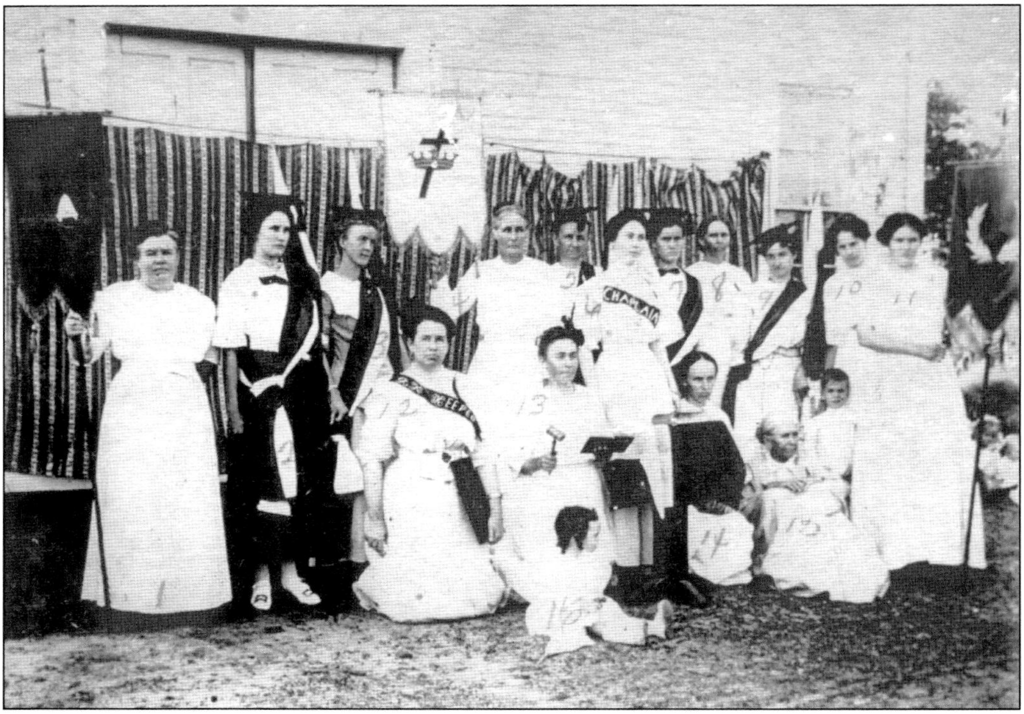

Organizations did not just provide support for their members. When someone in the community was sick, a family member had just died, or there was some other major setback in their lives, a member of WOW, IOOF, the Farmers Union, or Knights of the Modern Maccabees would be designated to help out that family for as long as was needed. Women also had their own organizations in the late 1800s and early 1900s. Above, the Ladies Auxiliary has gathered at the Bransford Lodge. Some organizations, including WOW, had special branches for women. The photograph below shows a WOW women's group in front of the Bransford Lodge building. (Both, courtesy of Tarrant County College Heritage Room.)

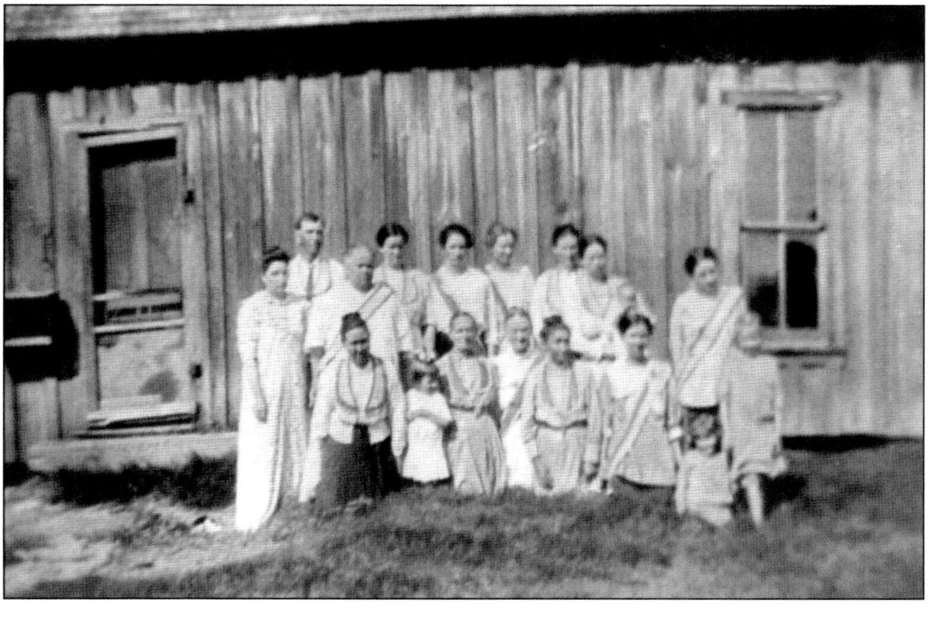

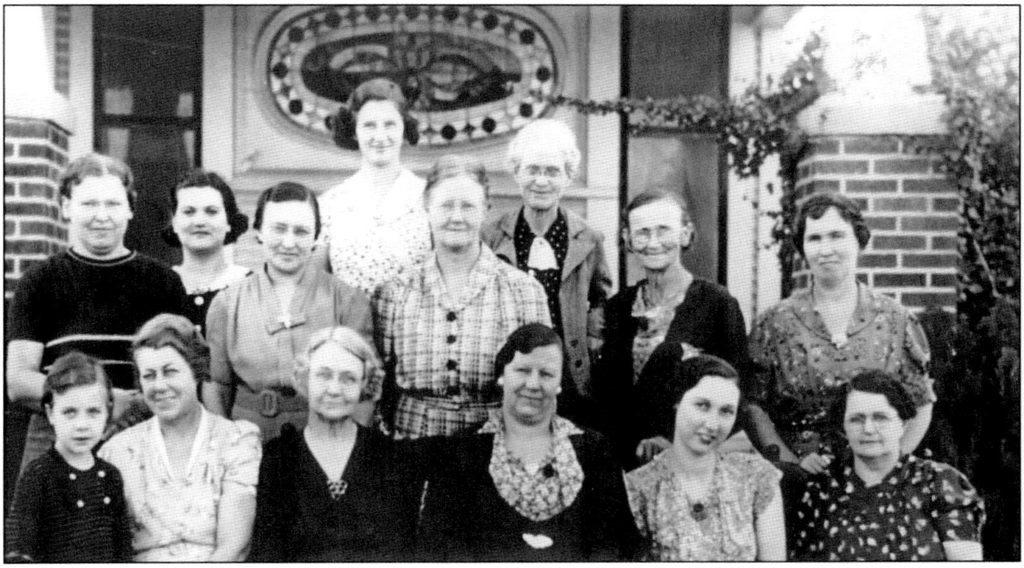

Running a home is not easy, even with all of today's technology. In the early and mid-1900s, the Home Demonstration Club helped mostly women organize their homes, manage their families, and support the community. There were even home-demonstration agents employed through the county by Texas A&M, the US Department of Agriculture, and the County Commissioners' Court. Above, Women's Club members stand in front of a home in Pleasant Run. Another group mainly for women, one of the earliest organizations in Colleyville, was the Colleyville Garden Club. The sign shown below, erected in 1965, welcomed drivers to Colleyville along present-day State Highway 26. (Above, courtesy of Tarrant County College Heritage Room; below, courtesy of Colleyville Historical Preservation Committee.)

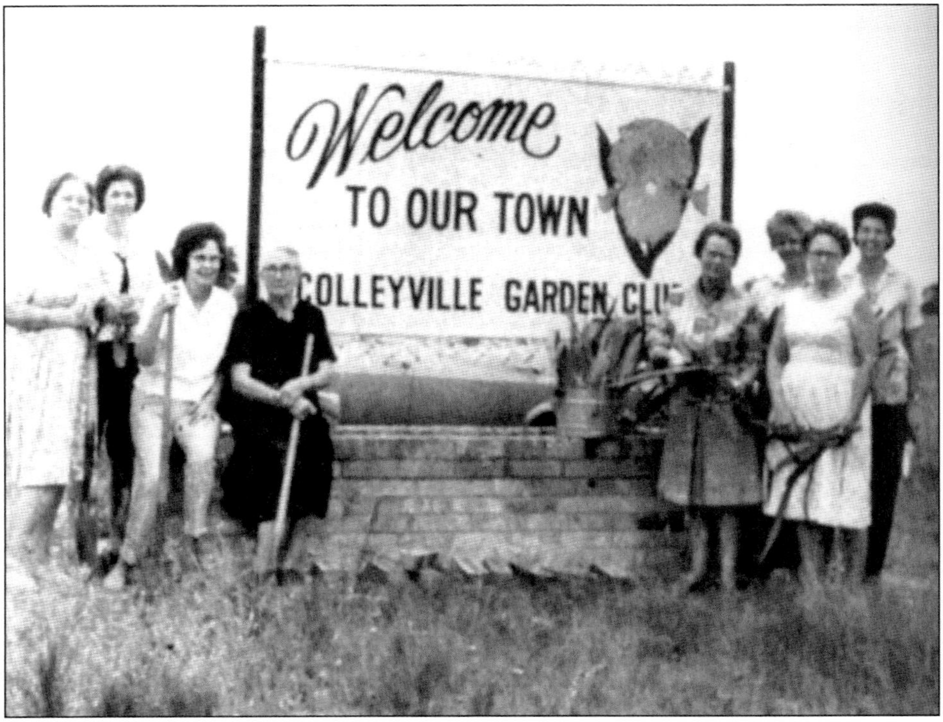

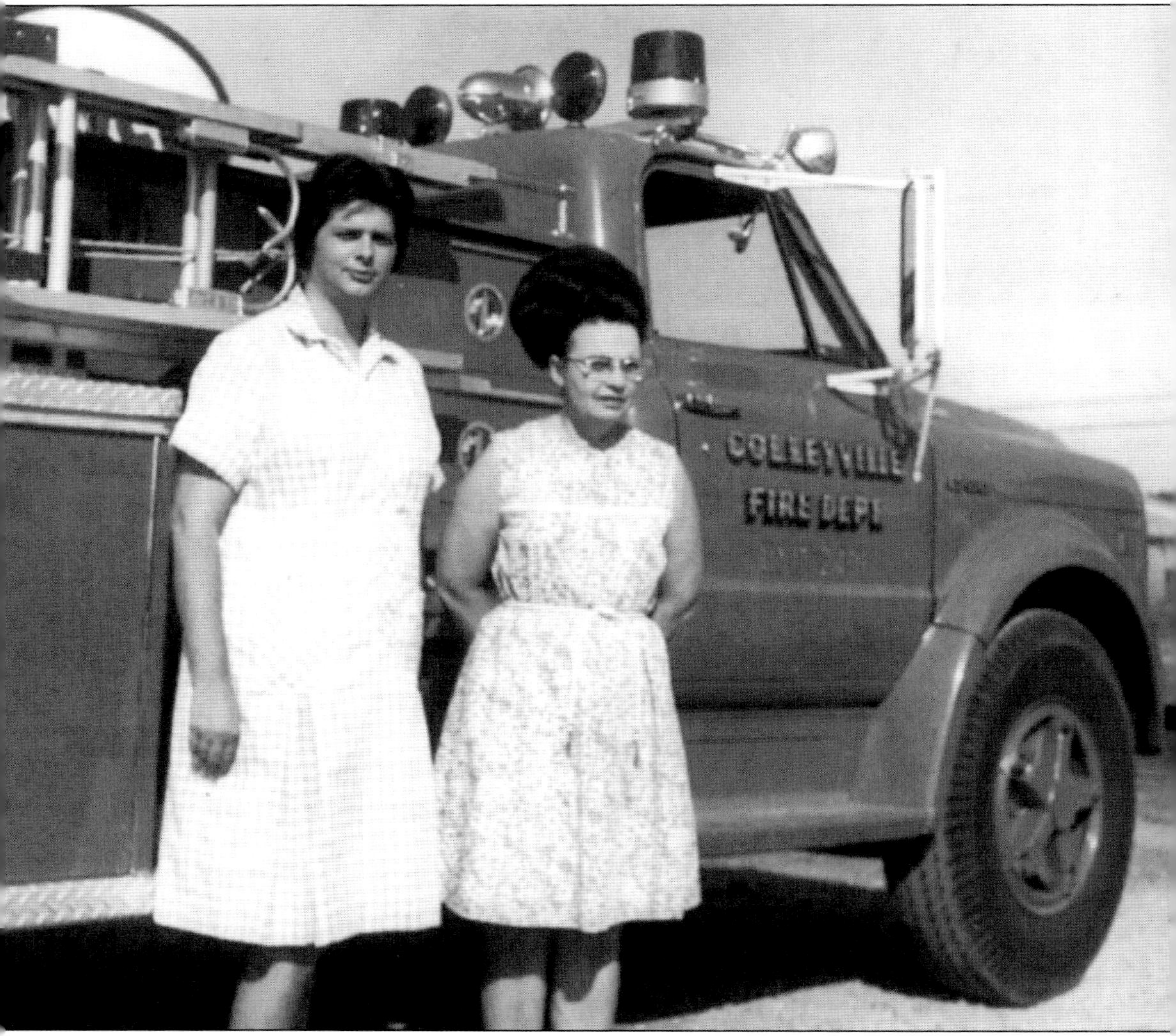

Another especially important women's group in the mid-1900s was the Ladies Fire Auxiliary. Perhaps more than anything else, this excerpt from the April 19, 1963, *Fort Worth Tribune* speaks to the group's importance: "Our Ladies Fire Auxiliary was called out Sunday morning April 7 to help in the search for bodies of the two men who were drowned last week in Grapevine Lake. . . . These ladies took food for 100 men and went to the lakeshore to prepare the food for the men who were working in the search operation. . . . The victims' families have been living on the lakeshore waiting for the finding of the bodies. These families are living in tents and friends from Fort Worth have come each day and helped them in the long vigil." Pictured in front of a new fire truck that the Ladies Fire Auxiliary was able to purchase for the fire department in 1968 using proceeds from a huge fish fry are Burnice "Bea" Davis (left) and Lauraine Rice. (Courtesy of Colleyville Historical Preservation Committee.)

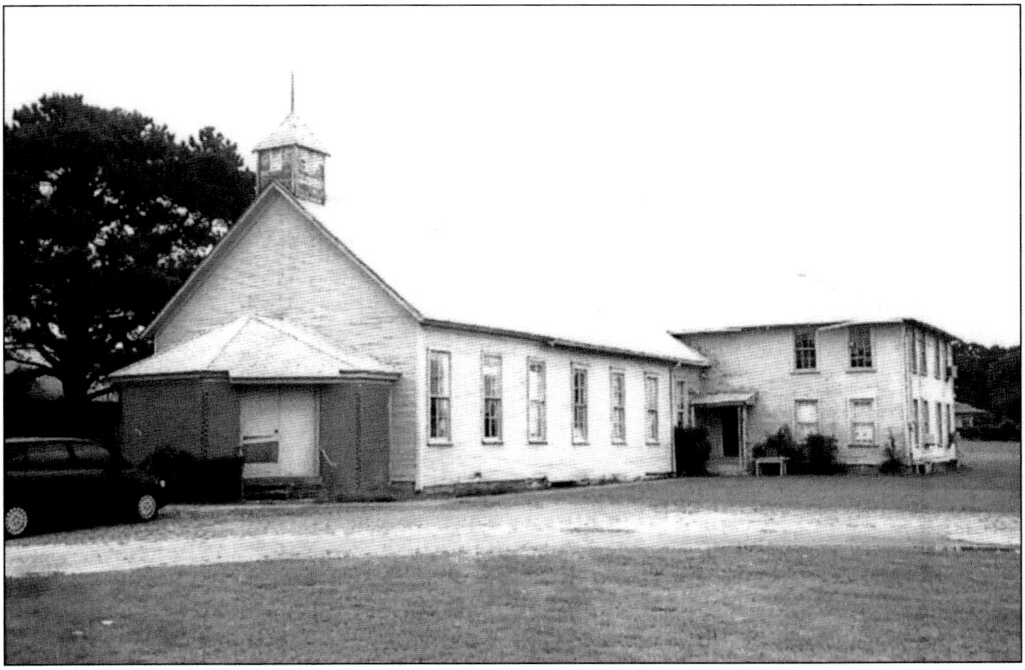

Pleasant Run Baptist Church was one of the first four churches organized in the pre-Colleyville period. Legend has it that when one of the wagons in a train carrying several Baptist families to the Pleasant Run community broke down, the families decided that the location was a perfect spot upon which to build their church. While services started out underneath the shade of a huge oak tree, a one-room building was soon erected in 1904. Pleasant Run Baptist Church expanded in terms of membership and the size of its campus over the years. The original building was enlarged to include four individual classrooms, a vestibule, a baptistery, and a two-story classroom before it was razed in 2004. Pictured below is the Pleasant Run Baptist Church congregation around 1955, in front of the parsonage on the occasion of its dedication. (Above, courtesy of Tarrant County College Heritage Room; below, courtesy of Colleyville Historical Preservation Committee.)

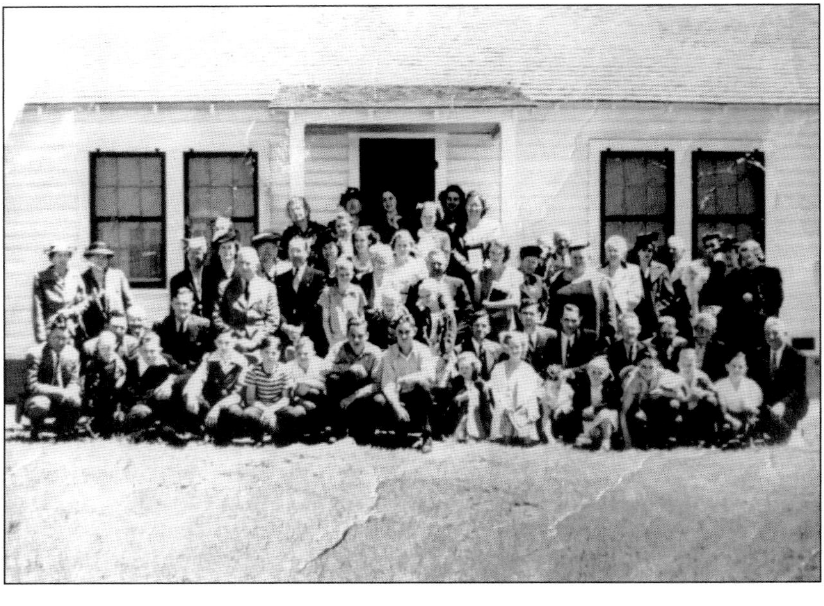

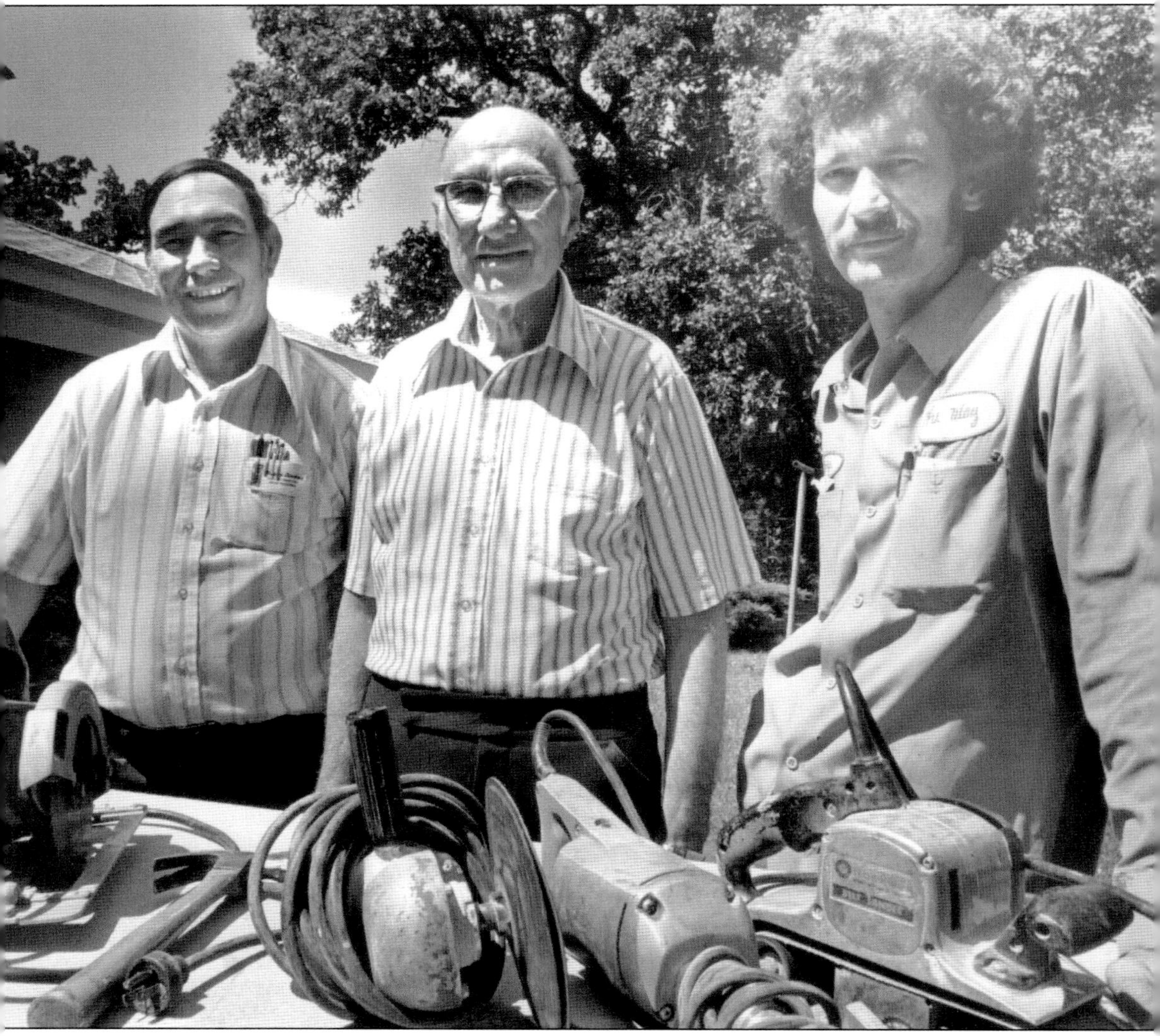

From left to right, J.C. Sullivan, Bob Sullivan, and Gary Vincent stand outside of the Nu-Way Foundation building. J.C. Sullivan, a former criminal, founded the Nu-Way Foundation, the first parole rehabilitation institution in the area on January 6, 1975. (Courtesy of Colleyville Historical Preservation Committee.)

Seven

Historical Markers and Places of Interest

The average American moves once every five years. While five years may seem like a long time, is it enough time for a place to leave a lasting impression on one's life? Furthermore, while mobility has allowed Americans to experience different parts of the country and the various cultures and traditions of new places, how much do people really know about the places they call home? Residents may not take the time to stop and think about the people in history who worked tirelessly to make that place what it is today. People become too occupied with day-to-day activities to notice a building that once upon a time housed the people and hosted the events that would influence life today. Many citizens too often fail to make the important connection bridging the present and the past.

The charter of the Society of Antiquaries of 1751 states, "The study of antiquity, and the history of former times, has ever been esteemed highly commendable and useful, not only to improve the lives of men, but also to incite them to virtuous and noble actions." The novelist Michael Crichton once stated, rather bluntly, that, "If you don't know history, you don't know anything. You are a leaf that doesn't know it is part of a tree." The last chapter of this book provides a visual tour of the historical markers and places of interest that capture the story of Colleyville. It is the responsibility of residents to take the time to stroll through the city's historical buildings or visit a few places of interest and consider what they meant to those citizens who passed there before. For those who call Colleyville home, that could mean having a picnic near the Dunn/Tirk Barn or riding a bike to the Webb House. By doing so, residents not only help maintain the connection between the past and the present, but also help themselves, their neighbors, and future citizens realize that they are all leaves on the tree that is Colleyville, Texas.

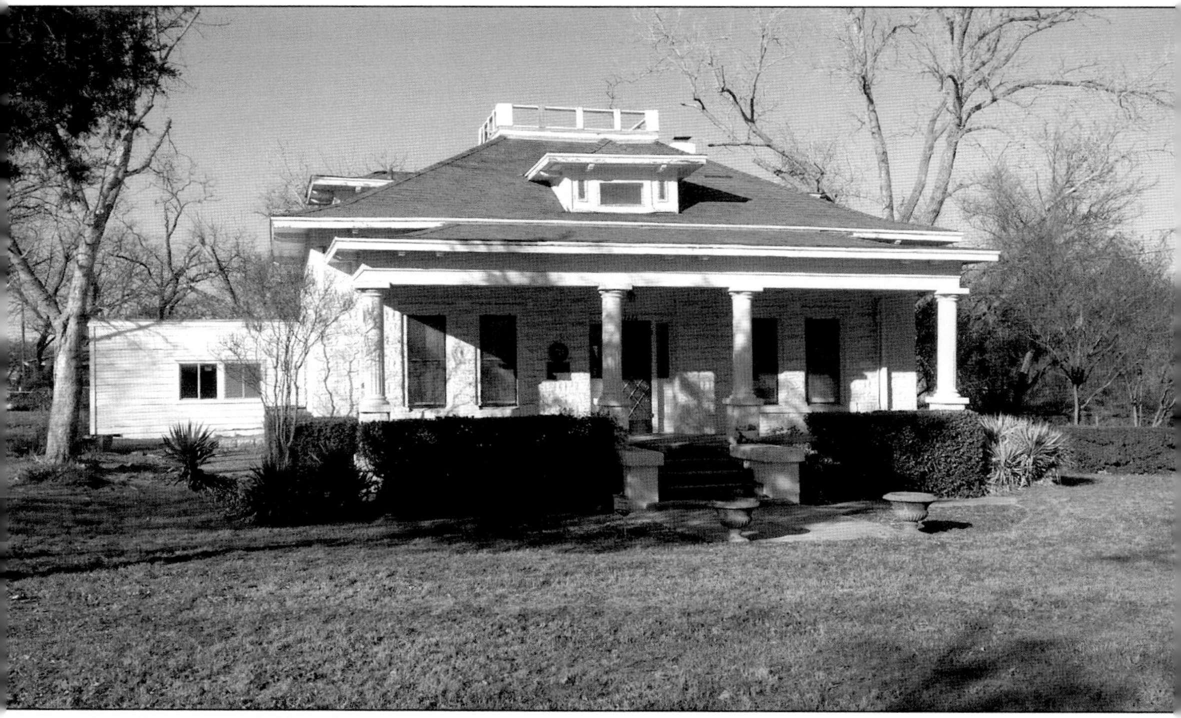

Standing atop a hill at the corner of Bluebonnet and Glade Roads, the Bidault House is one of the few historical buildings left in the city. Built of concrete, it took owner Anthelm Bidault and his family six years to complete, from 1905 to 1911. The concrete blocks were made by family members crushing native stones found around their farm and then combining that with sand inside molds bought from Sears Roebuck. Besides concrete, other materials used in the construction of the house were wood and tin hauled in from Fort Worth. (Courtesy of Mark Fadden.)

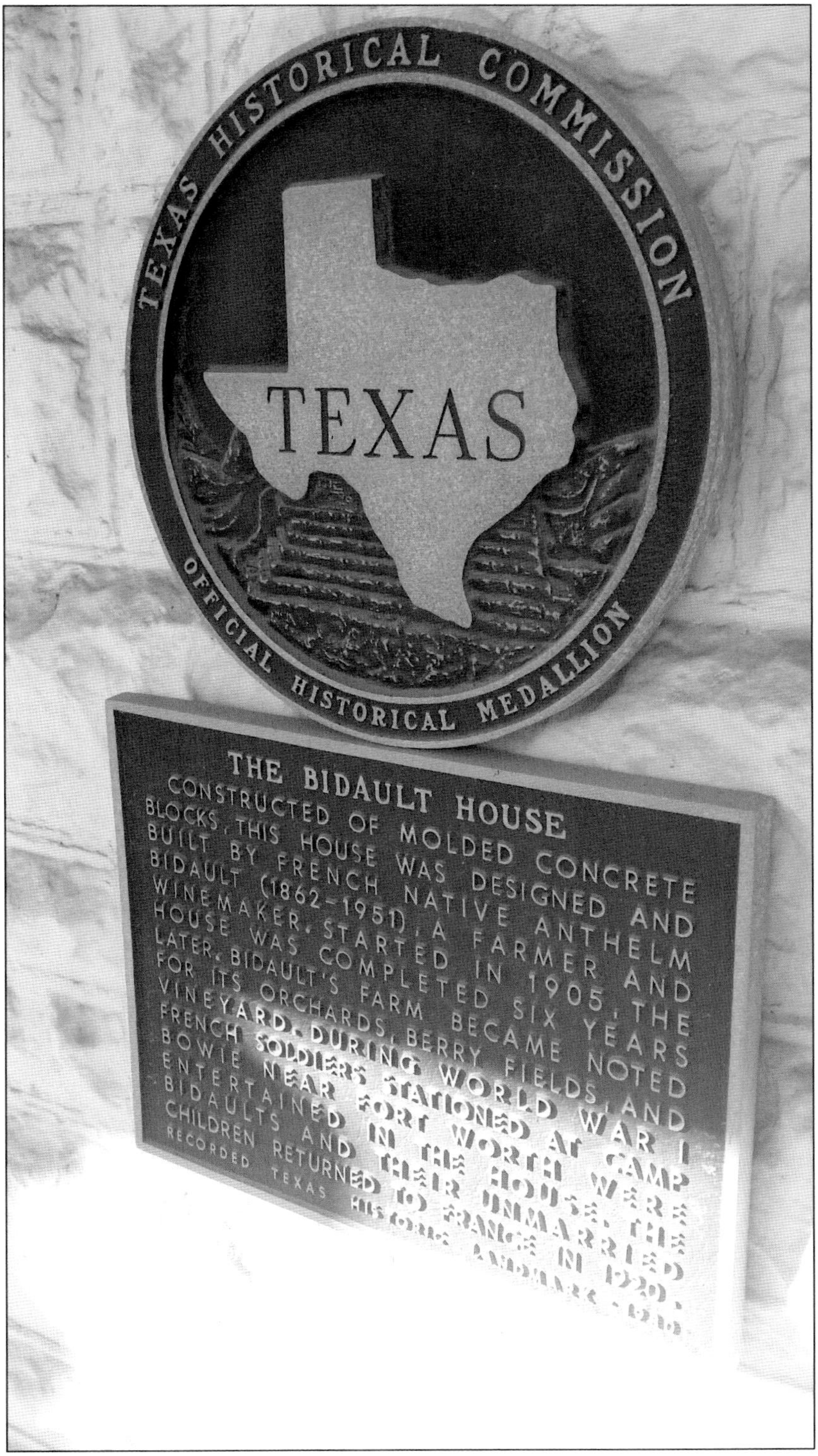

To help preserve it, the City of Colleyville bought the Bidault House in 2011. It was designated a Texas Historic Landmark in 1980. The previous photograph shows the house as it stands today. Shown here is a close-up of the Official Historical Medallion. (Courtesy of Mark Fadden.)

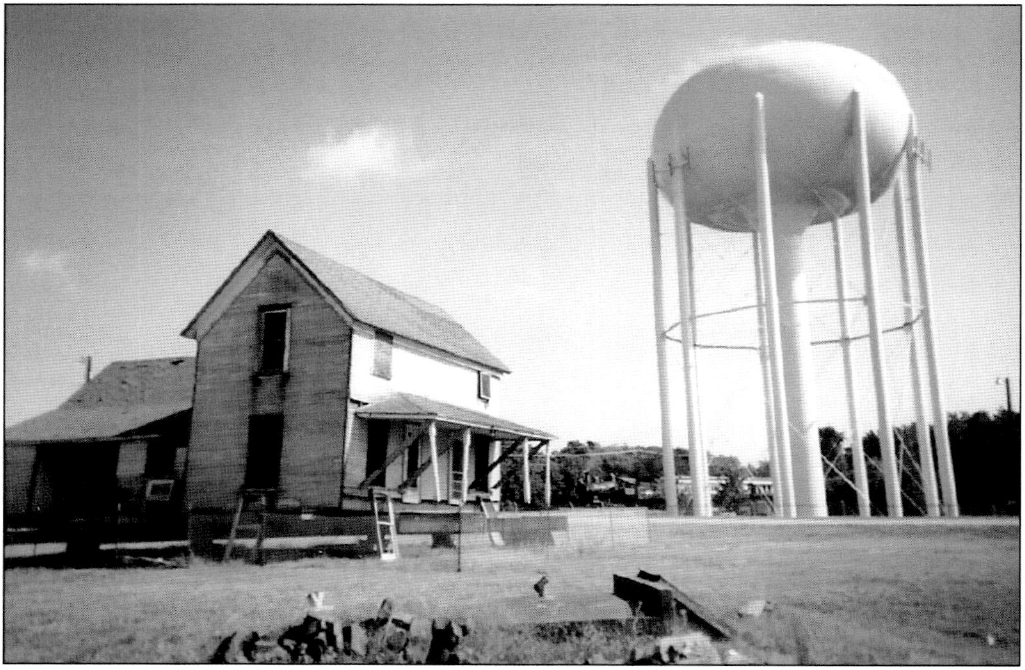

The Webb House was built in 1914 to replace the original one that burned down. The one-and-a-half-story house featured a gabled roof on the main body of the house, with a hipped roof porch with turned columns and a pair of central front doors flanked by double-hung windows with small space windows under the eaves. Such features were typical of early-20th-century architecture. (Courtesy of Colleyville Historical Preservation Committee.)

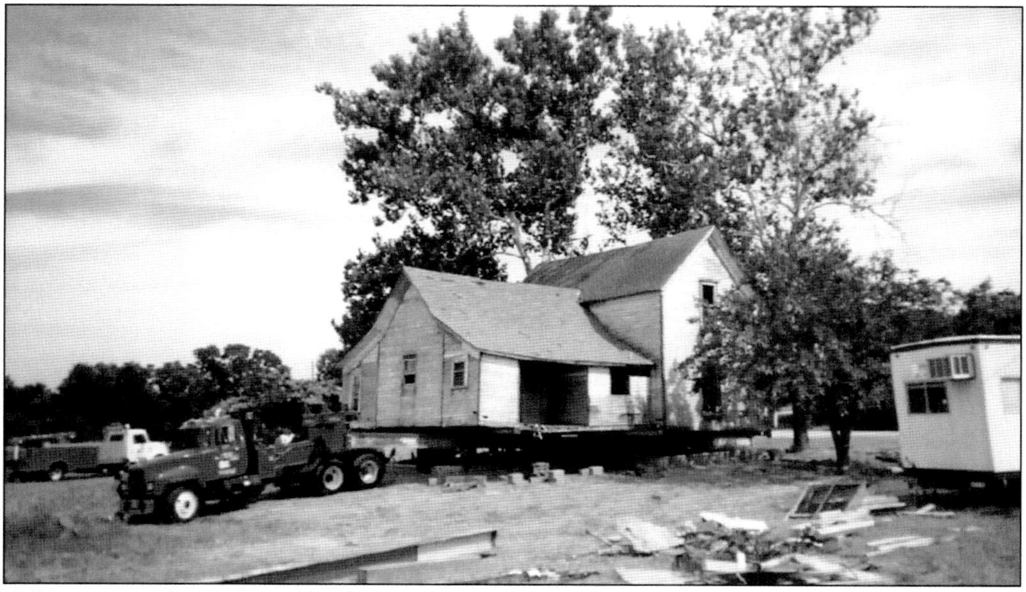

Following a study conducted by the Texas Historical Commission in 1985, it was determined that the Webb House was a significant building and needed to be preserved. The renovation project, which lasted from June to December 2002, was part of a master plan that included moving the house to a new location at the corner of Shelton Drive and Bransford Road. (Courtesy of Colleyville Historical Preservation Committee.)

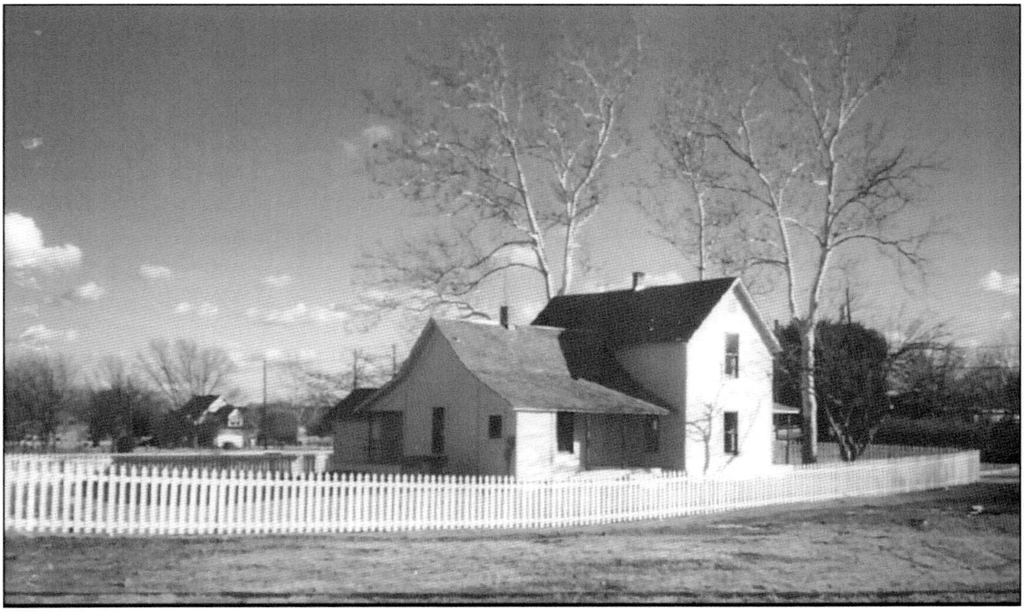

The Webb House (above) was restored to its former glory and dedicated on December 31, 2002. As part of Bransford Park, which was the last remaining part of the John R. Webb farm and purchased by the City of Colleyville in 1979, the house stands near another reminder of the Bransford community—the bright red Burlington Northern Santa Fe Railway caboose. The caboose (below) stands not only as a monument to one of the great railroad companies that helped build a transportation network across the nation, but as a reminder of how important the railroad was to the economic health of all of the communities in the Colleyville area. (Both, courtesy of Colleyville Historical Preservation Committee.)

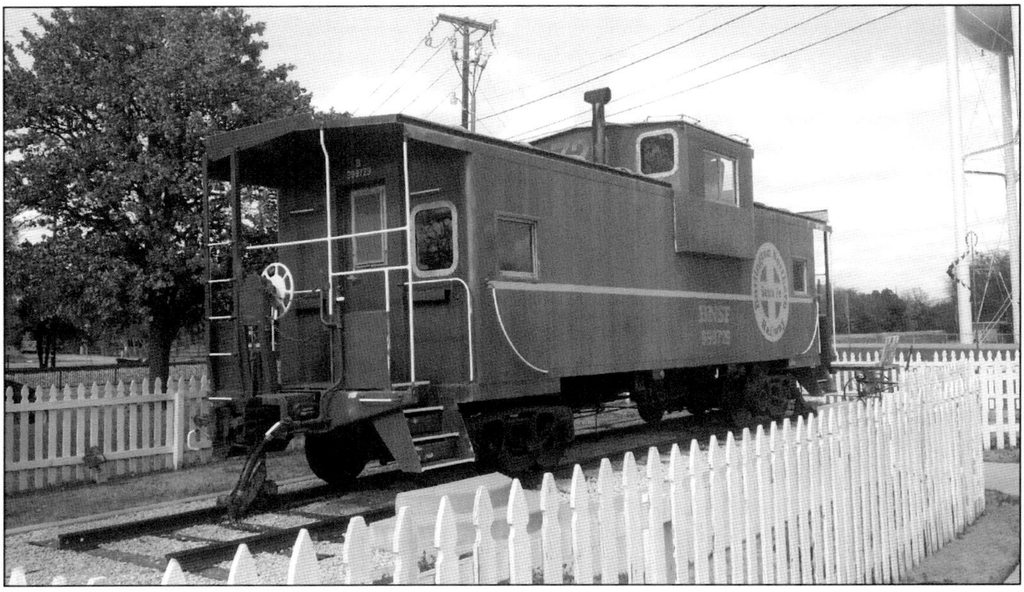

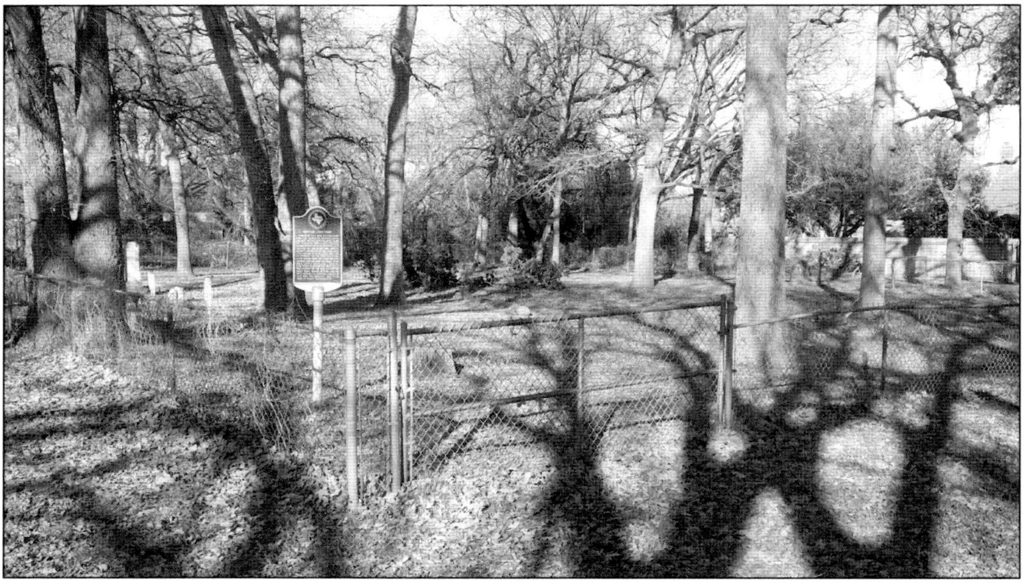

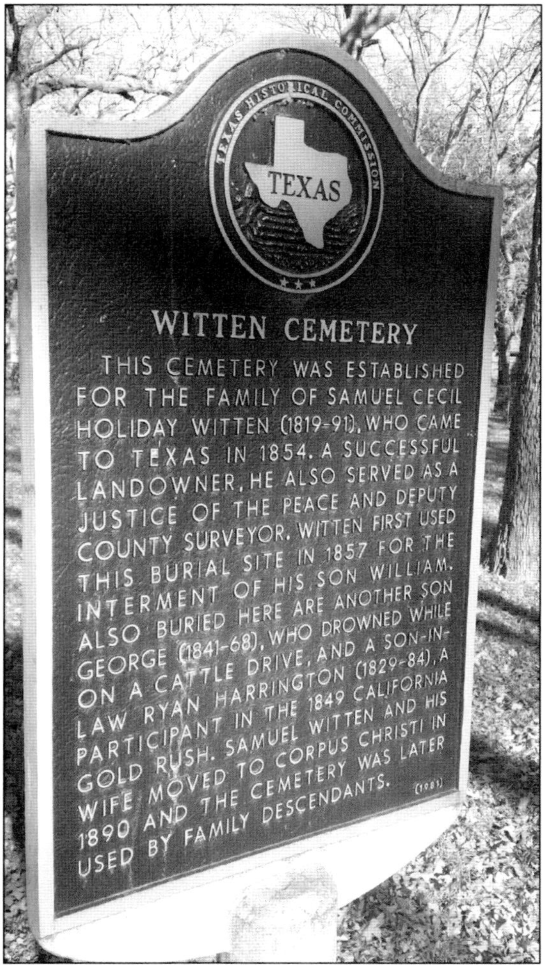

Samuel C.H. Witten, a farmer and rancher, also served as Tarrant County deputy land surveyor. His home off of Jackson Road, which was a large board house built for Witten, his wife, and their 11 children, was the first of its kind of that era among the typical log cabins and dugouts. Witten family descendants still live in the Colleyville area, and a private cemetery for the Witten family, which was awarded a Texas Historical Marker in 1981, still remains just off of Jackson Court in the Brook Meadows subdivision. (Both, courtesy of Mark Fadden.)

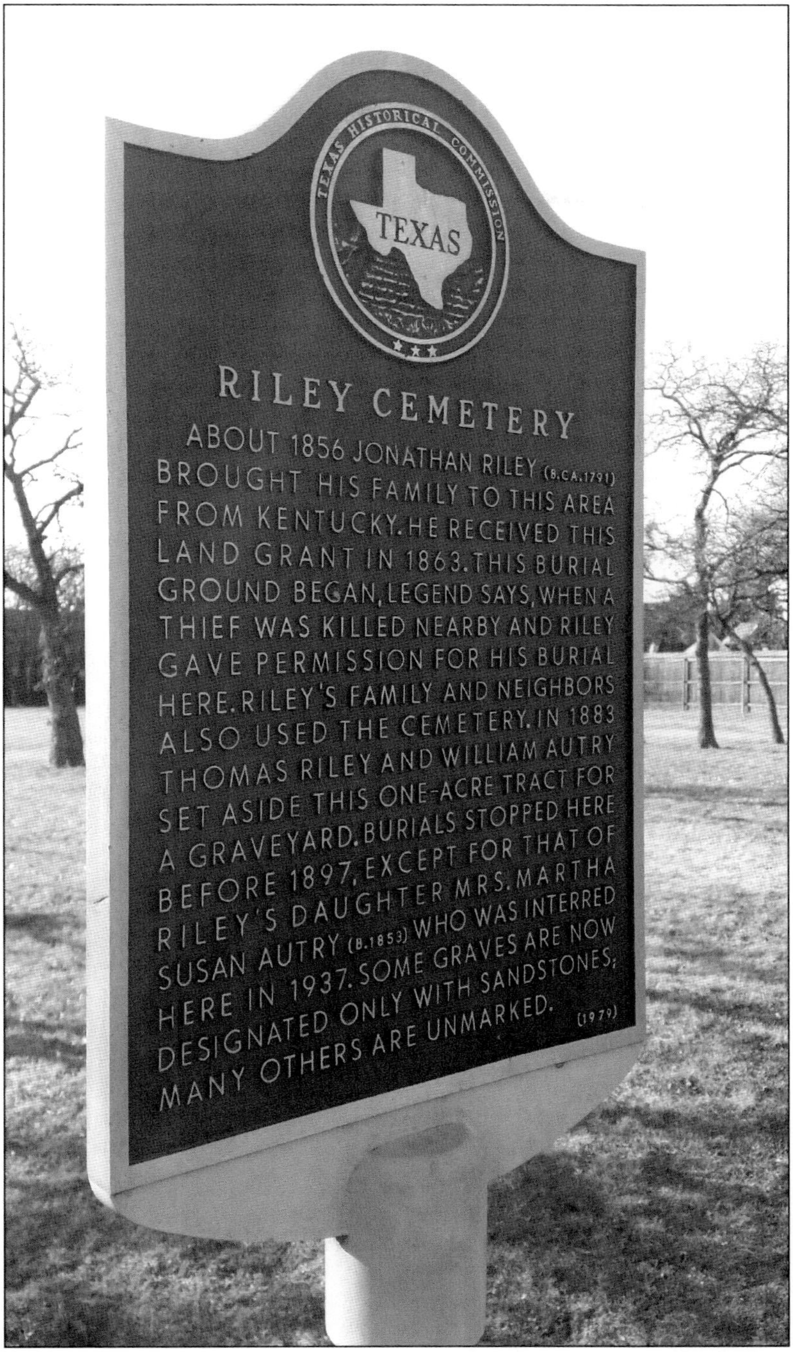

Located at Morning Glory Lane and Brown Trail, Riley Cemetery is one of the three pioneer cemeteries in Colleyville and one of two that still exist. Jonathan Riley brought his wife, Judy, and their family to the pre-Colleyville area and received a land grant in 1863. In 1877, the cemetery was created on a one-acre tract on Riley's property when he allowed a prisoner named John Alison Goldsmith to be buried there. Goldsmith was shot and killed nearby when he was attempting to escape Tarrant County sheriff's deputies while they were transporting him to Fort Worth. (Courtesy of Mark Fadden.)

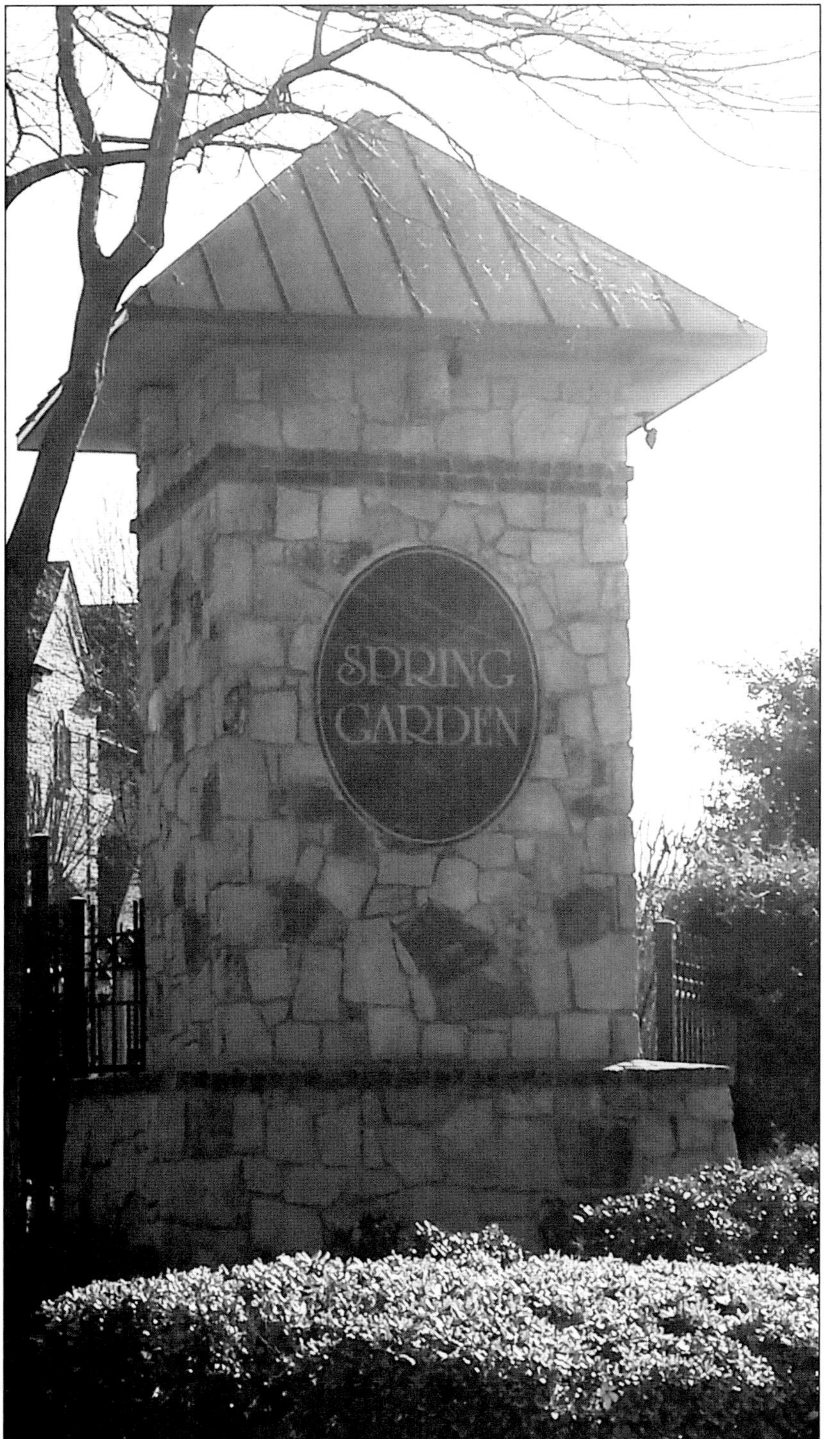

This Spring Garden sign marks the location of an enclave of townhomes on the corner of Jackson and Cheek-Sparger Roads. This location is near the site where the Spring Garden parent community flourished for two decades in the late 1800s. (Courtesy of Mark Fadden.)

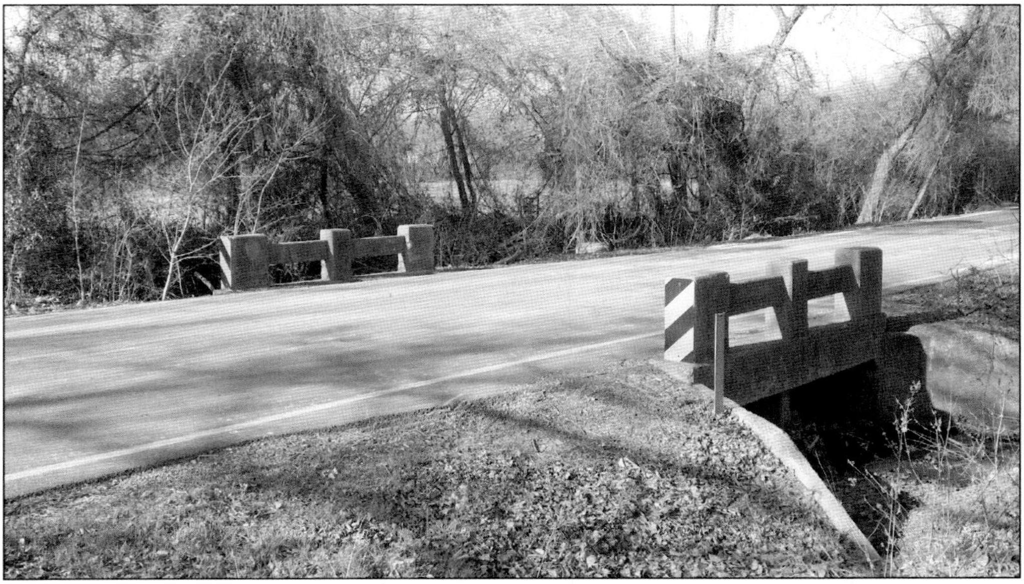

The WPA, which was created in 1935 under Pres. Franklin D. Roosevelt's New Deal initiative, was one of the largest and most ambitious programs in US history. As a way to help the nation recover from the Great Depression, the goal of public-building programs was to provide millions of people with work relief over public assistance, allowing beneficiaries to maintain self-respect, reinforce their work ethic, and keep their skills sharp. Nearly every community in the United States had a new park, bridge, or school constructed by the agency, which, at its peak in 1938, employed approximately three million men and women. The two bridges on Jackson Road were WPA projects. Shown below is one of the WPA plaques affixed to one of the bridges. (Both, courtesy of Mark Fadden.)

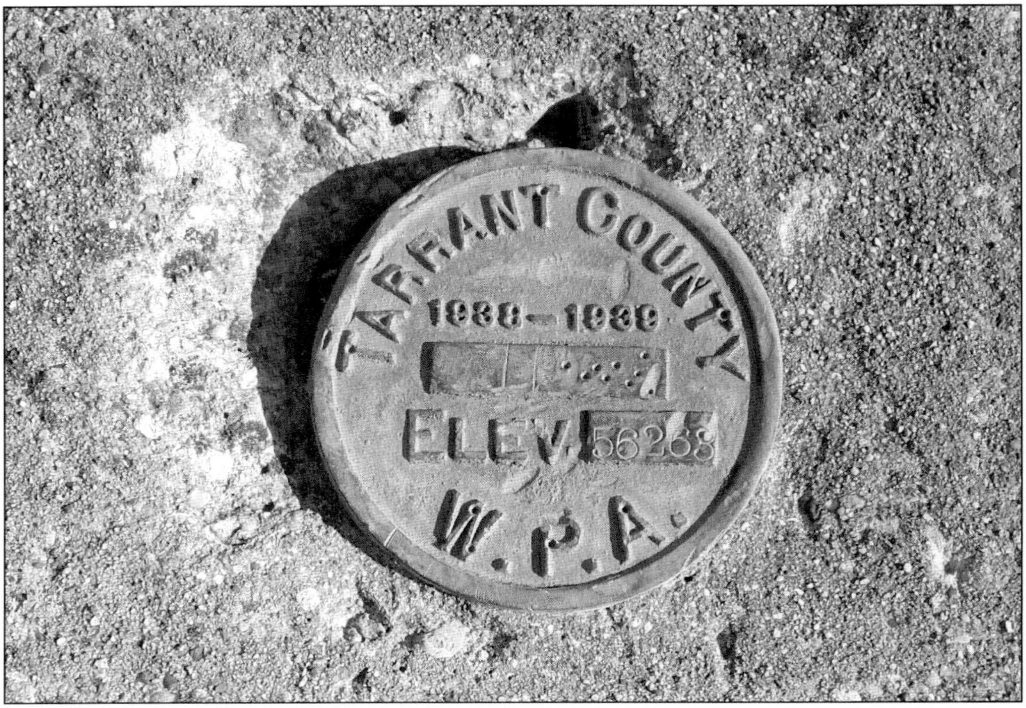

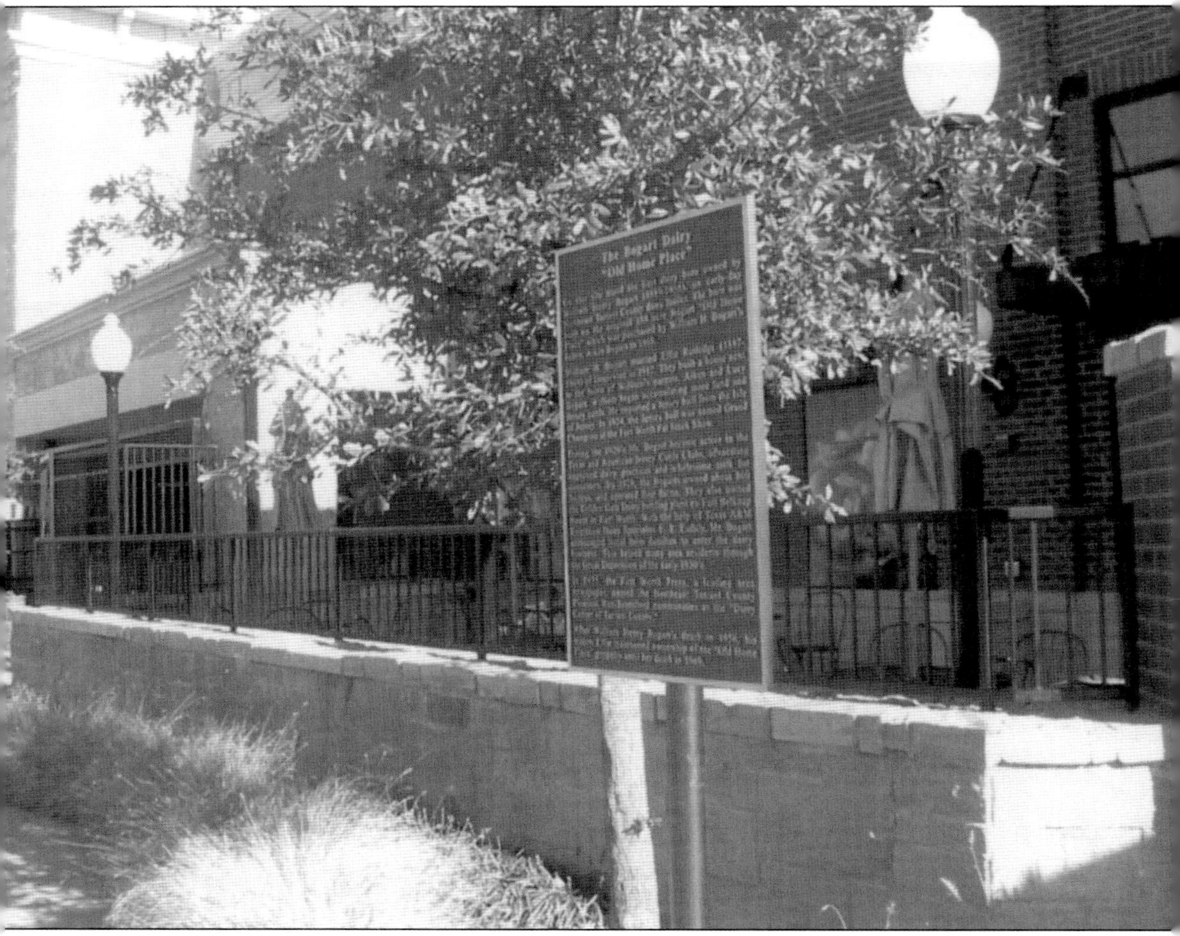

By 1929, William Henry Bogart was operating four dairy farms in Colleyville, with 800 head of Jersey cattle. As the largest dairy operation, the Bogart Dairy not only was the main reason why the Colleyville area was known as the "Dairy center of Tarrant County" at the time; it also took up a considerable stretch of land in Colleyville. When Cardinal Road was straightened to become present-day State Highway 26 in 1929, the new road split up several farms in the area, including the Bogart Dairy. If Bogart needed to move his dairy cows from a pasture on one side of the road to one on the other side, the road would have to be closed, a source of frustration for both drivers and Bogart and his workers. This marker stands in front of present-day Market Street grocery store at 5605 Colleyville Boulevard. Market Street is where the Bogart Dairy barn used to stand. (Courtesy of Mark Fadden.)

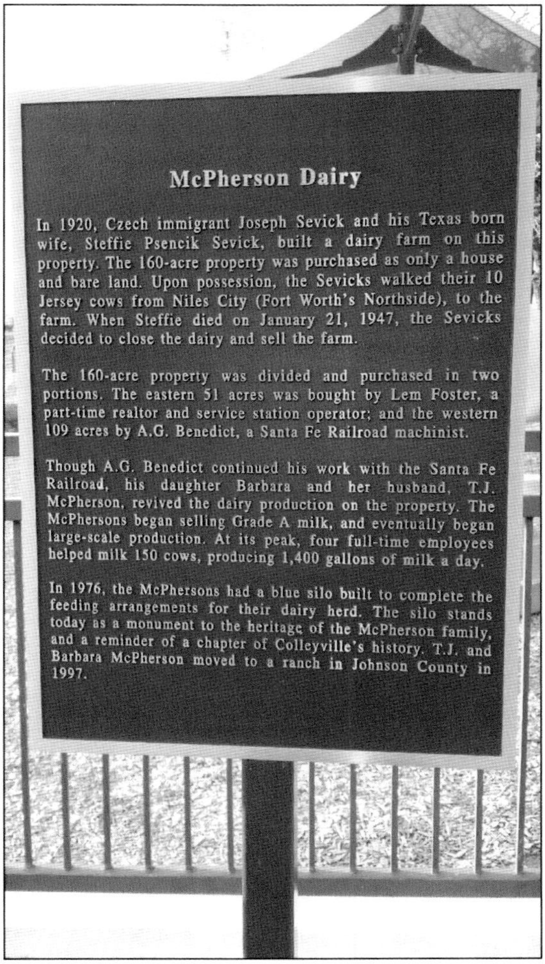

The McPherson Dairy started as a dairy owned by the Seviek family, who operated it from 1925 to 1947. It was sold to A.G. and Mabel Benedict, who in turn sold a portion of the land to her daughter and son-in-law, Barbara Jo and T.J. McPherson. The historical marker at right describes how the dairy passed down through the generations. The sign below shares information about dairy cows in particular. The signs are placed near a renovated dairy barn that features photographs and replicas of a milking operation that would have taken place at the McPherson Dairy. (Both, courtesy of Mark Fadden.)

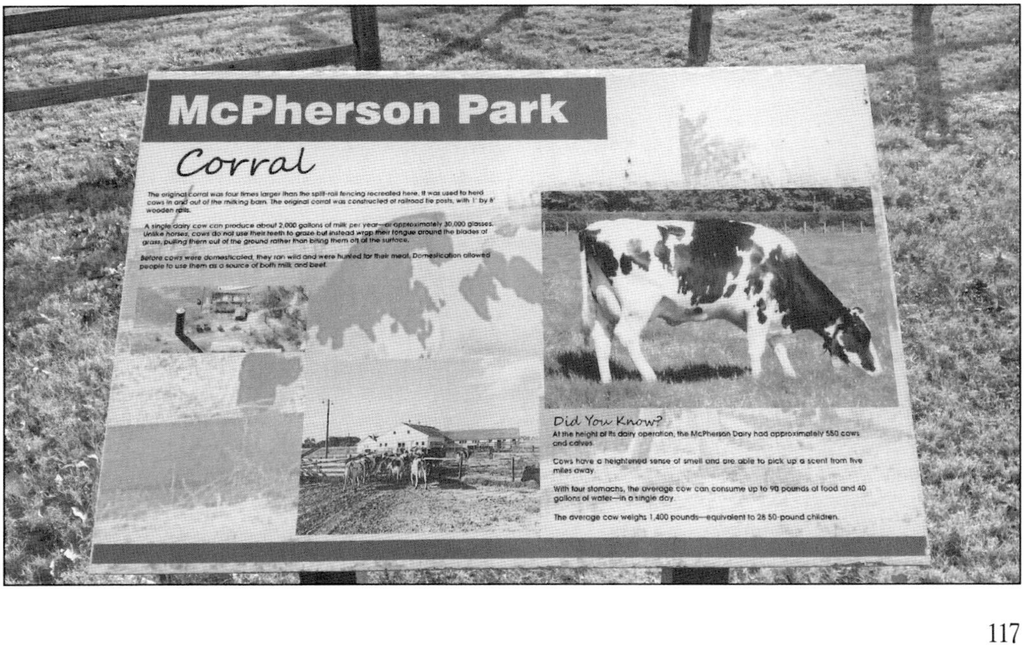

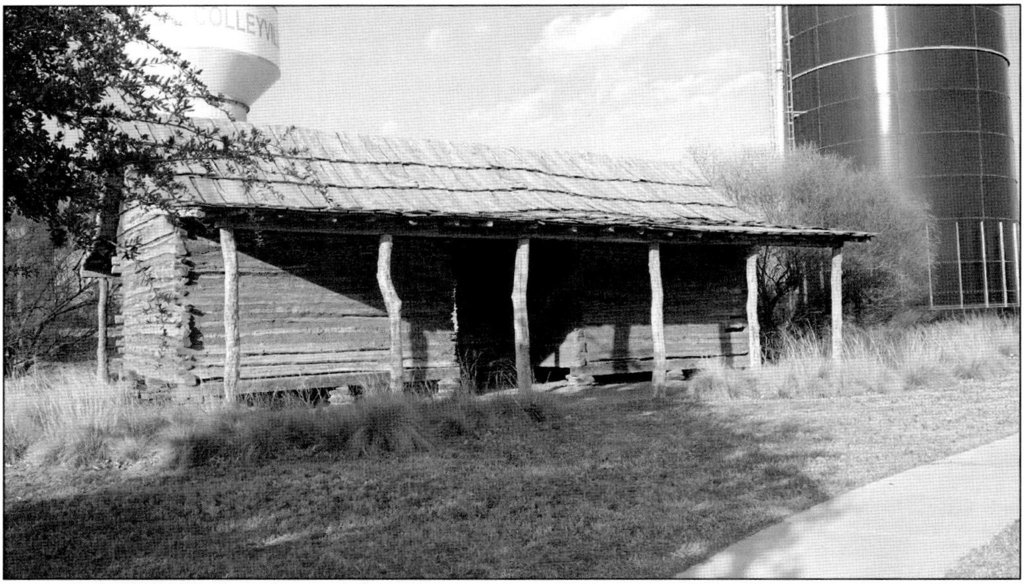

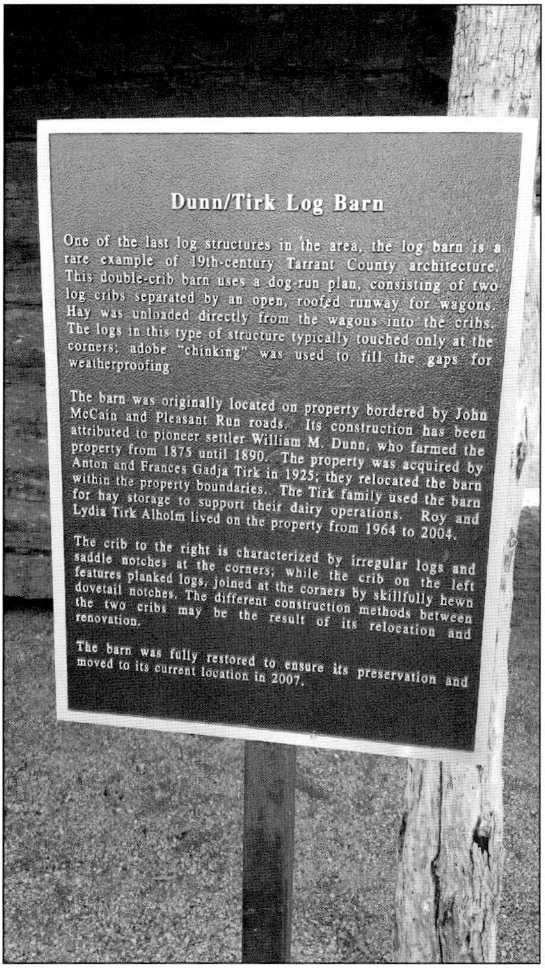

As one of the only original log-cabin structures left standing in Tarrant County from the late 1800s, the Dunn/Tirk Barn was used by generations of pioneers. Structures such as the one shown above were used both as hay barns, where wagons would offload their hay underneath the open middle, known as the dog run, and as houses, with a kitchen at one end and the sleeping quarters at the other. The Dunn/Tirk Barn historical marker (left) tells the tale of the architecture of the barn as well as how it changed hands over the years before being moved to its present location in 2007. (Both, courtesy of Mark Fadden.)

As the center of a large farming community, Bransford provided two important services for residents in the pre-Colleyville era. First, it had the area's only post office, which was named for pioneer Felix Grundy Bransford. Second, it was the only area stop for the St. Louis, Arkansas & Texas railroad, where residents could not only get supplies transported to them, but also ship the goods they produced to other markets. Located at the corner of L.D. Lockett and Bransford Roads, the Bransford historical marker (right) is displayed at the west end of the BNSF caboose. A little harder to find at that same corner, the Bransford Depot sign (below) is located just off the Cotton Belt hike and bike trail. (Both, courtesy of Mark Fadden.)

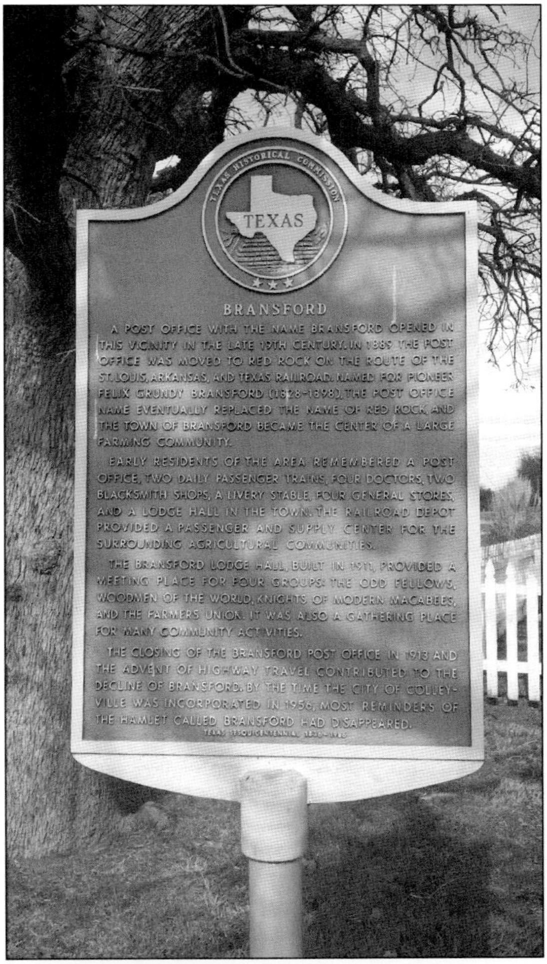

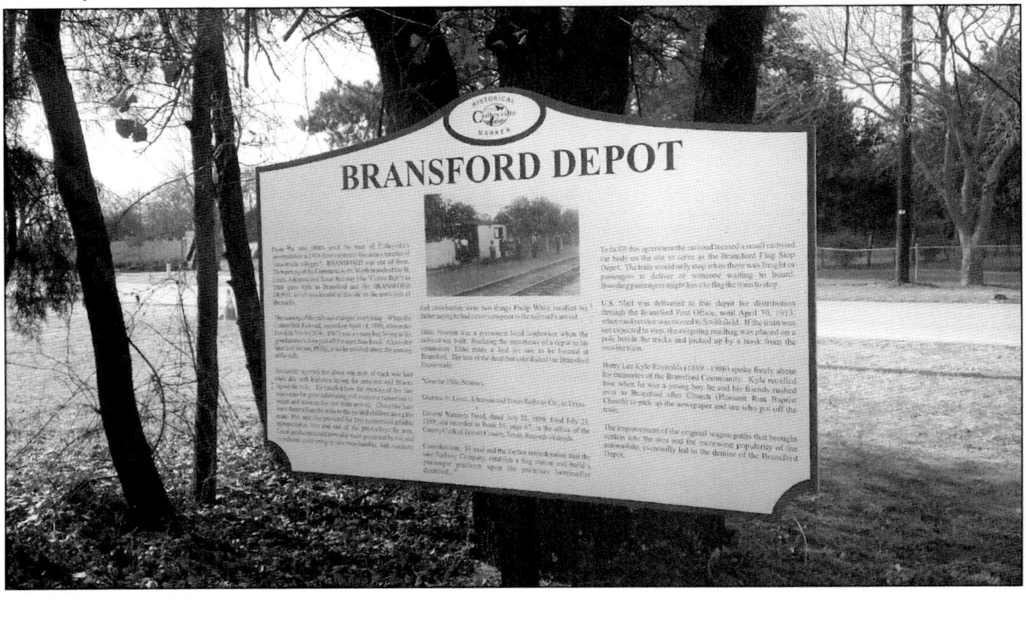

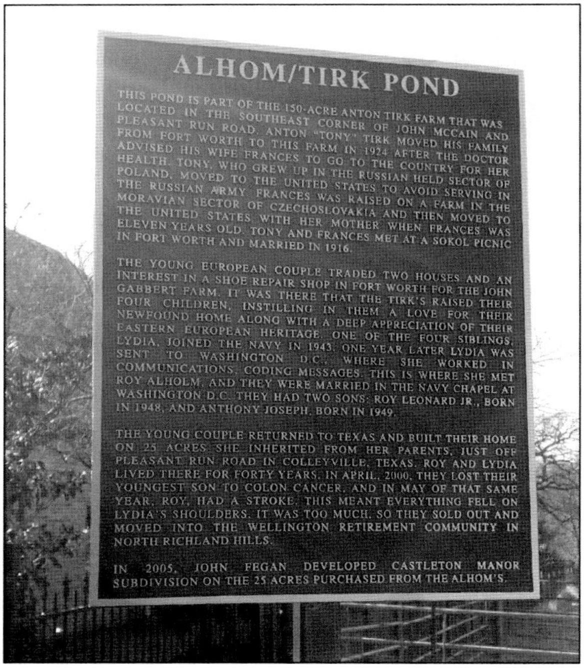

The Alhom/Tirk Pond marker stands just off of the hiking and biking trail that runs along the western edge of the Castleton Manor subdivision. It not only marks the pond to the northeast of it that provided a source of water on the Tirk farm, but tells the story of how the land around it was passed down through generations and was ultimately developed into an upscale neighborhood. (Courtesy of Mark Fadden.)

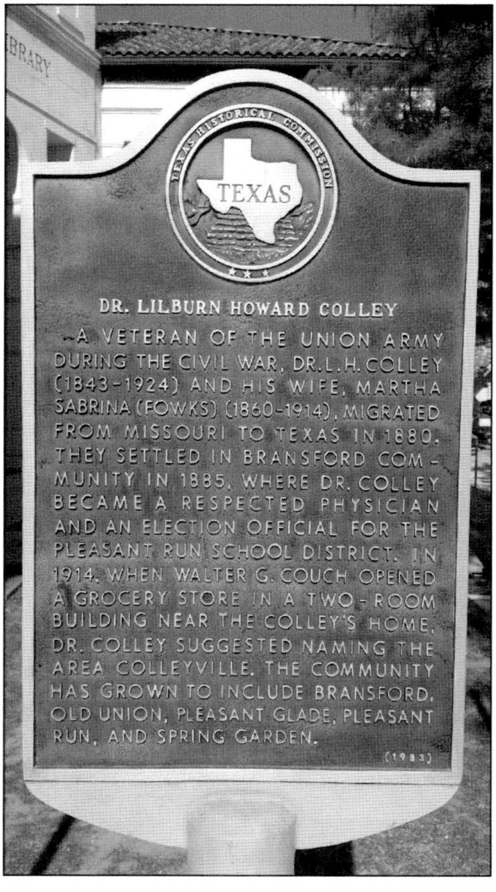

Located in front of Colleyville City Hall, this marker summarizes the story of the founder of Colleyville, Dr. Lilburn Howard Colley. As a country doctor who served a farming community, Colley traveled to the homes of his clients to care for the sick and tend to the births and deaths that marked major moments for the pioneer families. (Courtesy of Mark Fadden.)

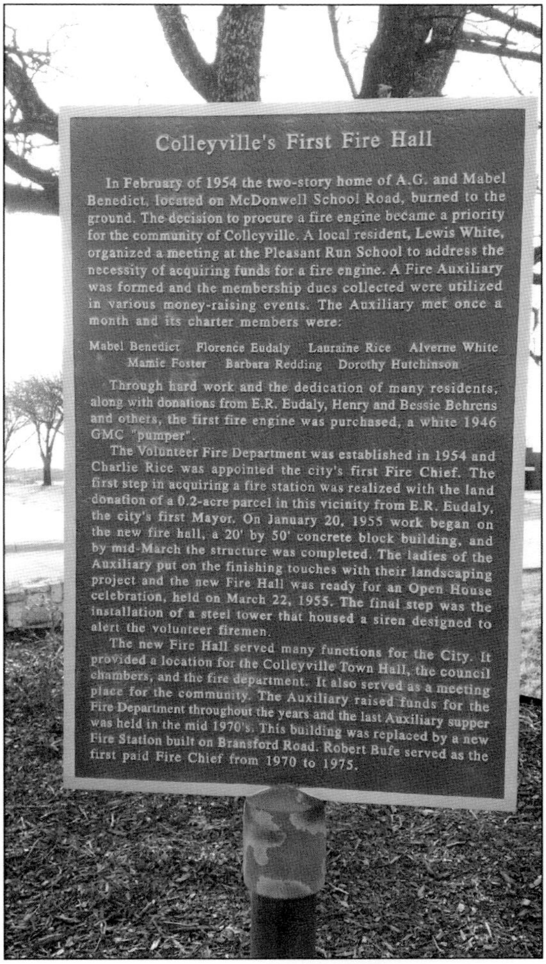

Colleyville's first publicly owned building was its fire hall. Built in 1955, it served other functions as well. It was a community center where residents could meet. It also served as the first City Hall, where the city's business took place. After Colleyville was incorporated in 1956, a small room was added on the back where the city council conducted business, making it Colleyville's first City Hall. Over the years, the building has gone from a place of politics to a place of business. Currently, it serves as a Compass Bank branch. Several historical photographs of Colleyville and its residents adorn the walls. (Both, courtesy of Mark Fadden.)

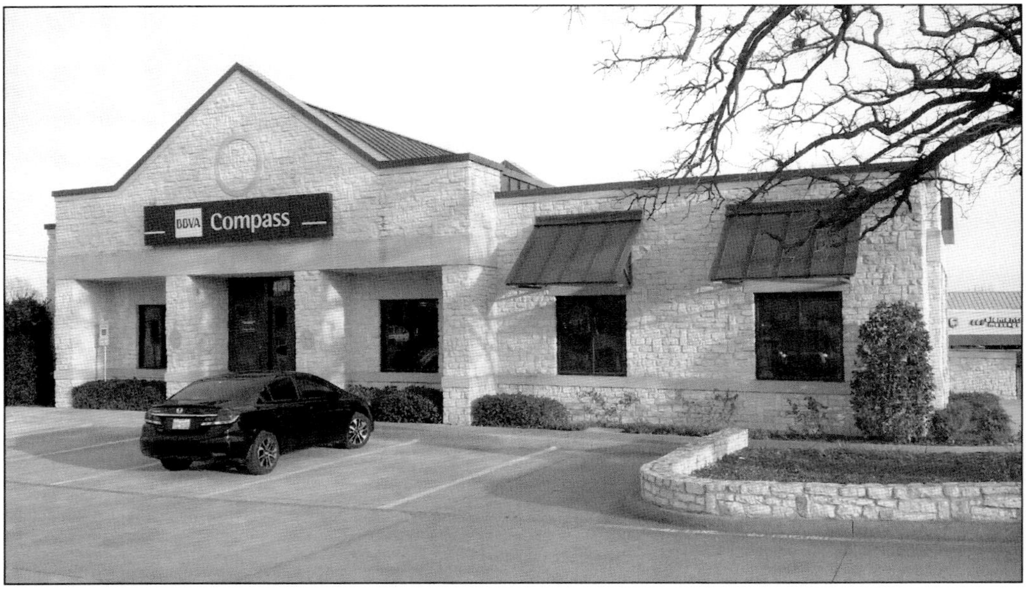

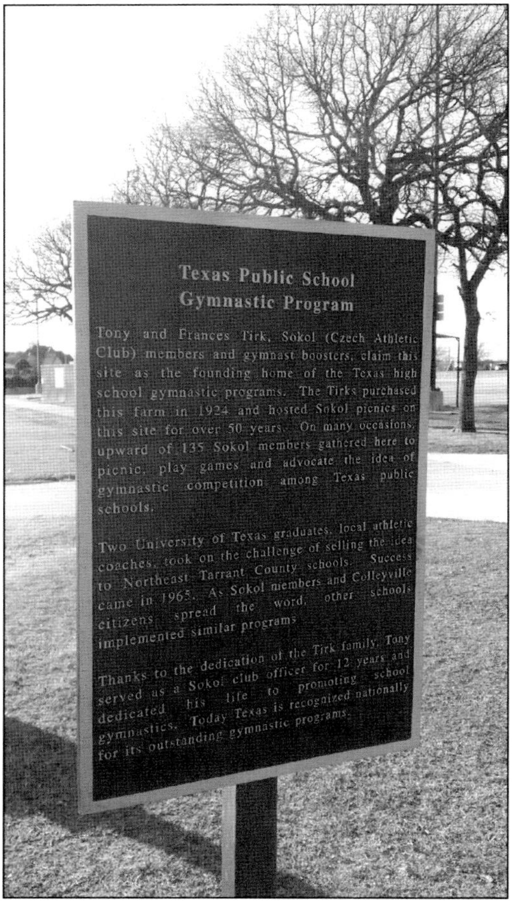

The Texas Public School Gymnastics Program marker celebrates the Tirks family, who hosted Sokol, the name of the Czech athletic club, and picnics at their farmland, on which the present-day Pleasant Run Soccer Complex and Park is situated. The picnics included food and gymnastics games. Keeping with that tradition, the site is currently used for recreational and competitive soccer games. (Courtesy of Mark Fadden.)

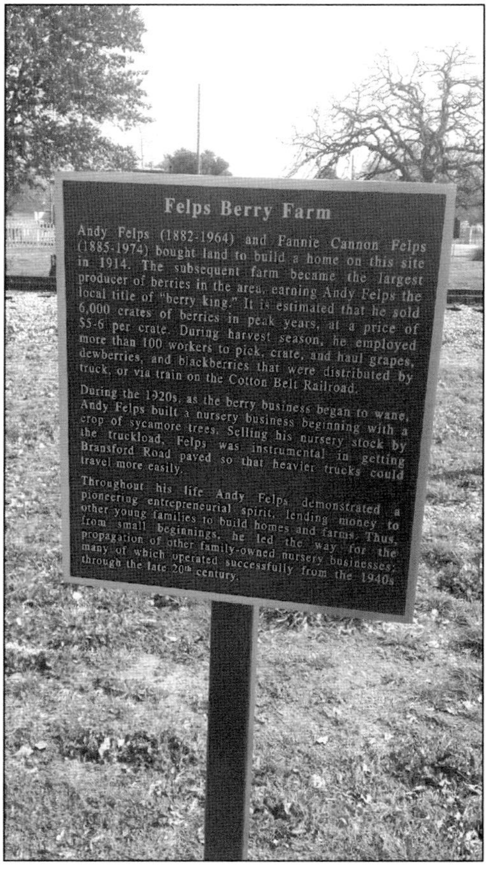

Andy and Fannie Cannon Felps bought land at the corner of present-day L.D. Lockett and Bransford Roads in 1914 and turned it into the largest-producing berry farm in the area. This marker to "The Berry King" stands just off of the Cotton Belt hike and bike trail, where the Felps farm once stood. (Courtesy of Mark Fadden.)

Pleasant Glade Baptist Church was organized on September 19, 1923, in the Pleasant Glade community. It continued to be the rock in people's lives through the Great Depression, World War II, and up to today, where it serves the people of Northeast Tarrant County. This marker stands in front of the church building at 3708 Glade Road. (Courtesy of Mark Fadden.)

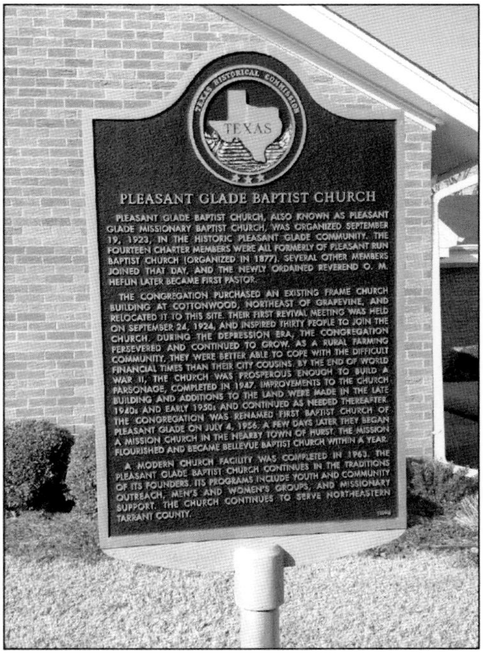

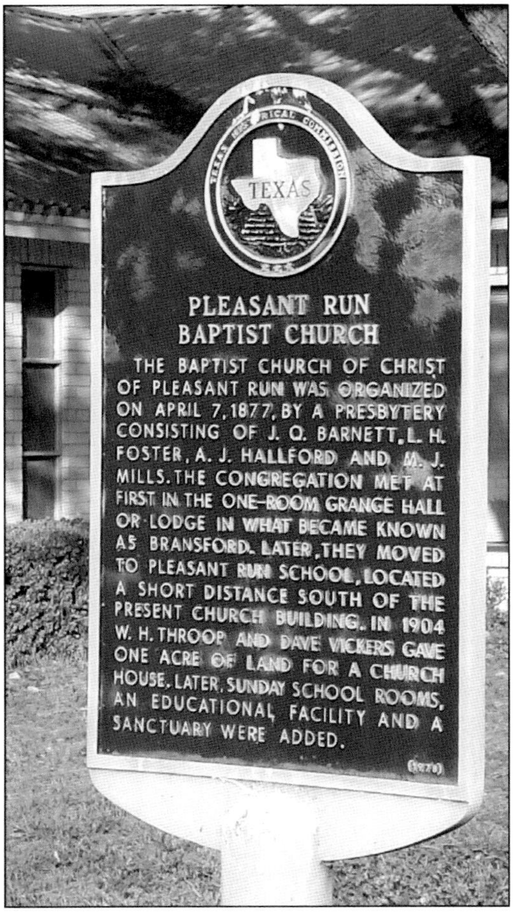

Pleasant Run Baptist Church was organized on April 7, 1877. The charter members first met at the lodge hall in Bransford before W.H. Throop and Dave Vickers donated an acre of land at 6000 Pleasant Run Road upon which to build the church. (Courtesy of Mark Fadden.)

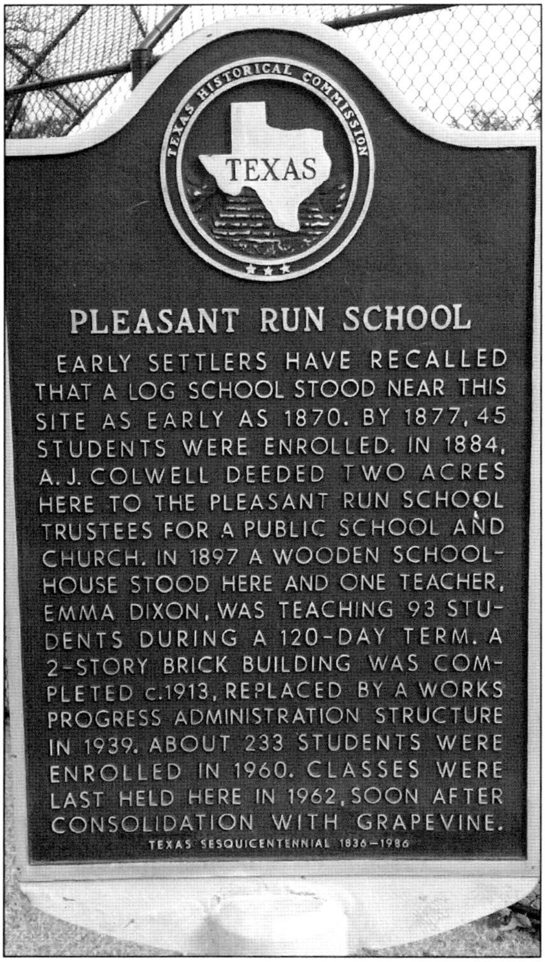

Located at the corner of Church Street and Pleasant Run Road, this marker tells the story of how the Pleasant Run School building provided a place to help generations of students get educated. The building is gone, but the location still serves children as game fields owned by the First Baptist Church of Colleyville. (Courtesy of Mark Fadden.)

Located behind the Colleyville Senior Center at 2512 Glade Road, three stone tablets commemorate Colleyville residents who enlisted in the armed forces and served in World War II. The World War II Memorial was placed at the entrance to the Village at Colleyville in 2002 and then moved to its present location. (Courtesy of Mark Fadden.)

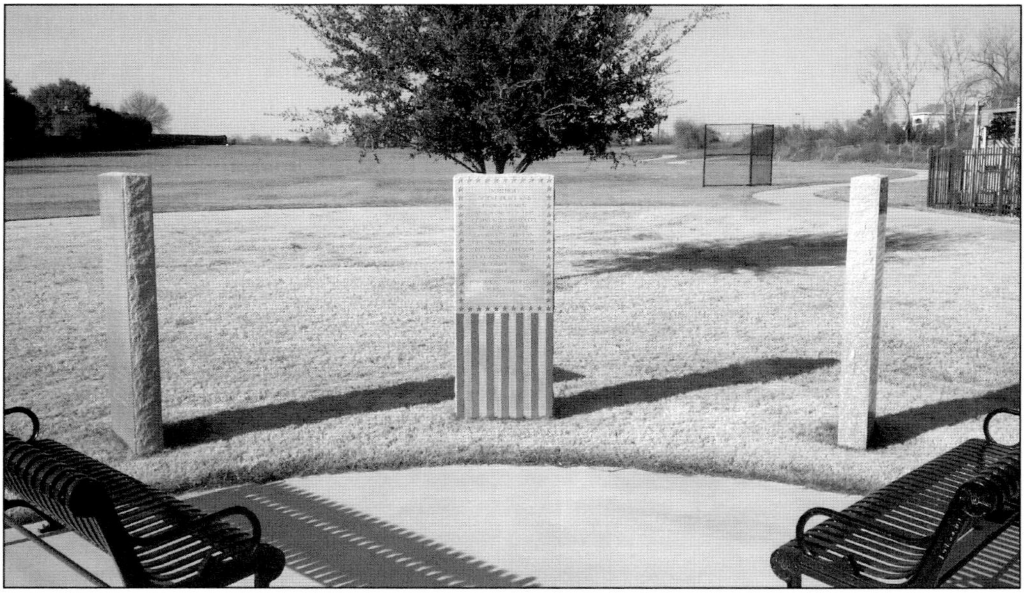

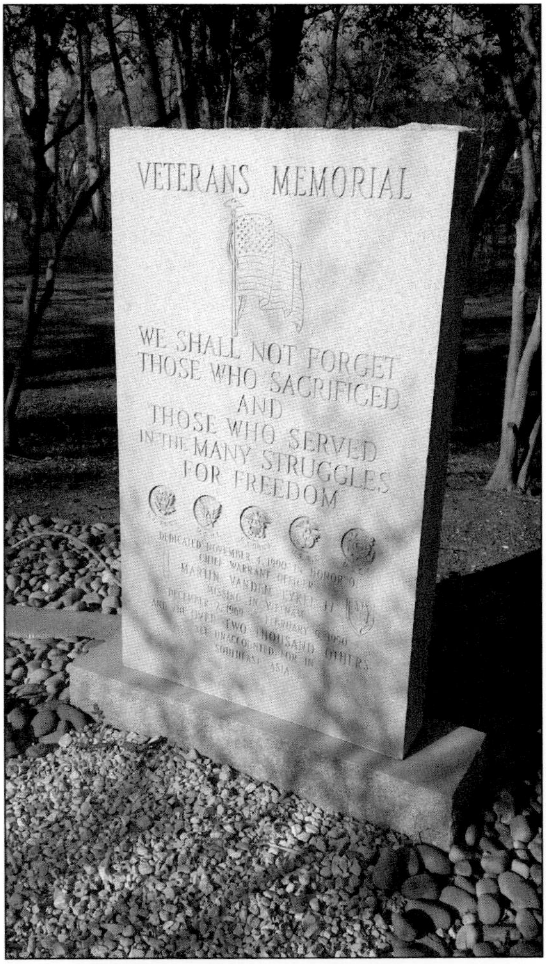

In a quiet corner of Sparger Park at 4301 Bedford Road stands the Veterans Memorial marker (right). Along with a flagpole bearing the United States, Texas, and POW-MIA flags, the marker was dedicated on November 4, 1990. It was designed by Mayor Chris Hawkins. Near that marker stands the Blue Star Memorial By-Way marker (below). The Blue Star Memorial By-Way was a program begun by the New Jersey Council of Garden Clubs in 1944 to honor all members of the armed forces. Blue Stars were displayed in the windows of homes where sons and daughters of the families living there were serving in World War II. Present-day State Highway 26 was designated a Blue Star Memorial Highway in 1992. (Both, courtesy of Mark Fadden.)

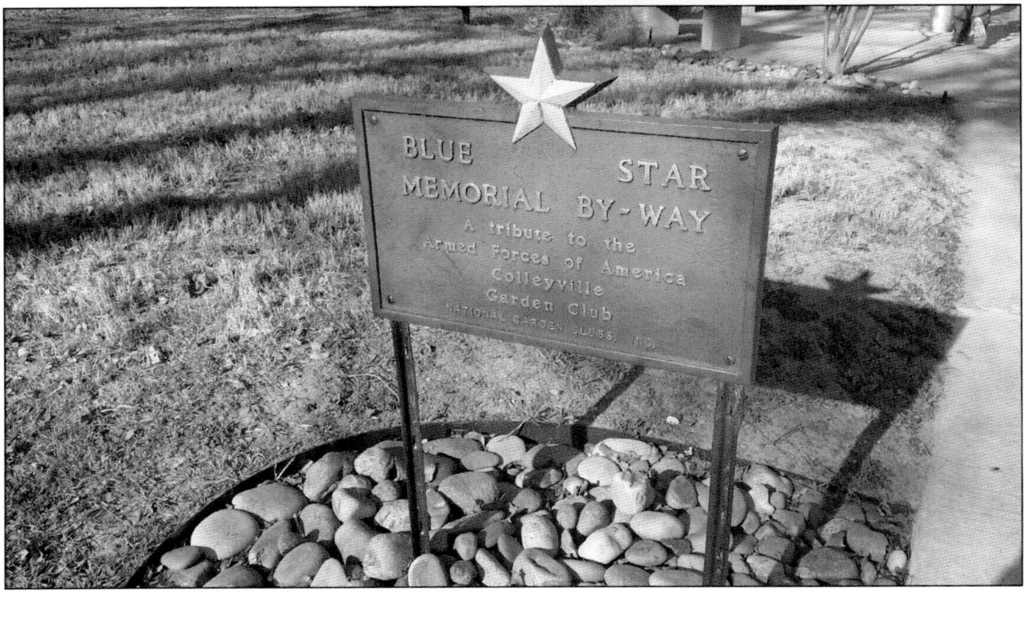

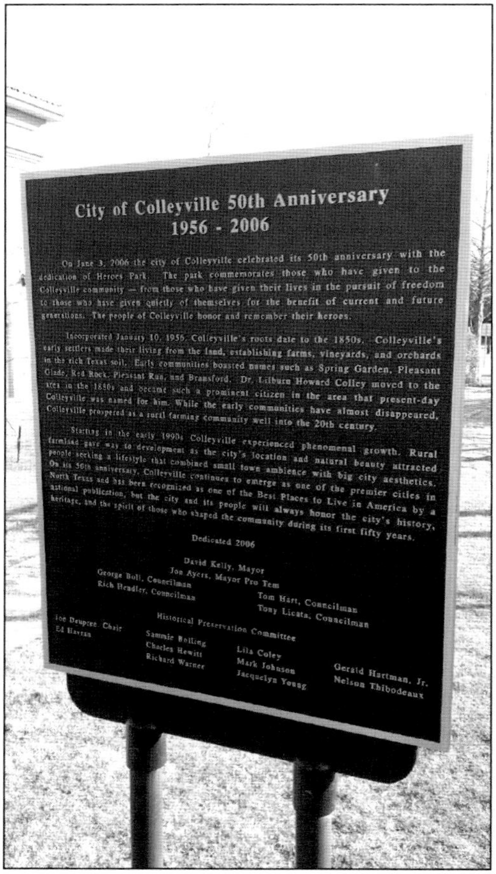

Heroes Park serves to commemorate the heroes who have helped to keep Colleyville, the state of Texas, and the United States of America places where freedom continues to reign. The stone wall that provides the northern border of the park is decorated with several plaques of our hometown heroes. The plaques honor eight Colleyville residents so far: Christian C. Schulz, Steven Charles Tucker, Frank Whitmire, Robert Wayne Bufe, Bobby Fitzgerald, Dennis Edward Harrell, James (Jim) Moore, and Jack Olsen. As Colleyville residents continue to dedicate countless hours and tireless energy to the city, room has been left along the wall to honor the efforts of current and future citizens. (Both, courtesy of Mark Fadden.)

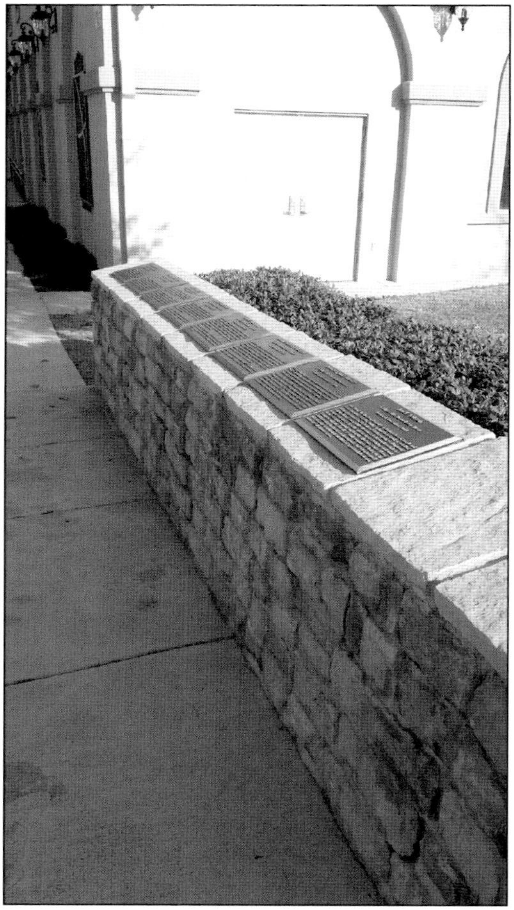

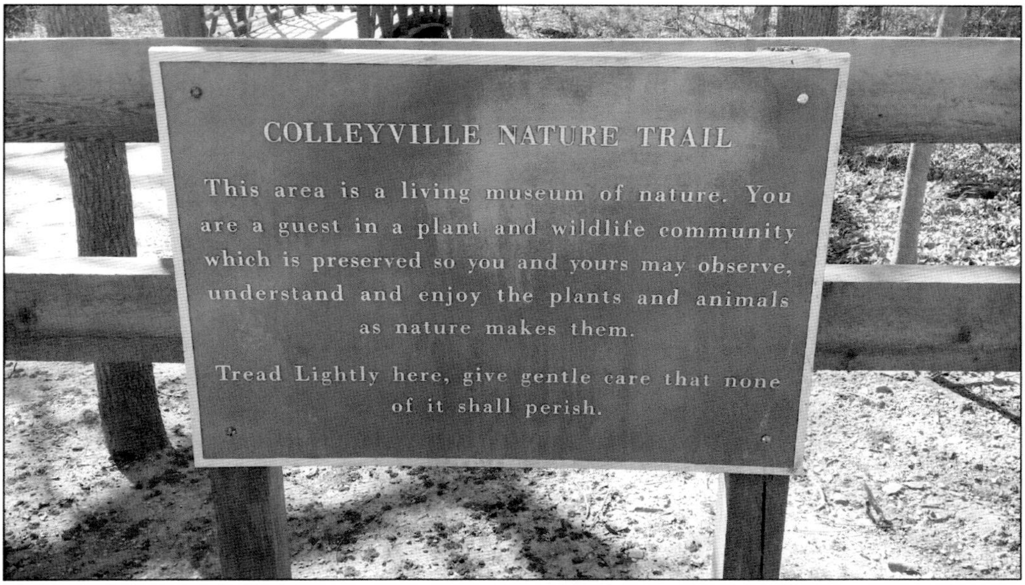

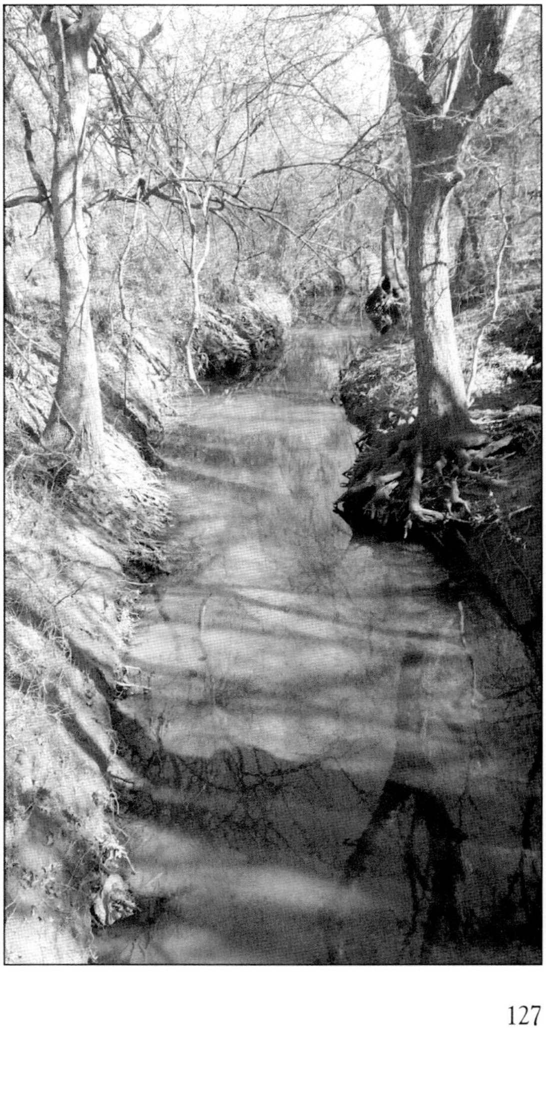

To mark the passage of history, monuments are chiseled with letters and set into place, buildings are saved and rehabilitated, and streets bear the names of heroes. However, the Earth has also borne witness to history. One only needs to take a walk in the woods of the Colleyville Nature Center or to gaze into the clear waters of Little Bear Creek to experience the sights and sounds experienced by their forefathers. Colleyville began as a rural community where nature provided nearly all of life's necessities for a pioneering family: the logs needed to build a cabin, animals for food, and even life-sustaining water. It should not be forgotten that nature, too, is history—perhaps the most accessible history of all. (Both, courtesy of Mark Fadden.)

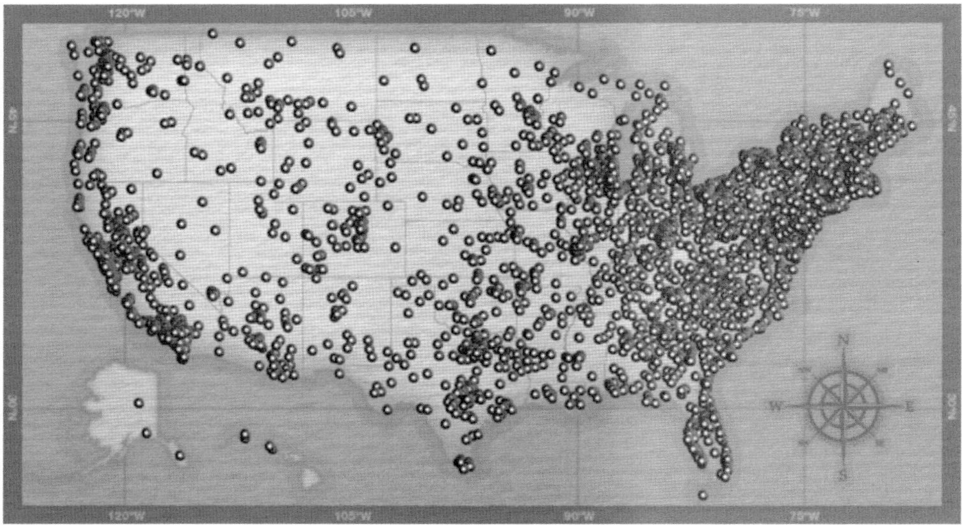